Contents

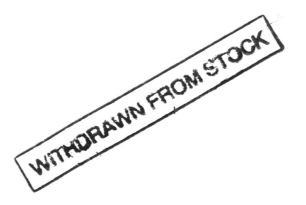

Getting the most from this book

Mathematics is not only a beautiful and exciting subject in its own right but also one that underpins many other branches of learning. It is consequently fundamental to our national wellbeing.

This book covers the compulsory core content of Year 1/AS Further Mathematics and so provides a course for the first of the two years of Advanced Level Further Mathematics study. The requirements of the compulsory core content for the second year are met in a second book, while the year one and year two optional applied content is covered in the Mechanics and Statistics books.

Between 2014 and 2016 A Level Mathematics and Further Mathematics were very substantially revised, for first teaching in 2017. Major changes included increased emphasis on

- Problem solving

- Mathematical proof

- Use of ICT

- Modelling

- Working with large data sets in statistics.

This book embraces these ideas. A large number of exercise questions involve elements of **problem solving**. The ideas of **mathematical proof**, rigorous logical argument and mathematical **modelling** are also included in suitable exercise questions throughout the book.

The use of **technology**, including graphing software, spreadsheets and high specification calculators, is encouraged wherever possible, for example in the Activities used to introduce some of the topics. In particular, readers are expected to have access to a calculator which handles matrices up to order 3×3. Places where ICT can be used are highlighted by a **T** icon. Margin boxes highlight situations where the use of technology – such as graphical calculators or graphing software – can be used to further explore a particular topic.

Throughout the book the emphasis is on understanding and interpretation rather than mere routine calculations, but the various exercises do nonetheless provide plenty of scope for practising basic techniques. The exercise questions are split into three bands. Band 1 questions are designed to reinforce basic understanding; Band 2 questions are broadly typical of what might be expected in an examination; Band 3 questions explore around the topic and some of them are rather more demanding. In addition, extensive online support tailored to the OCR specification, including further questions, is available by subscription to MEI's Integral website, integralmaths.org.

In addition to the exercise questions, there are two sets of Practice questions, covering groups of chapters. These include identified questions requiring **problem solving** **PS**, **mathematical proof** **MP**, use of ICT **T** and **modelling** **M**.

This book is written on the assumption that readers are studying or have studied AS Mathematics. It can be studied alongside the year 1/AS Mathematics book, or after studying AS or A Level Mathematics. There are places where the work depends on knowledge from earlier in the book or in the year 1/AS Mathematics book and this is flagged up in the Prior knowledge boxes. This should be seen as an invitation to those who have problems with the particular topic to revisit it. At the end of each chapter there is a list of key points covered as well as a summary of the new knowledge (learning outcomes) that readers should have gained.

Although, in general, knowledge of A Level Mathematics beyond AS Level is not required, there are two small topics from year 2 of A Level Mathematics that are needed in the study of the material in this book. These are radians (needed in the work on the argument of a complex number) and the compound angle formulae, which are helpful in understanding the multiplication and division of complex numbers in modulus-argument form. These two topics are introduced briefly at the back of the book, for the benefit of readers who have not yet studied year 2 of A Level Mathematics.

Two common features of the book are Activities and Discussion points. These serve rather different purposes. The Activities are designed to help readers get into the thought processes of the new work that they are about to meet; having done an Activity, what follows will seem much easier. The Discussion points invite readers to talk about particular points with their fellow students and their teacher and so enhance their understanding. Another feature is a Caution icon ❗, highlighting points where it is easy to go wrong.

Answers to all exercise questions and practice questions are provided at the back of the book, and also online at www.hoddereducation.co.uk/OCRFurtherMathsYear1

Catherine Berry

Roger Porkess

Prior knowledge

This book is designed so that it can be studied alongside OCR A Level Mathematics Year 1 (AS). There are some links with work in OCR A Level Mathematics Year 2, but it is not necessary to have covered this work before studying this book. Some essential background work on radians and compound angle formulae is covered in An introduction to radians and The identities $\sin(\theta \pm \phi)$ and $\cos(\theta \pm \phi)$ as well as in OCR A Level Mathematics Year 2.

- **Chapter 1: Complex numbers** uses work on solving quadratic equations, covered in chapter 3 of OCR A Level Mathematics Year 1 (AS).

- **Chapter 2: Matrices and transformations** builds on GCSE work on transformations.

- **Chapter 3: Roots of polynomials** uses work on solving polynomial equations using the factor theorem, covered in chapter 7 of OCR A Level Mathematics Year 1 (AS).

- **Chapter 4: Induction** builds on AS work on proof, covered in chapter 1 of OCR A level Mathematics Year 1 (AS).

- **Chapter 5: Complex numbers and geometry** develops the work in chapter 1. Knowledge of radians is assumed: this is covered in chapter 2 of OCR A Level Mathematics Year 2, but the required knowledge is also covered in An introduction to radians. It is also helpful to know the compound angle formulae which are introduced in chapter 8 of OCR A Level Mathematics Year 2; there is also a brief introduction in The identities $\sin(\theta \pm \phi)$ and $\cos(\theta \pm \phi)$.

- **Chapter 6: Matrices and their inverses** follows on from the work in chapter 2.

- **Chapter 7: Vectors and 3D space** builds on the vectors work covered in chapter 12 of OCR A Level Mathematics Year 1 (AS). Knowledge of 3D vectors is assumed, which are introduced in chapter 12 of OCR A Level Mathematics Year 2, but it is not necessary to have covered the Mathematics Year 2 chapter prior to this chapter. The work on the intersection of planes in 3D space, introduced in chapter 6, is also developed further in this chapter.

1 Complex numbers

... that wonder of analysis, that portent of the ideal world, that amphibian between being and not-being, which we call the imaginary root of negative unity.

Leibniz, 1702

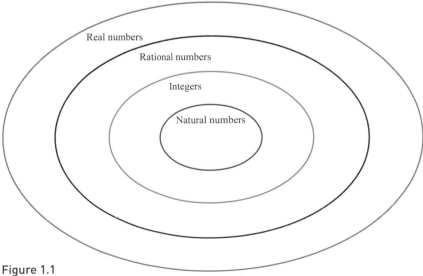

Figure 1.1

Discussion point

→ What is the meaning of each of the terms shown in Figure 1.1?

→ Suggest two numbers that could be placed in each part of the diagram.

1 Extending the number system

The number system we use today has taken thousands of years to develop. To classify the different types of numbers used in mathematics the following letter symbols are used:

$\mathbb{N}$	Natural numbers
$\mathbb{Z}$	Integers
$\mathbb{Q}$	Rational numbers
$\overline{\mathbb{Q}}$	Irrational numbers
$\mathbb{R}$	Real numbers

Discussion point

→ Why is there no set shown on the diagram for irrational numbers?

You may have noticed that some of these sets of numbers fit within the other sets. This can be seen in Figure 1.1.

ACTIVITY 1.1

On a copy of Figure 1.1 write the following numbers in the correct positions.

$7 \quad \sqrt{5} \quad -13 \quad \dfrac{227}{109} \quad -\sqrt{5} \quad 3.1415 \quad \pi \quad 0.33 \quad 0.\dot{3}$

What are complex numbers?

ACTIVITY 1.2

Solve each of these equations and decide which set of numbers the roots belong to in each case.

(i) $x + 7 = 9$ (ii) $7x = 9$ (iii) $x^2 = 9$

(iv) $x + 10 = 9$ (v) $x^2 + 7x = 0$ (vi) $x^2 = 5$

Now think about the equation $x^2 + 9 = 0$.

> Writing this quadratic equation as $x^2 + 0x + 9 = 0$ and calculating the discriminant for this quadratic gives $b^2 - 4ac = -36$ which is less than zero.

You could rewrite it as $x^2 = -9$. However, since the square of every real number is positive or zero, there is no real number with a square of -9. This is an example of a quadratic equation which, up to now, you would have classified as having 'no real roots'.

Prior knowledge

You should know how to solve quadratic equations using the quadratic formula.

The existence of such equations was recognised for hundreds of years, in the same way that Greek mathematicians had accepted that $x + 10 = 9$ had no solution; the concept of a negative number had yet to be developed. The number system has expanded as mathematicians increased the range of mathematical problems they wanted to tackle.

You can solve the equation $x^2 + 9 = 0$ by extending the number system to include a new number, i (sometimes written as j). This has the property that $i^2 = -1$ and it follows the usual laws of algebra. i is called an **imaginary** number.

The square root of any negative number can be expressed in terms of i. For example, the solution of the equation $x^2 = -9$ is $x = \pm\sqrt{-9}$. This can be written as $\pm\sqrt{9} \times \sqrt{-1}$ which simplifies to $\pm 3i$.

Example 1.1

Use the quadratic formula to solve the quadratic equation $z^2 - 6z + 58 = 0$, simplifying your answer as far as possible.

💻 TECHNOLOGY

If your calculator has an equation solver, find out if it will give you the complex roots of this quadratic equation.

Solution

$z^2 - 6z + 58 = 0$ ← Using the quadratic formula with $a = 1$, $b = -6$ and $c = 58$.

$$z = \frac{6 \pm \sqrt{(-6)^2 - 4 \times 1 \times 58}}{2 \times 1}$$

$$= \frac{6 \pm \sqrt{-196}}{2}$$

$$= \frac{6 \pm 14i}{2}$$ ← $\sqrt{-196} = \sqrt{196} \times \sqrt{-1} = 14i$.

$$= 3 \pm 7i$$

3 is called the real part of the complex number $3 + 7i$ and is denoted $\text{Re}(z)$.

You will have noticed that the roots $3 + 7i$ and $3 - 7i$ of the quadratic equation $z^2 - 6z + 58 = 0$ have both a **real part** and an **imaginary part**.

7 is called the imaginary part of the complex number and is denoted $\text{Im}(z)$.

Notation

Any number z of the form $x + yi$, where x and y are real, is called a **complex number**.

The letter z is commonly used for complex numbers, and w is also used. In this chapter a complex number z is often denoted by $x + yi$, but other letters are sometimes used, such as $a + bi$.

x is called the real part of the complex number, denoted by $\text{Re}(z)$, and y is called the imaginary part, denoted by $\text{Im}(z)$.

Working with complex numbers

Discussion point

➔ What are the values of i^3, i^4, i^5, i^6 and i^7?

➔ Explain how you could quickly work out the value of i^n for any positive integer value of n.

The general methods for addition, subtraction and multiplication of complex numbers are straightforward.

Addition: add the real parts and add the imaginary parts.

For example, $(3 + 4i) + (2 - 8i) = (3 + 2) + (4 - 8)i$
$$= 5 - 4i$$

Subtraction: subtract the real parts and subtract the imaginary parts.

For example, $(6 - 9i) - (1 + 6i) = 5 - 15i$

Multiplication: multiply out the brackets in the usual way and simplify.

For example, $(7 + 2i)(3 - 4i) = 21 - 28i + 6i - 8i^2$

$$= 21 - 22i - 8(-1)$$

$$= 29 - 22i$$

When simplifying it is important to remember that $i^2 = -1$.

Division of complex numbers follows later in this chapter.

Discussion point

➔ What answer do you think Gerolamo Cardano might have obtained to the calculation $(5 + \sqrt{-15})(5 - \sqrt{-15})$?

 Historical note

Gerolamo Cardano (1501–1576) was an Italian mathematician and physicist who was the first known writer to explore calculations involving the square roots of negative quantities, in his 1545 publication *Ars magna* ('The Great Art'). He wanted to calculate:

$$\left(5 + \sqrt{-15}\right)\left(5 - \sqrt{-15}\right)$$

Some years later, an Italian engineer named Rafael Bombelli introduced the words 'plus of minus' to indicate $\sqrt{-1}$ and 'minus of minus' to indicate $-\sqrt{-1}$.

However, the general mathematical community was slow to accept these 'fictional' numbers, with the French mathematician and philosopher René Descartes rather dismissively describing them as 'imaginary'. Similarly, Isaac Newton described the numbers as 'impossible' and the mystification of Gottfried Leibniz is evident in the quote at the beginning of the chapter! In the end it was Leonhard Euler who eventually began to use the symbol i, the first letter of 'imaginarius' (imaginary) instead of writing $\sqrt{-1}$.

Equality of complex numbers

Two complex numbers $z = x + yi$ and $w = u + vi$ are equal if both $x = u$ and $y = v$. If $x \neq u$ or $y \neq v$, or both, then z and w are not equal.

A complex number $z = x + yi$ is zero only if $x = 0$ and $y = 0$.

You may feel that this is obvious, but it is interesting to compare this situation with the equality of rational numbers.

Discussion point

➔ Are the rational numbers $\frac{x}{y}$ and $\frac{u}{v}$ equal if $x = u$ and $y = v$?

➔ Is it possible for the rational numbers $\frac{x}{y}$ and $\frac{u}{v}$ to be equal if $x \neq u$ and $y \neq v$?

For two complex numbers to be equal the real parts must be equal and the imaginary parts must be equal. Using this result is described as **equating real and imaginary parts**, as shown in the following example.

Example 1.2

The complex numbers z_1 and z_2 are given by

$$z_1 = (3 - a) + (2b - 4)i$$

and

$$z_2 = (7b - 4) + (3a - 2)i.$$

(i) Given than z_1 and z_2 are equal, find the values of a and b.

(ii) Check your answer by substituting your values for a and b into the expressions above.

Solution

(i) $(3 - a) + (2b - 4)i = (7b - 4) + (3a - 2)i$

Equating real parts: $3 - a = 7b - 4$

> Equating real and imaginary parts leads to two equations.

Equating imaginary parts: $2b - 4 = 3a - 2$

$$\begin{cases} 7b + a = 7 \\ 2b - 3a = 2 \end{cases}$$

> Simplifying the equations.

Solving simultaneously gives $b = 1$ and $a = 0$.

(ii) Substituting $a = 0$ and $b = 1$ gives $z_1 = 3 - 2i$ and $z_2 = 3 - 2i$ so z_1 and z_2 are indeed equal.

Example 1.3

Find the square roots of $21 - 20i$.

Solution

Let a square root be $a + bi$, where a and b are real.

Then $(a + bi)^2 = 21 - 20i$

$a^2 + 2iab - b^2 = 21 - 20i$

Equate real and imaginary parts:

$a^2 - b^2 = 21$ ①
$2ab = -20$ ②

$b = -\dfrac{20}{2a} = -\dfrac{10}{a}$

> Make b the subject of equation ②.

Substitute into equation ①: $a^2 - \left(-\dfrac{10}{a}\right)^2 = 21$

$a^4 - 100 = 21a^2$

> Multiply out and simplify.

$a^4 - 21a^2 - 100 = 0$

> Rearrange.

$(a^2 - 25)(a^2 + 4) = 0$

> This is a quadratic equation in a^2.

Therefore $a^2 = 25$ or -4.

> Factorise.

But a must be real, so $a^2 = 25$ only.

Therefore $a = 5$ or -5.

If $a = 5$, $b = -2$

> Substituting back into equation ②.

If $a = -5$, $b = 2$.

> Note that, just as with the square roots of real numbers, one answer is the negative of the other.

Therefore the two possible square roots of $21 + 20i$ are $5 - 2i$ and $-5 + 2i$.

Discussion point

→ What would have happened if a^2 had been taken to be -4?

Exercise 1.1

Do not use a calculator in this exercise

① Write down the values of
   (i) i^9 (ii) i^{14} (iii) i^{31} (iv) i^{100}

② Find the following:
   (i) $(6 + 4i) + (3 - 5i)$ (ii) $(-6 + 4i) + (-3 + 5i)$
   (iii) $(6 + 4i) - (3 - 5i)$ (iv) $(-6 + 4i) - (-3 + 5i)$

③ Find the following:
   (i) $3(6 + 4i) + 2(3 - 5i)$ (ii) $3i(6 + 4i) + 2i(3 - 5i)$
   (iii) $(6 + 4i)^2$ (iv) $(6 + 4i)(3 - 5i)$

④ (i) Find the following:
   (a) $(6 + 4i)(6 - 4i)$
   (b) $(3 - 5i)(3 + 5i)$
   (c) $(6 + 4i)(6 - 4i)(3 - 5i)(3 + 5i)$
   (ii) What do you notice about the answers in part (i)?

⑤ Find the following:
   (i) $(3 - 7i)(2 + 2i)(5 - i)$ (ii) $(3 - 7i)^3$

⑥ Solve each of the following equations.
   In each case, check your solutions are correct by substituting the values back into the equation.
   (i) $z^2 + 2z + 2 = 0$ (ii) $z^2 - 2z + 5 = 0$
   (iii) $z^2 - 4z + 13 = 0$ (iv) $z^2 + 6z + 34 = 0$
   (v) $4z^2 - 4z + 17 = 0$ (vi) $z^2 + 4z + 6 = 0$

⑦ Given that the complex numbers
   $$z_1 = a^2 + (3 + 2b)i$$
   $$z_2 = (5a - 4) + b^2 i$$
   are equal, find the possible values of a and b.
   Hence list the possible pairs of complex numbers z_1 and z_2.

⑧ A complex number $z = a + bi$, where a and b are real, is squared to give an answer of $-16 + 30i$. Find the possible values of a and b.

⑨ Find the square roots of the following complex numbers.
   (i) $3 + 4i$
   (ii) $40 - 42i$

⑩ Figure 1.2 shows the graph of $y = x^2 - 4x + 3$.

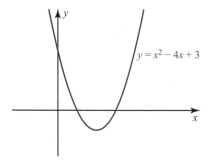

$y = x^2 - 4x + 3$

Figure 1.2

(i) Draw sketches of the curves $y = x^2 - 4x + 3$, $y = x^2 - 4x + 6$ and $y = x^2 - 4x + 8$ on the same axes.

(ii) Solve the equations

(a) $x^2 - 4x + 3 = 0$

(b) $x^2 - 4x + 6 = 0$

(c) $x^2 - 4x + 8 = 0$

(iii) Describe the relationship between the two roots for each of the three equations and how they relate to the graphs you sketched in part (i).

⑪ Given that $z = 2 + 3i$ is a root of the equation

$$z^2 + (a - i)z + 16 + bi = 0$$

where a and b are real, find a and b.

Explain why you cannot assume that the other root is $z = 2 - 3i$.

Given that the second root has the form $5 + ci$, find the other root of the equation.

2 Division of complex numbers

Complex conjugates

You have seen that the roots of a quadratic equation with real coefficients are almost the same, but have the opposite sign (+ and −) between the real and imaginary terms. For example, the roots of $x^2 - 4x + 13 = 0$ are $x = 2 + 3i$ and $x = 2 - 3i$. The pair of complex numbers $2 + 3i$ and $2 - 3i$ is called **a conjugate pair**. Each is the conjugate of the other.

In general the complex number $x - yi$ is called the **complex conjugate**, or just the conjugate, of $x + yi$. The conjugate of a complex number z is denoted by z^*.

Example 1.4

Given that $z = 3 + 5i$, find

(i) $z + z^*$ (ii) zz^*

Solution

(i) $z + z^* = (3 + 5i) + (3 - 5i)$

$= 6$

(ii) $zz^* = (3 + 5i)(3 - 5i)$

$= 9 + 15i - 15i - 25i^2$

$= 9 + 25$

$= 34$

ACTIVITY 1.3

Prove that $z + z^*$ and zz^* are both real for all complex numbers z.

You can see from the example above that $z + z^*$ and zz^* are both real. This is an example of an important general result: that the sum of two complex conjugates is real and that their product is also real.

Dividing complex numbers

You probably already know that you can write an expression like $\dfrac{2}{3 - \sqrt{2}}$

as a fraction with a rational denominator by multiplying the numerator and denominator by $3 + \sqrt{2}$.

$$\frac{2}{3 - \sqrt{2}} = \frac{2}{3 - \sqrt{2}} \times \frac{3 + \sqrt{2}}{3 + \sqrt{2}} = \frac{6 + 2\sqrt{2}}{9 - 2} = \frac{6 + 2\sqrt{2}}{7}$$

Because zz^* is always real, you can use a similar method to write an expression like $\dfrac{2}{3 - 5i}$ as a fraction with a real denominator, by multiplying the numerator and denominator by $3 + 5i$. ← 3 + 5i is the complex conjugate of 3 – 5i.

This is the basis for dividing one complex number by another.

Example 1.5

Find the real and imaginary parts of $\dfrac{1}{5 + 2i}$.

Solution

Multiply the numerator and denominator by $5 - 2i$. ← 5 – 2i is the complex conjugate of the denominator 5 + 2i.

$$\frac{1}{5 + 2i} = \frac{5 - 2i}{(5 + 2i)(5 - 2i)}$$

$$= \frac{5 - 2i}{25 + 4}$$

$$= \frac{5 - 2i}{29}$$

The real part is $\dfrac{5}{29}$ and the imaginary part is $-\dfrac{2}{29}$.

Example 1.6

Solve the equation $(2 + 3i)z = 9 - 4i$.

Solution

$$(2 + 3i)z = 9 - 4i$$

$$\Rightarrow z = \frac{9 - 4i}{2 + 3i}$$

Multiply top and bottom by 2 – 3i.

$$= \frac{(9 - 4i)(2 - 3i)}{(2 + 3i)(2 - 3i)}$$

$$= \frac{18 - 27i - 8i + 12i^2}{4 - 6i + 6i - 9i^2}$$

Notice how the –6i and + 6i terms will cancel to produce a real denominator.

$$= \frac{6 - 35i}{13}$$

Using 12i² = –12.

$$= \frac{6}{13} - \frac{35}{13}i$$

Discussion point

➜ What are the values of $\dfrac{1}{i}$, $\dfrac{1}{i^2}$, $\dfrac{1}{i^3}$ and $\dfrac{1}{i^4}$?

➜ Explain how you would work out the value of $\dfrac{1}{i^n}$ for any positive integer value n.

Exercise 1.2

TECHNOLOGY

If your calculator handles complex numbers, you can use it to check your answers.

① Express these complex numbers in the form $x + y\mathrm{i}$.

(i) $\dfrac{3}{7 - \mathrm{i}}$ (ii) $\dfrac{3}{7 + \mathrm{i}}$ (iii) $\dfrac{3\mathrm{i}}{7 - \mathrm{i}}$ (iv) $\dfrac{3\mathrm{i}}{7 + \mathrm{i}}$

② Express these complex numbers in the form $x + y\mathrm{i}$.

(i) $\dfrac{3 + 5\mathrm{i}}{2 - 3\mathrm{i}}$ (ii) $\dfrac{2 - 3\mathrm{i}}{3 + 5\mathrm{i}}$ (iii) $\dfrac{3 - 5\mathrm{i}}{2 + 3\mathrm{i}}$ (iv) $\dfrac{2 + 3\mathrm{i}}{3 - 5\mathrm{i}}$

③ Simplify the following, giving your answers in the form $x + y\mathrm{i}$.

(i) $\dfrac{(12 - 5\mathrm{i})(2 + 2\mathrm{i})}{4 - 3\mathrm{i}}$

(ii) $\dfrac{12 - 5\mathrm{i}}{(4 - 3\mathrm{i})^2}$

④ $z = 3 - 6\mathrm{i}$, $w = -2 + 9\mathrm{i}$ and $q = 6 + 3\mathrm{i}$.

Write down the values of the following:

(i) $z + z^*$ (ii) ww^* (iii) $q^* + q$

(iv) z^*z (v) $w + w^*$ (vi) qq^*

⑤ Given that $z = 2 + 3\mathrm{i}$ and $w = 6 - 4\mathrm{i}$, find the following:

(i) $\mathrm{Re}(z)$ (ii) $\mathrm{Im}(z)$ (iii) z^*

(iv) w^* (v) $z^* + w^*$ (vi) $z^* - w^*$

⑥ Given that $z = 2 + 3\mathrm{i}$ and $w = 6 - 4\mathrm{i}$, find the following:

(i) $\mathrm{Im}(z + z^*)$ (ii) $\mathrm{Re}(w - w^*)$ (iii) $zz^* - ww^*$

(iv) $(z^3)^*$ (v) $(z^*)^3$ (vi) $zw^* - z^*w$

⑦ Given that $z_1 = 2 - 5\mathrm{i}$, $z_2 = 4 + 10\mathrm{i}$ and $z_3 = 6 - 5\mathrm{i}$, find the following in the form $a + b\mathrm{i}$, where a and b are rational numbers.

(i) $\dfrac{z_1 z_2}{z_3}$ (ii) $\dfrac{(z_3)^2}{z_1}$ (iii) $\dfrac{z_1 + z_2 - z_3}{(z_3)^2}$

⑧ Solve these equations.

(i) $(1 + \mathrm{i})z = 3 + \mathrm{i}$

(ii) $(2 - \mathrm{i})z + (2 - 6\mathrm{i}) = 4 - 7\mathrm{i}$

(iii) $(3 - 4\mathrm{i})(z - 1) = 10 - 5\mathrm{i}$

(iv) $(3 + 5\mathrm{i})(z + 2 - 5\mathrm{i}) = 6 + 3\mathrm{i}$

⑨ Find the values of a and b such that $\dfrac{2 - 5\mathrm{i}}{3 + 2\mathrm{i}} = \dfrac{a + b\mathrm{i}}{1 - \mathrm{i}}$.

⑩ The complex number $w = a + b\mathrm{i}$, where a and b are real, satisfies the equation $(5 - 2\mathrm{i})w = 67 + 37\mathrm{i}$.

(i) Using the method of equating coefficients, find the values of a and b.

(ii) Using division of complex numbers, find the values of a and b.

⑪ (i) For $z = 5 - 8\mathrm{i}$ find $\dfrac{1}{z} + \dfrac{1}{z^*}$ in its simplest form.

(ii) Write down the value of $\dfrac{1}{z} + \dfrac{1}{z^*}$ for $z = 5 + 8\mathrm{i}$.

⑫ For $z = x + y\mathrm{i}$, find $\dfrac{1}{z} + \dfrac{1}{z^*}$ in terms of x and y.

⑬ Let $z_1 = x_1 + y_1\mathrm{i}$ and $z_2 = x_2 + y_2\mathrm{i}$.

Show that $(z_1 + z_2)^* = z_1^* + z_2^*$.

⑭ Find real numbers a and b such that $\dfrac{a}{3+i} + \dfrac{b}{1+2i} = 1 - i$.

⑮ Find all the numbers z, real or complex, for which $z^2 = 2z^*$.

⑯ The complex numbers z and w satisfy the following simultaneous equations.

$z + w\mathrm{i} = 13$

$3z - 4w = 2\mathrm{i}$

Find z and w, giving your answers in the form $a + b\mathrm{i}$.

Discussion point

→ Why is it not possible to show a complex number on a number line?

3 Representing complex numbers geometrically

A complex number $x + y\mathrm{i}$ can be represented by the point with cartesian coordinates (x, y).

For example, in Figure 1.3,

$2 + 3\mathrm{i}$ is represented by $(2, 3)$

$-5 - 4\mathrm{i}$ is represented by $(-5, -4)$

$2\mathrm{i}$ is represented by $(0, 2)$

7 is represented by $(7, 0)$.

All real numbers are represented by points on the x-axis, which is therefore called the **real axis**. Purely imaginary numbers which have no real part (so they are of the form $0 + y\mathrm{i}$) give points on the y-axis, which is called the **imaginary axis**.

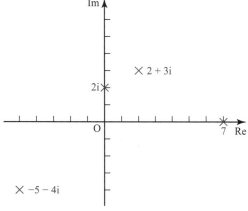

Figure 1.3

These axes are labelled as Re and Im.

This geometrical illustration of complex numbers is called the **complex plane** or the **Argand diagram**.

The Argand diagram is named after Jean-Robert Argand (1768–1822), a self-taught Swiss book-keeper who published an account of it in 1806.

ACTIVITY 1.4

(i) Copy Figure 1.3.

For each of the four given points z, mark also the point $-z$.

Describe the geometrical transformation which maps the point representing z to the point representing $-z$.

(ii) For each of the points z, mark the point z^*, the complex conjugate of z.

Describe the geometrical transformation which maps the point representing z to the point representing z^*.

Representing the sum and difference of complex numbers

In Figure 1.4 the complex number $z = x + y\mathrm{i}$ is shown as a vector on an Argand diagram.

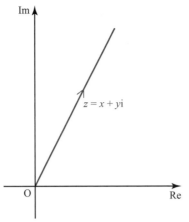

Figure 1.4

The use of vectors can be helpful in illustrating addition and subtraction of complex numbers on an Argand diagram. Figure 1.5 shows that the position vectors representing z_1 and z_2 form two sides of a parallelogram, the diagonal of which is the vector $z_1 + z_2$.

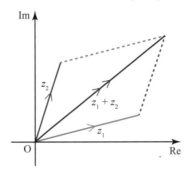

Figure 1.5

The addition can also be shown as a triangle of vectors, as in Figure 1.6.

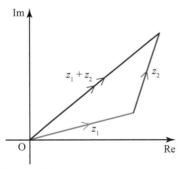

Figure 1.6

In Figure 1.7 you can see that $z_2 + w = z_1$ and so $w = z_1 - z_2$.

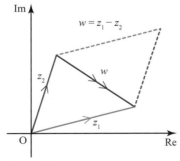

Figure 1.7

This shows that the complex number $z_1 - z_2$ is represented by the vector from the point representing z_2 to the point representing z_1, as shown in Figure 1.8.

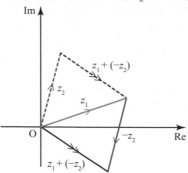

Figure 1.8

Notice the order of the points: the vector representing $z_1 - z_2$ starts at the point representing z_2 and goes to the point representing z_1.

Exercise 1.3

① Represent each of the following complex numbers on a single Argand diagram.

(i) $3 + 2i$ (ii) $4i$ (iii) $-5 + i$

(iv) -2 (v) $-6 - 5i$ (vi) $4 - 3i$

② Given that $z = 2 - 4i$, represent the following by points on a single Argand diagram.

(i) z (ii) $-z$ (iii) z^* (iv) $-z^*$

(v) iz (vi) $-iz$ (vii) iz^* (viii) $(iz)^*$

What is the geometrical relationship between a point representing z and a point representing z^* on the Argand diagram?

③ Given that $z = 10 + 5i$ and $w = 1 + 2i$, represent the following complex numbers on an Argand diagram.

(i) z (ii) w (iii) $z + w$

(iv) $z - w$ (v) $w - z$

④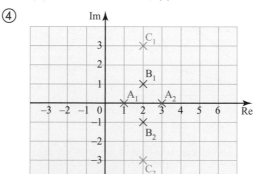

Figure 1.9

(i) Find the quadratic equation which has roots A_1 and A_2.

(ii) Find the quadratic equation which has roots B_1 and B_2.

(iii) Find the quadratic equation which has roots C_1 and C_2.

(iv) What do you notice about your answers to (i), (ii) and (iii)?

⑤ Give a geometrical proof that $(-z)^* = -(z^*)$.

⑥ Let $z = 1 + i$.

(i) Find z^n for $n = -1, 0, 1, 2, 3, 4, 5$

(ii) Plot each of the points z^n from part (i) on a single Argand diagram. Join each point to its predecessor and to the origin.

(iii) Find the distance of each point from the origin.

(iv) What do you notice?

⑦ Figure 1.10 shows the complex number $z = a + ib$. The distance of the point representing z from the origin is denoted by r.

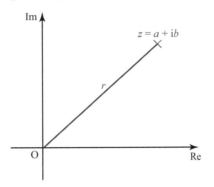

Figure 1.10

(i) Find an expression for r, and hence prove that $r^2 = zz^*$.

A second complex number, w, is given by $w = c + di$. The distance of the point representing w from the origin is denoted by s.

(ii) Write down an expression for s.

(iii) Find zw, and prove that the distance of the point representing zw from the origin is given by rs.

LEARNING OUTCOMES

When you have completed this chapter you should be able to:

➤ understand how complex numbers extend the number system

➤ solve quadratic equations with complex roots

➤ know what is meant by the terms real part, imaginary part and complex conjugate

➤ add, subtract, multiply and divide complex numbers

➤ solve problems involving complex numbers by equating real and imaginary parts

➤ find the two square roots of a complex number, using an algebraic method

➤ represent a complex number on an Argand diagram

➤ represent addition and subtraction of two complex numbers on an Argand diagram.

KEY POINTS

1 Complex numbers are of the form $z = x + y\text{i}$, where x and y are real numbers, with $\text{i}^2 = -1$.

   x is called the real part, $\text{Re}(z)$, and y is called the imaginary part, $\text{Im}(z)$.

2 The conjugate of $z = x + y\text{i}$ is $z^* = x - y\text{i}$.

3 To add or subtract complex numbers, add or subtract the real and imaginary parts separately.

   $$(x_1 + y_1\text{i}) + (x_2 + y_2\text{i}) = (x_1 + x_2) + (y_1 + y_2)\text{i}$$

   $$(x_1 + y_1\text{i}) - (x_2 + y_2\text{i}) = (x_1 - x_2) + (y_1 - y_2)\text{i}$$

4 To multiply complex numbers, expand the brackets then simplify using the fact that $\text{i}^2 = -1$.

5 To divide complex numbers, write as a fraction, then multiply top and bottom by the conjugate of the bottom and simplify the answer.

6 Two complex numbers $z_1 = x_1 + y_1\text{i}$ and $z_2 = x_2 + y_2\text{i}$ are equal only if $x_1 = x_2$ and $y_1 = y_2$.

7 The complex number $z = x + y\text{i}$ can be represented geometrically as the point (x, y).

   This geometrical representation is called an Argand diagram.

8 The point representing z^* on an Argand diagram is the reflection in the real axis of the point representing z.

FUTURE USES

■ In Chapter 5 you will look at how complex numbers can be used to describe sets of points in the Argand diagram.

2 Matrices and transformations

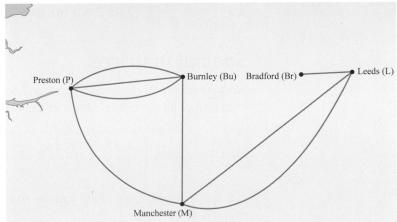

Figure 2.1 Illustration of some major roads and motorways joining some towns and cities in the north of England.

Discussion point

→ How many direct routes (without going through any other town) are there from Preston to Burnley? What about Manchester to Leeds? Preston to Manchester? Burnley to Leeds?

1 Matrices

You can represent the number of direct routes between each pair of towns (shown in Figure 2.1) in an array of numbers like this:

This array is called a **matrix** (the plural is **matrices**) and is usually written inside curved brackets.

	Br	Bu	L	M	P
Br	0	0	1	0	0
Bu	0	0	0	1	3
L	1	0	0	2	0
M	0	1	2	0	1
P	0	3	0	1	0

$$\begin{pmatrix} 0 & 0 & 1 & 0 & 0 \\ 0 & 0 & 0 & 1 & 3 \\ 1 & 0 & 0 & 2 & 0 \\ 0 & 1 & 2 & 0 & 1 \\ 0 & 3 & 0 & 1 & 0 \end{pmatrix}$$

It is usual to represent matrices by capital letters, often in bold print.

A matrix consists of rows and columns, and the entries in the various cells are known as **elements**.

The matrix $\mathbf{M} = \begin{pmatrix} 0 & 0 & 1 & 0 & 0 \\ 0 & 0 & 0 & 1 & 3 \\ 1 & 0 & 0 & 2 & 0 \\ 0 & 1 & 2 & 0 & 1 \\ 0 & 3 & 0 & 1 & 0 \end{pmatrix}$ representing the routes between the

towns and cities has 25 elements, arranged in five rows and five columns. $\mathbf{M}$ is described as a 5×5 matrix, and this is the **order** of the matrix. You state the number of rows first, then the number of columns. So, for example, the matrix

$\mathbf{A} = \begin{pmatrix} 3 & -1 & 4 \\ 2 & 0 & 5 \end{pmatrix}$ is a 2×3 matrix and $\mathbf{B} = \begin{pmatrix} 4 & -4 \\ 3 & 4 \\ 0 & -2 \end{pmatrix}$ is a 3×2 matrix.

Special matrices

Some matrices are described by special names which relate to the number of rows and columns or the nature of the elements.

Matrices such as $\begin{pmatrix} 4 & 2 \\ 1 & 0 \end{pmatrix}$ and $\begin{pmatrix} 3 & 5 & 1 \\ 2 & 0 & -4 \\ 1 & 7 & 3 \end{pmatrix}$ which have the same number

of rows as columns are called **square matrices** (as opposed to **rectangular matrices**).

The matrix $\begin{pmatrix} 1 & 0 \\ 0 & 1 \end{pmatrix}$ is called the 2×2 **identity matrix** or **unit matrix**, and

similarly $\begin{pmatrix} 1 & 0 & 0 \\ 0 & 1 & 0 \\ 0 & 0 & 1 \end{pmatrix}$ is called the 3×3 identity matrix. Identity matrices must

be square, and are usually denoted by I.

The matrix $\mathbf{O} = \begin{pmatrix} 0 & 0 \\ 0 & 0 \end{pmatrix}$ is called the 2×2 **zero matrix** or **null matrix**.

Zero matrices can be of any order.

Two matrices are said to be **equal** if and only if they have the same order and each element in one matrix is equal to the corresponding element in the other matrix. So, for example, the matrices $\mathbf{A}$ and $\mathbf{D}$ below are equal, but $\mathbf{B}$ and $\mathbf{C}$ are not equal to any of the other matrices.

$$\mathbf{A} = \begin{pmatrix} 1 & 3 \\ 2 & 4 \end{pmatrix} \qquad \mathbf{B} = \begin{pmatrix} 1 & 2 \\ 3 & 4 \end{pmatrix} \qquad \mathbf{C} = \begin{pmatrix} 1 & 3 & 0 \\ 2 & 4 & 0 \end{pmatrix} \qquad \mathbf{D} = \begin{pmatrix} 1 & 3 \\ 2 & 4 \end{pmatrix}$$

The **transpose** of a matrix is obtained by writing its rows as columns, and vice versa. In the above examples, the transpose of $\mathbf{A}$, denoted by $\mathbf{A}^T$, is $\begin{pmatrix} 1 & 2 \\ 3 & 4 \end{pmatrix}$ and

the transpose of $\mathbf{C}$ is $\mathbf{C}^T = \begin{pmatrix} 1 & 2 \\ 3 & 4 \\ 0 & 0 \end{pmatrix}$.

Working with matrices

Matrices can be added or subtracted if they are of the same order.

$$\begin{pmatrix} 2 & 4 & 0 \\ -1 & 3 & 5 \end{pmatrix} + \begin{pmatrix} 1 & -1 & 4 \\ 2 & 0 & -5 \end{pmatrix} = \begin{pmatrix} 3 & 3 & 4 \\ 1 & 3 & 0 \end{pmatrix}$$

← Add the elements in corresponding positions.

$$\begin{pmatrix} 2 & -3 \\ 4 & 1 \end{pmatrix} - \begin{pmatrix} 7 & -3 \\ -1 & 2 \end{pmatrix} = \begin{pmatrix} -5 & 0 \\ 5 & -1 \end{pmatrix}$$

← Subtract the elements in corresponding positions.

But $\begin{pmatrix} 2 & 4 & 0 \\ -1 & 3 & 5 \end{pmatrix} + \begin{pmatrix} 2 & -3 \\ 4 & 1 \end{pmatrix}$ cannot be evaluated because the matrices are

not of the same order. These matrices are **non-conformable** for addition.

If you add a zero matrix to any matrix $\mathbf{A}$ of the same order, then $\mathbf{A}$ is unchanged:

$$\begin{pmatrix} 0 & 0 \\ 0 & 0 \end{pmatrix} + \begin{pmatrix} 1 & 2 \\ -3 & 4 \end{pmatrix} = \begin{pmatrix} 1 & 2 \\ -3 & 4 \end{pmatrix}$$

You can also multiply a matrix by a **scalar** number:

$$2\begin{pmatrix} 3 & -4 \\ 0 & 6 \end{pmatrix} = \begin{pmatrix} 6 & -8 \\ 0 & 12 \end{pmatrix}$$

← Multiply each of the elements by 2.

☐ TECHNOLOGY

You can use a calculator to add and subtract matrices of the same order and to multiply a matrix by a number. For your calculator, find out:

- the method for inputting matrices
- how to add and subtract matrices
- how to multiply a matrix by a number for matrices of varying sizes.

Associativity and commutativity

When working with numbers the properties of **associativity** and **commutativity** are often used.

Associativity

Addition of numbers is **associative**.

$$(3 + 5) + 8 = 3 + (5 + 8)$$

When you add any three numbers, it does not matter how the numbers are grouped, the answer will be the same.

Commutativity

Addition of numbers is **commutative**.

$$4 + 5 = 5 + 4$$

When you add any two numbers, the order of the numbers can be reversed and the answer will still be the same.

Discussion points

→ Give examples to show that subtraction of numbers is not commutative or associative.

→ Are matrix addition and matrix subtraction associative and/or commutative?

Exercise 2.1

① Write down the order of these matrices.

(i) $\begin{pmatrix} 2 & 4 \\ 6 & 0 \\ -3 & 7 \end{pmatrix}$ (ii) $\begin{pmatrix} 0 & 8 & 4 \\ -2 & -3 & 1 \\ 5 & 3 & -2 \end{pmatrix}$ (iii) $\begin{pmatrix} 7 & -3 \end{pmatrix}$ (iv) $\begin{pmatrix} 1 \\ 2 \\ 3 \\ 4 \\ 5 \end{pmatrix}$

(v) $\begin{pmatrix} 2 & -6 & 4 & 9 \\ 5 & 10 & 11 & -4 \end{pmatrix}$ (vi) $\begin{pmatrix} 8 & 5 \\ -2 & 0 \\ 3 & -9 \end{pmatrix}$

② For the matrices

$$\mathbf{A} = \begin{pmatrix} 2 & -3 \\ 0 & 4 \end{pmatrix} \quad \mathbf{B} = \begin{pmatrix} 7 & -3i \\ i & 4 \end{pmatrix} \quad \mathbf{C} = \begin{pmatrix} 3 & 5 & -9 \\ 2 & 1 & 4 \end{pmatrix} \quad \mathbf{D} = \begin{pmatrix} 0 & -4 & 5 \\ 2 & 1 & 8 \end{pmatrix}$$

$$\mathbf{E} = \begin{pmatrix} -3 & 5 \\ -2 & 7 \end{pmatrix} \quad \mathbf{F} = \begin{pmatrix} 1 \\ 3 \\ 5 \end{pmatrix}$$

find, where possible

(i) $\mathbf{A} - \mathbf{E}$ (ii) $\mathbf{C} + \mathbf{D}$ (iii) $\mathbf{E} + \mathbf{A} - \mathbf{B}$ (iv) $\mathbf{F} + \mathbf{D}$ (v) $\mathbf{D} - \mathbf{C}$
(vi) $4\mathbf{F}$ (vii) $3\mathbf{C} + 2\mathbf{D}$ (viii) $\mathbf{B} + 2\mathbf{F}$ (ix) $\mathbf{E} - (2\mathbf{B} - \mathbf{A})$
(x) $\mathbf{A}^T$ (xi) $\mathbf{C}^T$ (xii) $\mathbf{F}^T$

③ The diagram in Figure 2.2 shows the number of direct flights on one day offered by an airline between cities P, Q, R and S.

The same information is also given in the partly-completed matrix **X**.

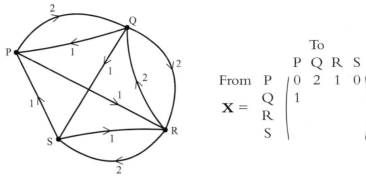

$$\text{From} \quad \begin{matrix} \\ P \\ Q \\ R \\ S \end{matrix} \quad \mathbf{X} = \begin{array}{c} \text{To} \\ \begin{matrix} P & Q & R & S \end{matrix} \\ \begin{pmatrix} 0 & 2 & 1 & 0 \\ 1 & & & \\ & & & \\ & & & \end{pmatrix} \end{array}$$

Figure 2.2

(i) Copy and complete the matrix **X**.

A second airline also offers flights between these four cities. The following matrix represents the total number of direct flights offered by the two airlines.

$$\begin{pmatrix} 0 & 2 & 3 & 2 \\ 2 & 0 & 2 & 1 \\ 2 & 2 & 0 & 3 \\ 1 & 0 & 3 & 0 \end{pmatrix}$$

(ii) Find the matrix **Y** representing the flights offered by the second airline.

(iii) Draw a diagram similar to the one in Figure 2.2, showing the flights offered by the second airline.

④ Find the values of w, x, y and z such that

$$\begin{pmatrix} 3 & w \\ -1 & 4 \end{pmatrix} + x \begin{pmatrix} 2 & -1 \\ y & z \end{pmatrix} = \begin{pmatrix} -9 & 8 \\ 11 & -8 \end{pmatrix}.$$

⑤ Find the possible values of p and q such that

$$\begin{pmatrix} p^2 & -3 \\ 2 & 9 \end{pmatrix} - \begin{pmatrix} 5p & -2 \\ -7 & q^2 \end{pmatrix} = \begin{pmatrix} 6 & -1 \\ 9 & 4 \end{pmatrix}.$$

⑥ Four local football teams took part in a competition in which they each played each other twice, once at home and once away. Figure 2.3 shows the results matrix after half of the games had been played.

	Win	Draw	Lose	Goals for	Goals against
City	2	1	0	6	3
Rangers	0	0	3	2	8
Town	2	0	1	4	3
United	1	1	1	5	3

Figure 2.3

(i) The results of the next three matches are as follows:

City 2   Rangers 0

Town 3   United 3

City 2   Town 4

Find the results matrix for these three matches and hence find the complete results matrix for all the matches so far.

(ii) Here is the complete results matrix for the whole competition.

$$\begin{pmatrix} 4 & 1 & 1 & 12 & 8 \\ 1 & 1 & 4 & 5 & 12 \\ 3 & 1 & 2 & 12 & 10 \\ 1 & 3 & 2 & 10 & 9 \end{pmatrix}$$

Find the results matrix for the last three matches (City vs United, Rangers vs Town and Rangers vs United) and deduce the result of each of these three matches.

⑦ A mail-order clothing company stocks a jacket in three different sizes and four different colours.

The matrix $\mathbf{P} = \begin{pmatrix} 17 & 8 & 10 & 15 \\ 6 & 12 & 19 & 3 \\ 24 & 10 & 11 & 6 \end{pmatrix}$ represents the number of jackets in

stock at the start of one week.

The matrix $\mathbf{Q} = \begin{pmatrix} 2 & 5 & 3 & 0 \\ 1 & 3 & 4 & 6 \\ 5 & 0 & 2 & 3 \end{pmatrix}$ represents the number of orders for

jackets received during the week.

(i) Find the matrix $\mathbf{P} - \mathbf{Q}$.

What does this matrix represent? What does the negative element in the matrix mean?

A delivery of jackets is received from the manufacturers during the week.

The matrix $\mathbf{R} = \begin{pmatrix} 5 & 10 & 10 & 5 \\ 10 & 10 & 5 & 15 \\ 0 & 0 & 5 & 5 \end{pmatrix}$ shows the number of jackets received.

(ii) Find the matrix which represents the number of jackets in stock at the end of the week after all the orders have been dispatched.

(iii) Assuming that this week is typical, find the matrix which represents sales of jackets over a six-week period. How realistic is this assumption?

2 Multiplication of matrices

When you multiply two matrices you do not just multiply corresponding terms. Instead you follow a slightly more complicated procedure. The following example will help you to understand the rationale for the way it is done.

There are four ways of scoring points in rugby: a try (five points), a conversion (two points), a penalty (three points) and a drop goal (three points). In a match Tonga scored three tries, one conversion, two penalties and one drop goal.

So their score was

$3 \times 5 + 1 \times 2 + 2 \times 3 + 1 \times 3 = 26$.

You can write this information using matrices. The tries, conversions, penalties and drop goals that Tonga scored are written as the 1×4 row matrix $(3 \; 1 \; 2 \; 1)$ and

the points for the different methods of scoring as the 4×1 column matrix $\begin{pmatrix} 5 \\ 2 \\ 3 \\ 3 \end{pmatrix}$.

These are combined to give the 1×1 matrix $(3 \times 5 + 1 \times 2 + 2 \times 3 + 1 \times 3) = (26)$.

Combining matrices in this way is called **matrix multiplication** and this

example is written as $(3 \quad 1 \quad 2 \quad 1) \times \begin{pmatrix} 5 \\ 2 \\ 3 \\ 3 \end{pmatrix} = (26)$.

The use of matrices can be extended to include the points scored by the other team, Japan. They scored two tries, two conversions, four penalties and one drop goal. This information can be written together with Tonga's scores as a 2×4 matrix, with one row for Tonga and the other for Japan. The multiplication is then written as:

$$\begin{pmatrix} 3 & 1 & 2 & 1 \\ 2 & 2 & 4 & 1 \end{pmatrix} \times \begin{pmatrix} 5 \\ 2 \\ 3 \\ 3 \end{pmatrix} = \begin{pmatrix} 26 \\ 29 \end{pmatrix}.$$

So Japan scored 29 points and won the match.

This example shows you two important points about matrix multiplication. Look at the orders of the matrices involved.

The two 'middle' numbers, in this case 4, must be the same for it to be possible to multiply two matrices. If two matrices can be multiplied, they are **conformable for multiplication**.

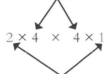

$2 \times 4 \; \times \; 4 \times 1$

The two 'outside' numbers give you the order of the product matrix, in this case 2 x 1.

You can see from the previous example that multiplying matrices involves multiplying each element in a row of the left-hand matrix by each element in a column of the right-hand matrix and then adding these products.

Multiplication of matrices

Example 2.1

Find $\begin{pmatrix} 10 & 3 \\ -2 & 7 \end{pmatrix} \begin{pmatrix} 5 \\ 2 \end{pmatrix}$.

Solution

The product will have order 2 × 1.

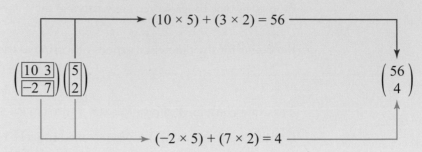

$$(10 \times 5) + (3 \times 2) = 56$$

$$\begin{pmatrix} \boxed{10\ \ 3} \\ \boxed{-2\ \ 7} \end{pmatrix} \begin{pmatrix} \boxed{5} \\ \boxed{2} \end{pmatrix} \qquad \begin{pmatrix} 56 \\ 4 \end{pmatrix}$$

$$(-2 \times 5) + (7 \times 2) = 4$$

Figure 2.4

Example 2.2

Find $\begin{pmatrix} 1 & 3 \\ -2 & 5 \end{pmatrix} \begin{pmatrix} 4 & 3 & 0 \\ -2 & -3 & 1 \end{pmatrix}$.

Solution

The order of this product is 2 × 3.

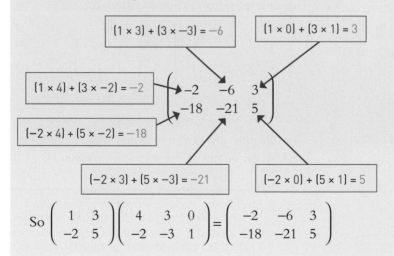

$(1 \times 3) + (3 \times -3) = -6$

$(1 \times 0) + (3 \times 1) = 3$

$(1 \times 4) + (3 \times -2) = -2$

$\begin{pmatrix} -2 & -6 & 3 \\ -18 & -21 & 5 \end{pmatrix}$

$(-2 \times 4) + (5 \times -2) = -18$

$(-2 \times 3) + (5 \times -3) = -21$

$(-2 \times 0) + (5 \times 1) = 5$

So $\begin{pmatrix} 1 & 3 \\ -2 & 5 \end{pmatrix} \begin{pmatrix} 4 & 3 & 0 \\ -2 & -3 & 1 \end{pmatrix} = \begin{pmatrix} -2 & -6 & 3 \\ -18 & -21 & 5 \end{pmatrix}$

Discussion point

➜ if $\mathbf{A} = \begin{pmatrix} 1 & 3 & 5 \\ -2 & 4 & 1 \\ 0 & 3 & 7 \end{pmatrix}$, $\mathbf{B} = \begin{pmatrix} 8 & -1 \\ -2 & 3 \\ 4 & 0 \end{pmatrix}$ and $\mathbf{C} = \begin{pmatrix} 5 & 0 \\ 3 & -4 \end{pmatrix}$

➜ which of the products **AB**, **BA**, **AC**, **CA**, **BC** and **CB** exist?

Example 2.3

Find $\begin{pmatrix} 3 & 2 \\ -1 & 4 \end{pmatrix}\begin{pmatrix} 1 & 0 \\ 0 & 1 \end{pmatrix}$.

What do you notice?

The matrix $\begin{pmatrix} 1 & 0 \\ 0 & 1 \end{pmatrix}$ is called **the 2 × 2 identity matrix**.

Solution

The order of this product is 2 × 2.

$$\begin{pmatrix} 3 & 2 \\ -1 & 4 \end{pmatrix}\begin{pmatrix} 1 & 0 \\ 0 & 1 \end{pmatrix} = \begin{pmatrix} 3 & 2 \\ -1 & 4 \end{pmatrix}$$

$(3 \times 1) + (2 \times 0) = 3$

$(3 \times 0) + (2 \times 1) = 2$

$(-1 \times 0) + (4 \times 1) = 4$

$(-1 \times 1) + (4 \times 0) = -1$

Multiplying a matrix by the identity matrix has no effect.

Multiplying a matrix by a compatible zero matrix gives the zero matrix.

$$\begin{pmatrix} 0 & 0 \\ 0 & 0 \end{pmatrix} \times \begin{pmatrix} 1 & 2 \\ -3 & 4 \end{pmatrix} = \begin{pmatrix} 0 & 0 \\ 0 & 0 \end{pmatrix}$$

Properties of matrix multiplication

In this section you will look at whether matrix multiplication is:

■ commutative

■ associative.

On page 18 you saw that for numbers, addition is both associative and commutative. Multiplication is also both associative and commutative. For example:

$(3 \times 4) \times 5 = 3 \times (4 \times 5)$

and

$3 \times 4 = 4 \times 3$

ACTIVITY 2.1

Using $\mathbf{A} = \begin{pmatrix} 2 & -1 \\ 3 & 4 \end{pmatrix}$ and $\mathbf{B} = \begin{pmatrix} -4 & 0 \\ -2 & 1 \end{pmatrix}$ find the products **AB** and **BA** and hence comment on whether or not matrix multiplication is commutative. Find a different pair of matrices, **C** and **D**, such that **CD = DC**.

ACTIVITY 2.2

Using $\mathbf{A} = \begin{pmatrix} 2 & -1 \\ 3 & 4 \end{pmatrix}$, $\mathbf{B} = \begin{pmatrix} -4 & 0 \\ -2 & 1 \end{pmatrix}$ and $\mathbf{C} = \begin{pmatrix} 1 & 2 \\ 2 & 3 \end{pmatrix}$, find the matrix products:

(i)   **AB**

(ii) **BC**

(iii) **(AB)C**

(iv) **A(BC)**

Does your answer suggest that matrix multiplication is associative?

Is this true for all 2 × 2 matrices? How can you prove your answer?

Exercise 2.2

In this exercise, do not use a calculator unless asked to. A calculator can be used for checking answers.

① Write down the orders of these matrices.

(i)   (a) $\mathbf{A} = \begin{pmatrix} 3 & 4 & -1 \\ 0 & 2 & 3 \\ 1 & 5 & 0 \end{pmatrix}$ (b) $\mathbf{B} = \begin{pmatrix} 2 & 3 & 6 \end{pmatrix}$

(c) $\mathbf{C} = \begin{pmatrix} 4 & 9 & 2 \\ 1 & -3 & 0 \end{pmatrix}$ (d) $\mathbf{D} = \begin{pmatrix} 0 & 2 & 4 & 2 \\ 0 & -3 & -8 & 1 \end{pmatrix}$

(e) $\mathbf{E} = \begin{pmatrix} 3 \\ 6 \end{pmatrix}$ (f) $\mathbf{F} = \begin{pmatrix} 2 & 5 & 0 & -4 & 1 \\ -3 & 9 & -3 & 2 & 2 \\ 1 & 0 & 0 & 10 & 4 \end{pmatrix}$

(ii) Which of the following matrix products can be found? For those that can state the order of the matrix product.

(a) **AE**   (b) **AF**   (c) **FA**   (d) **CA**   (e) **DC**

② Calculate these products.

(i) $\begin{pmatrix} 3 & 0 \\ 5 & -1 \end{pmatrix}\begin{pmatrix} 7 & 2 \\ 4 & -3 \end{pmatrix}$

(ii) $\begin{pmatrix} 2 & -3 & 5 \end{pmatrix}\begin{pmatrix} 0 & 2 \\ 5 & 8 \\ -3 & 1 \end{pmatrix}$

(iii) $\begin{pmatrix} 2 & 5 & -1 & 0 \\ 3 & 6 & 4 & -3 \end{pmatrix}\begin{pmatrix} 1 \\ -9 \\ 11 \\ -2 \end{pmatrix}$

Check your answers using the matrix function on a calculator if possible.

③ Using the matrices $\mathbf{A} = \begin{pmatrix} 5 & 9 \\ -2 & 7 \end{pmatrix}$ and $\mathbf{B} = \begin{pmatrix} -3 & 5 \\ 2 & -9 \end{pmatrix}$, confirm that matrix multiplication is not commutative.

④ For the matrices

$$\mathbf{A} = \begin{pmatrix} 3 & 1 \\ 2 & 4 \end{pmatrix} \quad \mathbf{B} = \begin{pmatrix} -3 & 7 \\ 2 & 5 \end{pmatrix} \quad \mathbf{C} = \begin{pmatrix} 2 & 3 & 4 \\ 5 & 7 & 1 \end{pmatrix}$$

$$\mathbf{D} = \begin{pmatrix} 3 & 4 \\ 7 & 0 \\ 1 & -2 \end{pmatrix} \quad \mathbf{E} = \begin{pmatrix} 4 & 7 \\ 3 & -2 \\ 1 & 5 \end{pmatrix} \quad \mathbf{F} = \begin{pmatrix} 3 & 7 & -5 \\ 2 & 6 & 0 \\ -1 & 4 & 8 \end{pmatrix}$$

calculate, where possible, the following:

(i) **AB**   (ii) **BA**   (iii) **CD**   (iv) **DC**   (v) **EF**   (vi) **FE**

⑤ For the matrices

$$\mathbf{I} = \begin{pmatrix} i & 0 \\ 0 & i \end{pmatrix} \quad \mathbf{J} = \begin{pmatrix} 0 & -i \\ i & 0 \end{pmatrix} \quad \mathbf{K} = \begin{pmatrix} 2i & 1+i \\ 1-i & i \end{pmatrix}$$

calculate the following:

(i) **IJ**   (ii) **JI**   (iii) **JK**   (iv) **KJ**

⑥ Using the matrix function on a calculator, find $\mathbf{M}^4$ for the matrix

$$\mathbf{M} = \begin{pmatrix} 2 & 0 & -1 \\ 3 & 1 & 2 \\ -1 & 4 & 3 \end{pmatrix}.$$

> **Note**
>
> $\mathbf{M}^4$ means $\mathbf{M} \times \mathbf{M} \times \mathbf{M} \times \mathbf{M}$

⑦ $\mathbf{A} = \begin{pmatrix} x & 3 \\ 0 & -1 \end{pmatrix} \quad \mathbf{B} = \begin{pmatrix} 2x & 0 \\ 4 & -3 \end{pmatrix}.$

(i) Find the matrix product **AB** in terms of x.

(ii) If $\mathbf{AB} = \begin{pmatrix} 10x & -9 \\ -4 & 3 \end{pmatrix}$, find the possible values of x.

(iii) Find the possible matrix products **BA**.

⑧ (i) For the matrix $\mathbf{A} = \begin{pmatrix} 2 & 1 \\ 0 & 1 \end{pmatrix}$, find

    (a) $\mathbf{A}^2$

    (b) $\mathbf{A}^3$

    (c) $\mathbf{A}^4$

(ii) Suggest a general form for the matrix $\mathbf{A}^n$ in terms of n.

(iii) Verify your answer by finding $\mathbf{A}^{10}$ on your calculator and confirming it gives the same answer as using (ii).

⑨ The map in Figure 2.5 below shows the bus routes in a holiday area. Lines represent routes that run each way between the resorts. Arrows indicated one-way scenic routes.

$\mathbf{M}$ is the partly completed 4×4 matrix which shows the number of direct routes between the various resorts.

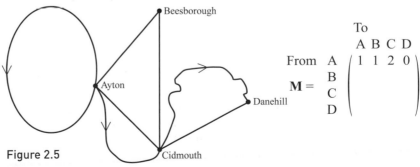

Figure 2.5

(i) Copy and complete the matrix **M**.

(ii) Calculate **M²** and explain what information it contains.

(iii) What information would **M³** contain?

⑩ $\mathbf{A} = \begin{pmatrix} 4 & x & 0 \\ 2 & -3 & 1 \end{pmatrix} \mathbf{B} = \begin{pmatrix} 2 & -5 \\ 4 & x \\ x & 7 \end{pmatrix}$.

(i) Find the product **AB** in terms of x.

A symmetric matrix is one in which the entries are symmetrical about the leading diagonal, for example $\begin{pmatrix} 2 & 5 \\ 5 & 0 \end{pmatrix}$ and $\begin{pmatrix} 3 & 4 & -6 \\ 4 & 2 & 5 \\ -6 & 5 & 1 \end{pmatrix}$.

(ii) Given that the matrix **AB** is symmetric, find the possible values of x.

(iii) Write down the possible matrices **AB**.

⑪ The matrix **A**, in Figure 2.6, shows the number of sales of five flavours of ice cream: Vanilla(V), Strawberry(S), Chocolate(C), Toffee(T) and Banana(B), from an ice cream shop on each of Wednesday(W), Thursday(Th), Friday(F) and Saturday(S) during one week.

$$\mathbf{A} = \begin{array}{c} \\ W \\ T \\ F \\ S \end{array} \begin{array}{ccccc} V & S & C & T & B \\ \left(\begin{array}{ccccc} 63 & 49 & 55 & 44 & 18 \\ 58 & 52 & 66 & 29 & 26 \\ 77 & 41 & 81 & 39 & 25 \\ 101 & 57 & 68 & 63 & 45 \end{array} \right) \end{array}$$

Figure 2.6

(i) Find a matrix **D** such that the product **DA** shows the total number of sales of each flavour of ice cream during the four-day period and find the product **DA**.

(ii) Find a matrix **F** such that the product **AF** gives the total number of ice cream sales each day during the four-day period and find the product **AF**.

The Vanilla and Banana ice creams are served with strawberry sauce; the other three ice creams are served with chocolate sprinkles.

(iii) Find two matrices, **S** and **C**, such that the product **DAS** gives the total number of servings of strawberry sauce needed and the product **DAC** gives the total number of servings of sprinkles needed during the four-day period. Find the matrices **DAS** and **DAC**.

The price of Vanilla and Strawberry ice creams is 95p, Chocolate ice creams cost £1.05 and Toffee and Banana ice creams cost £1.15 each.

(iv) Using only matrix multiplication, find a way of calculating the total cost of all of the ice creams sold during the four-day period.

⑫ Figure 2.7 shows the start of the plaiting process for producing a leather bracelet from three leather strands a, b and c.

The process has only two steps, repeated alternately:

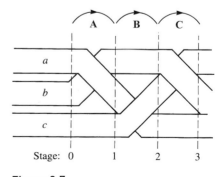

Figure 2.7

Step 1: cross the top strand over the middle strand

Step 2: cross the middle strand under the bottom strand.

At the start of the plaiting process, Stage 0, the order of the strands is given by $S_0 = \begin{pmatrix} a \\ b \\ c \end{pmatrix}$.

> Pre-multiplying **P** by **Q** means calculating **QP**.

(i) Show that pre-multiplying S_0 by the matrix $A = \begin{pmatrix} 0 & 1 & 0 \\ 1 & 0 & 0 \\ 0 & 0 & 1 \end{pmatrix}$

gives S_1, the matrix which represents the order of the strands at Stage 1.

(ii) Find the 3×3 matrix **B** which represents the transition from Stage 1 to Stage 2.

(iii) Find matrix $M = BA$ and show that MS_0 gives S_2, the matrix which represents the order of the strands at Stage 2.

(iv) Find M^2 and hence find the order of the strands at Stage 4.

(v) Calculate M^3. What does this tell you?

3 Transformations

You are already familiar with several different types of transformation, including reflections, rotations and enlargements.

■ The original point, or shape, is called the **object**.

■ The new point, or shape, after the transformation, is called the **image**.

■ A transformation is a **mapping** of an object onto its image.

Some examples of transformations are illustrated in Figures 2.8 to 2.10 (note that the vertices of the image are denoted by the same letters with a dash, e.g. A′, B′).

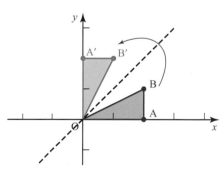

Figure 2.8 Reflection in the line $y = x$

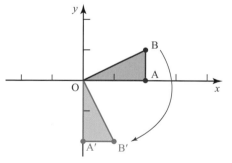

Figure 2.9 Rotation through 90° clockwise, centre O

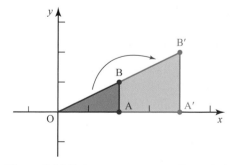

Figure 2.10 Enlargement centre O, scale factor 2

In this section, you will also meet the idea of

■   a **stretch** parallel to the x-axis or y-axis
■   a **shear**

and three-dimensional transformations where

■   a shape is reflected in the planes $x = 0$, $y = 0$ or $z = 0$
■   a shape is rotated about one of the three coordinate axes.

A transformation maps an object according to a rule and can be represented by a matrix (see next section). The effect of a transformation on an object can be found by looking at the effect it has on the **position vector** of the point $\begin{pmatrix} x \\ y \end{pmatrix}$,

i.e. the vector from the origin to the point (x, y). So, for example, to find the effect of a transformation on the point $(2, 3)$ you would look at the effect that the transformation matrix has on the position vector $\begin{pmatrix} 2 \\ 3 \end{pmatrix}$.

Vectors that have length or **magnitude** of 1 are called **unit vectors**.

In two dimensions, two unit vectors that are of particular interest are

$$\mathbf{i} = \begin{pmatrix} 1 \\ 0 \end{pmatrix} - \text{a unit vector in the direction of the } x\text{-axis}$$

$$\mathbf{j} = \begin{pmatrix} 0 \\ 1 \end{pmatrix} - \text{a unit vector in the direction of the } y\text{-axis.}$$

The equivalent unit vectors in three dimensions are

$$\mathbf{i} = \begin{pmatrix} 1 \\ 0 \\ 0 \end{pmatrix} - \text{a unit vector in the direction of the } x\text{-axis}$$

$$\mathbf{j} = \begin{pmatrix} 0 \\ 1 \\ 0 \end{pmatrix} - \text{a unit vector in the direction of the } y\text{-axis}$$

$$\mathbf{k} = \begin{pmatrix} 0 \\ 0 \\ 1 \end{pmatrix} - \text{a unit vector in the direction of the } z\text{-axis.}$$

Finding the transformation represented by a given matrix

Start by looking at the effect of multiplying the unit vectors $\mathbf{i} = \begin{pmatrix} 1 \\ 0 \end{pmatrix}$ and $\mathbf{j} = \begin{pmatrix} 0 \\ 1 \end{pmatrix}$ by the matrix $\begin{pmatrix} -1 & 0 \\ 0 & -1 \end{pmatrix}$.

The image of $\begin{pmatrix} 1 \\ 0 \end{pmatrix}$ under this transformation is given by

$$\begin{pmatrix} -1 & 0 \\ 0 & -1 \end{pmatrix}\begin{pmatrix} 1 \\ 0 \end{pmatrix} = \begin{pmatrix} -1 \\ 0 \end{pmatrix}.$$

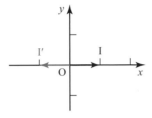

Figure 2.11

The image of $\begin{pmatrix} 0 \\ 1 \end{pmatrix}$ under the transformation is given by

$$\begin{pmatrix} -1 & 0 \\ 0 & -1 \end{pmatrix}\begin{pmatrix} 0 \\ 1 \end{pmatrix} = \begin{pmatrix} 0 \\ -1 \end{pmatrix}.$$

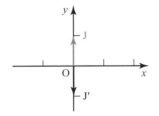

Figure 2.12

You can see from this that the matrix $\begin{pmatrix} -1 & 0 \\ 0 & -1 \end{pmatrix}$ represents a rotation, centre the origin, through 180°.

Example 2.4

Describe the transformations represented by the following matrices.

(i) $\begin{pmatrix} 0 & 1 \\ 1 & 0 \end{pmatrix}$ (ii) $\begin{pmatrix} 2 & 0 \\ 0 & 2 \end{pmatrix}$

Solution

(i) $\begin{pmatrix} 0 & 1 \\ 1 & 0 \end{pmatrix}\begin{pmatrix} 1 \\ 0 \end{pmatrix} = \begin{pmatrix} 0 \\ 1 \end{pmatrix}$ $\begin{pmatrix} 0 & 1 \\ 1 & 0 \end{pmatrix}\begin{pmatrix} 0 \\ 1 \end{pmatrix} = \begin{pmatrix} 1 \\ 0 \end{pmatrix}$

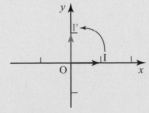

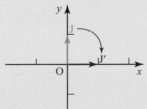

Figure 2.13   **Figure 2.14**

The matrix $\begin{pmatrix} 0 & 1 \\ 1 & 0 \end{pmatrix}$ represents a reflection in the line $y = x$.

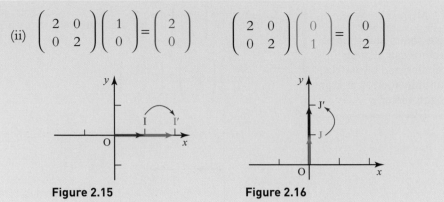

(ii) $\begin{pmatrix} 2 & 0 \\ 0 & 2 \end{pmatrix}\begin{pmatrix} 1 \\ 0 \end{pmatrix} = \begin{pmatrix} 2 \\ 0 \end{pmatrix}$ $\begin{pmatrix} 2 & 0 \\ 0 & 2 \end{pmatrix}\begin{pmatrix} 0 \\ 1 \end{pmatrix} = \begin{pmatrix} 0 \\ 2 \end{pmatrix}$

Figure 2.15   **Figure 2.16**

The matrix $\begin{pmatrix} 2 & 0 \\ 0 & 2 \end{pmatrix}$ represents an enlargement, centre the origin, scale factor 2.

You can see that the images of $\mathbf{i} = \begin{pmatrix} 1 \\ 0 \end{pmatrix}$ and $\mathbf{j} = \begin{pmatrix} 0 \\ 1 \end{pmatrix}$ are the two columns of the transformation matrix.

Finding the matrix that represents a given transformation

The connection between the images of the unit vectors $\mathbf{i}$ and $\mathbf{j}$ and the matrix representing the transformation provides a quick method for finding the matrix representing a transformation.

It is common to use the unit square with coordinates O(0, 0), I(1, 0), P(1, 1) and J(0, 1).

You can think about the images of the points I and J, and from this you can write down the images of the unit vectors $\mathbf{i}$ and $\mathbf{j}$.

This is done in the next example.

> **Hint**
>
> You may find it easier to see what the transformation is when you use a shape, like the unit square, rather than points or lines.

Example 2.5

By drawing a diagram to show the image of the unit square, find the matrices which represent each of the following transformations:

(i) a reflection in the x-axis

(ii) an enlargement of scale factor 3, centre the origin.

Solution

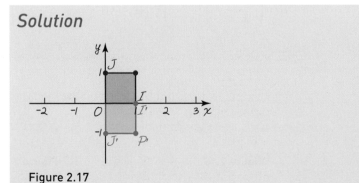

Figure 2.17

(i) You can see from Figure 2.17 that I $(1, 0)$ is mapped to itself and J $(0, 1)$ is mapped to J′ $(0, -1)$.

So the image of I is $(1, 0)$

and the image of J is $(0, -1)$.

So the matrix which represents a reflection in the x-axis is $\begin{pmatrix} 1 & 0 \\ 0 & -1 \end{pmatrix}$.

(ii)

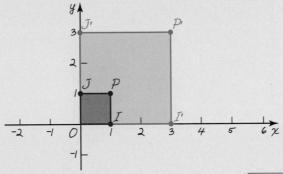

Figure 2.18

So the image of I is $(3, 0)$

You can see from Figure 2.18 that I $(1, 0)$ is mapped to I′ $(3, 0)$, and J $(0, 1)$ is mapped to J′ $(0, 3)$.

and the image of J is $(0, 3)$.

So the matrix which represents an enlargement, centre the origin, scale factor 3 is $\begin{pmatrix} 3 & 0 \\ 0 & 3 \end{pmatrix}$.

Discussion point

➜ For a general transformation represented by the matrix $\begin{pmatrix} a & b \\ c & d \end{pmatrix}$, what are the images of the unit vectors $\begin{pmatrix} 1 \\ 0 \end{pmatrix}$ and $\begin{pmatrix} 0 \\ 1 \end{pmatrix}$?

ACTIVITY 2.3

Using the image of the unit square, find the matrix which represents a rotation of 45° anticlockwise about the origin.

Use a similar method to find the matrices which represent the following transformations:

(i) a rotation of 45° clockwise about the origin

(ii) a rotation of 135° anticlockwise about the origin.

Example 2.6

(i) Find the matrix which represents a rotation through angle θ anticlockwise about the origin.

(ii) Use your answer to find the matrix which represents a rotation of 60° anticlockwise about the origin.

Solution

(i) Figure 2.19 shows a rotation of angle θ about the origin.

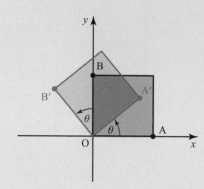

Figure 2.19

Call the coordinates of the point A' (p, q). Since the lines OA and OB are perpendicular, the coordinates of B' will be $(-q, p)$.

From the right-angled triangle with OA' as the hypotenuse, $\cos\theta = \dfrac{p}{1}$ and so $p = \cos\theta$.

Similarly, from the right-angled triangle with OB' as the hypotenuse, $\sin\theta = \dfrac{q}{1}$ so $q = \sin\theta$.

So, the image point A' (p, q) has position vector $\begin{pmatrix} \cos\theta \\ \sin\theta \end{pmatrix}$ and the

image point B' $(-q, p)$ has position vector $\begin{pmatrix} -\sin\theta \\ \cos\theta \end{pmatrix}$.

Therefore, the matrix that represents a rotation of angle θ about the origin is $\begin{pmatrix} \cos\theta & -\sin\theta \\ \sin\theta & \cos\theta \end{pmatrix}$.

(ii) The matrix that represents an anticlockwise rotation of 60° about the

origin is $\begin{pmatrix} \cos 60° & -\sin 60° \\ \sin 60° & \cos 60° \end{pmatrix} = \begin{pmatrix} \dfrac{1}{2} & -\dfrac{\sqrt{3}}{2} \\ \dfrac{\sqrt{3}}{2} & \dfrac{1}{2} \end{pmatrix}$.

Note

The direction of a positive rotation is taken to be anticlockwise unless you are told otherwise.

Discussion point

➜ What matrix would represent a rotation through angle θ clockwise about the origin?

ACTIVITY 2.4

Investigate the effect of the matrices:

(i) $\begin{pmatrix} 2 & 0 \\ 0 & 1 \end{pmatrix}$ (ii) $\begin{pmatrix} 1 & 0 \\ 0 & 5 \end{pmatrix}$

Describe the general transformation represented by the

matrices $\begin{pmatrix} m & 0 \\ 0 & 1 \end{pmatrix}$ and $\begin{pmatrix} 1 & 0 \\ 0 & n \end{pmatrix}$.

Activity 2.4 illustrates two important general results.

A matrix of the form $\begin{pmatrix} m & 0 \\ 0 & n \end{pmatrix}$ represents a **two-way stretch**, scale factor m parallel to the x-axis and scale factor n parallel to the y-axis.

- The matrix $\begin{pmatrix} m & 0 \\ 0 & 1 \end{pmatrix}$ represents a stretch of scale factor m parallel to the x-axis.

- The matrix $\begin{pmatrix} 1 & 0 \\ 0 & n \end{pmatrix}$ represents a stretch of scale factor n parallel to the y-axis.

Shears

Figure 2.20 shows the unit square and its image under the transformation

represented by the matrix $\begin{pmatrix} 1 & 3 \\ 0 & 1 \end{pmatrix}$. The matrix $\begin{pmatrix} 1 & 3 \\ 0 & 1 \end{pmatrix}$ transforms the unit

vector $\mathbf{i} = \begin{pmatrix} 1 \\ 0 \end{pmatrix}$ to the vector $\begin{pmatrix} 1 \\ 0 \end{pmatrix}$ and transforms the

unit vector $\mathbf{j} = \begin{pmatrix} 0 \\ 1 \end{pmatrix}$ to the vector $\begin{pmatrix} 3 \\ 1 \end{pmatrix}$.

The point with position vector $\begin{pmatrix} 1 \\ 1 \end{pmatrix}$ is transformed to the point with

position vector $\begin{pmatrix} 4 \\ 1 \end{pmatrix}$.

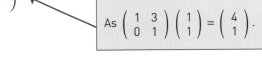
As $\begin{pmatrix} 1 & 3 \\ 0 & 1 \end{pmatrix} \begin{pmatrix} 1 \\ 1 \end{pmatrix} = \begin{pmatrix} 4 \\ 1 \end{pmatrix}$.

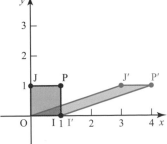

Figure 2.20

This transformation is called a **shear**. Notice that the points on the x-axis stay the same, and the points J and P move parallel to the x-axis to the right.

This shear can be described fully by saying that the x-axis is **invariant**, and giving the image of one point not on the x-axis, e.g. (0, 1) is mapped to (3, 1).

Generally, a shear with an invariant x-axis has the form $\begin{pmatrix} 1 & k \\ 0 & 1 \end{pmatrix}$ and a shear with an invariant y-axis has the form $\begin{pmatrix} 1 & 0 \\ k & 1 \end{pmatrix}$.

Example 2.7

Find the image of the rectangle with vertices A(-1, 2), B(1, 2), C(1, -1) and D(-1, -1) under the shear $\begin{pmatrix} 1 & 3 \\ 0 & 1 \end{pmatrix}$ and show the rectangle and its image on a diagram.

Solution

$$\begin{pmatrix} 1 & 3 \\ 0 & 1 \end{pmatrix}\begin{pmatrix} -1 & 1 & 1 & -1 \\ 2 & 2 & -1 & -1 \end{pmatrix} = \begin{pmatrix} 5 & 7 & -2 & -4 \\ 2 & 2 & -1 & -1 \end{pmatrix}$$

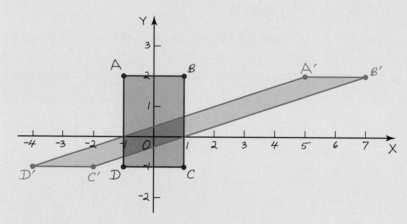

Figure 2.21

The effect of this shear is to transform the sides of the rectangle parallel to the y-axis into sloping lines. Notice that the gradient of the side A′D′ is $\frac{1}{3}$ which is the reciprocal of the top right-hand element of the matrix $\begin{pmatrix} 1 & 3 \\ 0 & 1 \end{pmatrix}$.

> **Note**
> Notice that under the shear transformation, points above the x-axis move to the right and points below the x-axis move to the left.

ACTIVITY 2.5

For each of the points A, B, C and D in Example 2.7, find

$$\frac{\text{distance between the point and its image}}{\text{distance of original point from } x\text{-axis}}.$$

What do you notice?

You should have found that dividing the distance between the point and its image by the distance of the original point from the x-axis (which is invariant), gives the answer 3 for all points, which is the number in the top right of the matrix. This is called the **shear factor** for the shear.

TECHNOLOGY

If you have access to geometrical software, investigate how shears are defined.

> **!** There are different conventions about the sign of a shear factor, and for this reason shear factors are not used to define a shear in this book. It is possible to show the effect of matrix transformations using some geometrical computer software packages. You might find that some packages use different approaches towards shears and define them in different ways.

Example 2.8

In a shear, S, the y-axis is invariant, and the image of the point $(1, 0)$ is the point $(1, 5)$.

(i) Draw a diagram showing the image of the unit square under the transformation S.

(ii) Find the matrix that represents the shear S.

Solution

(i)

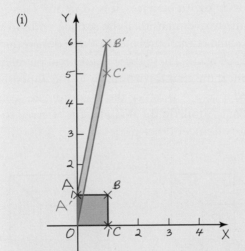

Figure 2.22

(ii) Under S $\begin{pmatrix} 1 \\ 0 \end{pmatrix} \rightarrow \begin{pmatrix} 1 \\ 5 \end{pmatrix}$

and $\begin{pmatrix} 0 \\ 1 \end{pmatrix} \rightarrow \begin{pmatrix} 0 \\ 1 \end{pmatrix}$ ← since the y-axis is invariant.

So the matrix representing S is $\begin{pmatrix} 1 & 0 \\ 5 & 1 \end{pmatrix}$.

Notice that this matrix is of the form $\begin{pmatrix} 1 & 0 \\ k & 1 \end{pmatrix}$ for shears with the y-axis invariant.

Summary of transformations in two dimensions

Reflection in the x-axis	$\begin{pmatrix} 1 & 0 \\ 0 & -1 \end{pmatrix}$	Reflection in the y-axis	$\begin{pmatrix} -1 & 0 \\ 0 & 1 \end{pmatrix}$
Reflection in the line $y = x$	$\begin{pmatrix} 0 & 1 \\ 1 & 0 \end{pmatrix}$	Reflection in the line $y = -x$	$\begin{pmatrix} 0 & -1 \\ -1 & 0 \end{pmatrix}$
Rotation anticlockwise about the origin through angle θ	$\begin{pmatrix} \cos\theta & -\sin\theta \\ \sin\theta & \cos\theta \end{pmatrix}$	Enlargement, centre the origin, scale factor k	$\begin{pmatrix} k & 0 \\ 0 & k \end{pmatrix}$
Stretch parallel to the x-axis, scale factor k	$\begin{pmatrix} k & 0 \\ 0 & 1 \end{pmatrix}$	Stretch parallel to the y-axis, scale factor k	$\begin{pmatrix} 1 & 0 \\ 0 & k \end{pmatrix}$
Shear, x-axis invariant, with $(0, 1)$ mapped to $(k, 1)$	$\begin{pmatrix} 1 & k \\ 0 & 1 \end{pmatrix}$	Shear, y-axis invariant, with $(1, 0)$ mapped to $(1, k)$	$\begin{pmatrix} 1 & 0 \\ k & 1 \end{pmatrix}$

Transformations in three dimensions

When working with matrices, it is sometimes necessary to refer to a 'plane' – this is an infinite two-dimensional flat surface with no thickness. Figure 2.23 below illustrates some common planes in three dimensions – the XY plane, the XZ plane and YZ plane. These three planes will be referred to when using matrices to represent some transformations in three dimensions. The plane XY can also be referred to as $z = 0$, since the z-coordinate would be zero for all points in the XY plane. Similarly, the XZ plane is referred to as $y = 0$ and the YZ plane as $x = 0$. You will meet other planes later in A Level Further Mathematics.

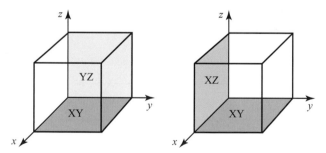

Figure 2.23

So far you have looked at transformations of sets of points from a plane (i.e. two dimensions) to the same plane. You can transform a set of points within three-dimensional space. You will look at reflections in the planes $x = 0$, $y = 0$ or $z = 0$, and rotations about one of the coordinate axes. Again, the matrix can be found algebraically or by considering the effect of the transformation on the three unit vectors

$$\mathbf{i} = \begin{pmatrix} 1 \\ 0 \\ 0 \end{pmatrix}, \mathbf{j} = \begin{pmatrix} 0 \\ 1 \\ 0 \end{pmatrix} \text{ and } \mathbf{k} = \begin{pmatrix} 0 \\ 0 \\ 1 \end{pmatrix}.$$

Think about reflecting an object in the plane $y = 0$. The plane $y = 0$ is the plane which contains the x- and z-axes. Figure 2.24 shows the effect of a reflection in the plane $y = 0$.

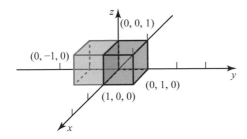

Figure 2.24

$$\mathbf{i} = \begin{pmatrix} 1 \\ 0 \\ 0 \end{pmatrix} \text{ maps to } \begin{pmatrix} 1 \\ 0 \\ 0 \end{pmatrix}, \mathbf{j} = \begin{pmatrix} 0 \\ 1 \\ 0 \end{pmatrix} \text{ maps to } \begin{pmatrix} 0 \\ -1 \\ 0 \end{pmatrix} \text{ and } \mathbf{k} = \begin{pmatrix} 0 \\ 0 \\ 1 \end{pmatrix} \text{ maps}$$

to $\begin{pmatrix} 0 \\ 0 \\ 1 \end{pmatrix}$.

The images of $\mathbf{i}$, $\mathbf{j}$ and $\mathbf{k}$ form the columns of the 3×3 transformation matrix.

It is $\begin{pmatrix} 1 & 0 & 0 \\ 0 & -1 & 0 \\ 0 & 0 & 1 \end{pmatrix}$.

Example 2.9

Find the matrix that represents a rotation of $75°$ anticlockwise about the x-axis.

Solution

A rotation of $75°$ anticlockwise about the x-axis is shown in Figure 2.25.

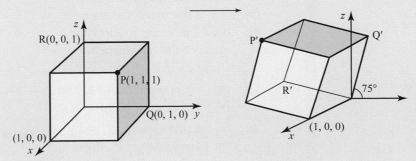

Figure 2.25

> **Note**
>
> Rotations are taken to be anticlockwise about the axis of rotation when looking along the axis from the positive end towards the origin.

Look at the effect of the transformation on the unit vectors $\mathbf{i}, \mathbf{j}$ and $\mathbf{k}$. $\mathbf{i}$ is invariant, but $\mathbf{j}$ and $\mathbf{k}$ rotate in the YZ plane, as shown in Figure 2.26.

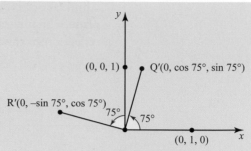

$$\mathbf{i} = \begin{pmatrix} 1 \\ 0 \\ 0 \end{pmatrix} \text{ maps to } \begin{pmatrix} 1 \\ 0 \\ 0 \end{pmatrix},$$

Figure 2.26

$$\mathbf{j} = \begin{pmatrix} 0 \\ 1 \\ 0 \end{pmatrix} \text{ maps to } \begin{pmatrix} 0 \\ \cos 75° \\ \sin 75° \end{pmatrix} \text{ and } \mathbf{k} = \begin{pmatrix} 0 \\ 0 \\ 1 \end{pmatrix} \text{ maps to } \begin{pmatrix} 0 \\ -\sin 75° \\ \cos 75° \end{pmatrix}.$$

The images of $\mathbf{i}, \mathbf{j}$ and $\mathbf{k}$ form the columns of the 3×3 transformation matrix.

The matrix is $\begin{pmatrix} 1 & 0 & 0 \\ 0 & \cos 75° & -\sin 75° \\ 0 & \sin 75° & \cos 75° \end{pmatrix}$.

(You may like to compare this with the matrix for a rotation of $\theta°$ in two dimensions on page 36.)

A rotation of θ anticlockwise about the x-axis is represented by $\begin{pmatrix} 1 & 0 & 0 \\ 0 & \cos\theta & -\sin\theta \\ 0 & \sin\theta & \cos\theta \end{pmatrix}$

A rotation of θ anticlockwise about the y-axis is represented by $\begin{pmatrix} \cos\theta & 0 & \sin\theta \\ 0 & 1 & 0 \\ -\sin\theta & 0 & \cos\theta \end{pmatrix}$

A rotation of θ anticlockwise about the z-axis is represented by $\begin{pmatrix} \cos\theta & -\sin\theta & 0 \\ \sin\theta & \cos\theta & 0 \\ 0 & 0 & 1 \end{pmatrix}$

Exercise 2.3

① Figure 2.27 shows a triangle with vertices at O, A(1, 2) and B(0, 2).
For each of the transformations below

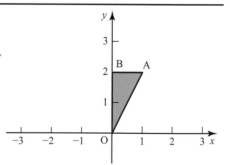

(a) draw a diagram to show the effect of the transformation on triangle OAB

(b) give the coordinates of A′ and B′, the images of points A and B

(c) find expressions for x' and y', the coordinates of P′, the image of a general point P(x, y)

Figure 2.27

(d) find the matrix which represents the transformation.

(i) Enlargement, centre the origin, scale factor 3

(ii) Reflection in the x-axis

(iii) Reflection in the line $x + y = 0$

(iv) Rotation 90° clockwise about O

(v) Two-way stretch, scale factor 3 horizontally and scale factor $\frac{1}{2}$ vertically.

② Describe the geometrical transformations represented by these matrices.

(i) $\begin{pmatrix} 1 & 0 \\ 0 & -1 \end{pmatrix}$ (ii) $\begin{pmatrix} 0 & -1 \\ -1 & 0 \end{pmatrix}$ (iii) $\begin{pmatrix} 2 & 0 \\ 0 & 3 \end{pmatrix}$

(iv) $\begin{pmatrix} 4 & 0 \\ 0 & 4 \end{pmatrix}$ (v) $\begin{pmatrix} 0 & 1 \\ -1 & 0 \end{pmatrix}$

③ Each of the following matrices represents a rotation about the origin. Find the angle and direction of rotation in each case.

(i) $\begin{pmatrix} \dfrac{1}{2} & -\dfrac{\sqrt{3}}{2} \\ \dfrac{\sqrt{3}}{2} & \dfrac{1}{2} \end{pmatrix}$ (ii) $\begin{pmatrix} 0.574 & -0.819 \\ 0.819 & 0.574 \end{pmatrix}$

(iii) $\begin{pmatrix} -\dfrac{1}{\sqrt{2}} & \dfrac{1}{\sqrt{2}} \\ -\dfrac{1}{\sqrt{2}} & -\dfrac{1}{\sqrt{2}} \end{pmatrix}$ (iv) $\begin{pmatrix} -\dfrac{\sqrt{3}}{2} & -\dfrac{1}{2} \\ \dfrac{1}{2} & -\dfrac{\sqrt{3}}{2} \end{pmatrix}$

④ Figure 2.28 shows a square with vertices at the points $A(1, 1), B(1, -1), C(-1, -1)$ and $D(-1,1)$.

(i) Draw a diagram to show the image of this square under the transformation matrix $\mathbf{M} = \begin{pmatrix} 1 & 4 \\ 0 & 1 \end{pmatrix}$.

(ii) Describe fully the transformation represented by the matrix $\mathbf{M}$. State the fixed line and the image of the point A.

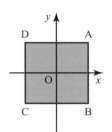

Figure 2.28

⑤ (i) Find the image of the unit square under the transformations represented by the matrices

(a) $\mathbf{A} = \begin{pmatrix} 1 & 0 \\ 5 & 1 \end{pmatrix}$ (b) $\mathbf{B} = \begin{pmatrix} 1 & 0.5 \\ 0 & 1 \end{pmatrix}$

(ii) Use your answers to part (i) to describe fully the transformations represented by each of the matrices $\mathbf{A}$ and $\mathbf{B}$.

⑥ Find the matrix that represents each of the following transformations in three dimensions.

(i) Rotation of 90° anticlockwise about the z-axis

(ii) Reflection in the plane $y = 0$

(iii) Rotation of 180° about the x-axis

(iv) Rotation of 270° anticlockwise about the y-axis

(v) Rotation of 45° anticlockwise about the z-axis

(vi) Rotation of 60° anticlockwise about the x-axis

(vii) Rotation of 120° clockwise about the y-axis

⑦ Figure 2.29 shows a shear that maps the rectangle ABCD to the parallelogram A′B′C′D′.

The angle A′DA is 60°.

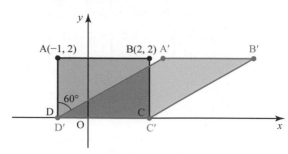

Figure 2.29

(i) Find the coordinates of A′.

(ii) Find the matrix that represents the shear.

⑧ The unit square OABC has its vertices at $(0, 0)$, $(1, 0)$, $(1, 1)$ and $(0, 1)$.

OABC is mapped to OA'B'C' by the transformation defined by the matrix $\begin{pmatrix} 4 & 3 \\ 5 & 4 \end{pmatrix}$.

Find the coordinates of A', B' and C' and show that the area of the shape has not been changed by the transformation.

⑨ The transformation represented by the matrix $\mathbf{M} = \begin{pmatrix} 1 & 2 \\ 0 & 1 \end{pmatrix}$ is applied to the triangle ABC with vertices $A(-1, 1)$, $B(1, -1)$ and $C(-1, -1)$.

(i) Draw a diagram showing the triangle ABC and its image A′B′C′.

(ii) Find the gradient of the line A′C′ and explain how this relates to the matrix $\mathbf{M}$.

⑩ Describe the transformations represented by these matrices.

(i) $\begin{pmatrix} 1 & 0 & 0 \\ 0 & 0 & 1 \\ 0 & -1 & 0 \end{pmatrix}$
(ii) $\begin{pmatrix} 3 & 0 & 0 \\ 0 & 3 & 0 \\ 0 & 0 & 3 \end{pmatrix}$
(iii) $\begin{pmatrix} 1 & 0 & 0 \\ 0 & 1 & 0 \\ 0 & 0 & -1 \end{pmatrix}$
(iv) $\begin{pmatrix} 0.8 & 0 & 0.6 \\ 0 & 1 & 0 \\ -0.6 & 0 & 0.8 \end{pmatrix}$

⑪ Find the matrices that would represent

(i) a reflection in the plane $x = 0$

(ii) a rotation of 180° about the y-axis.

⑫ A transformation maps P to P' as follows:

■ Each point is mapped on to the line $y = x$.

■ The line joining a point to its image is parallel to the y-axis.

Find the coordinates of the image of the point (x, y) and hence show that this transformation can be represented by means of a matrix.

What is that matrix?

⑬ A square has corners with coordinates $A(1, 0)$, $B(1, 1)$, $C(0, 1)$ and $O(0, 0)$. It is to be transformed into another quadrilateral in the first quadrant of the coordinate grid.

Find a matrix which would transform the square into

(i)   a rectangle with one vertex at the origin and one side of length 5 units

(ii) a rhombus with one vertex at the origin, two angles of 45° and side lengths of $\sqrt{2}$ units; one of the sides lies along an axis

(iii) a parallelogram with one vertex at the origin and two angles of 30°; one of the longest sides lies along an axis and has length 7 units; the shortest sides have length 3 units.

Is there more than one possibility for any of these matrices? If so, write down alternative matrices that satisfy the same description.

4 Successive transformations

Figure 2.30 shows the effect of two successive transformations on a triangle. The transformation A represents a reflection in the *x*-axis. A maps the point P to the point A(P).

The transformation B represents a rotation of 90° anticlockwise about O. When you apply B to the image formed by A, the point A(P) is mapped to the point B(A(P)). This is abbreviated to BA(P).

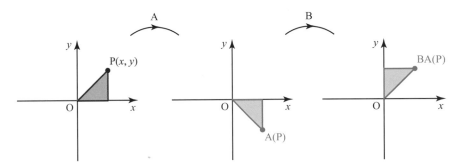

Figure 2.30

Note

Notice that a transformation written as BA means 'carry out A, then carry out B'. This process is sometimes called **composition of transformations**.

Discussion point

➜ Look at Figure 2.30 and compare the original triangle with the final image after both transformations.

(i) Describe the single transformation represented by BA.

(ii) Write down the matrices which represent the transformations A and B. Calculate the matrix product **BA** and comment on your answer.

Note

A transformation is often denoted by a capital letter. The matrix representing this transformation is usually denoted by the same letter, in bold.

In general, the matrix for a composite transformation is found by multiplying the matrices of the individual transformations in the reverse order to that which they are written. (As previously discussed, BA means carry out A then carry out B). So, for two transformations the matrix representing the first transformation is on the right and the matrix for the second transformation is on the left. For n transformations $T_1, T_2, \ldots, T_{n-1}, T_n$, being applied in the order T_1, then T_2, etc, the matrix representing the composition of the n transformations is given by $\mathbf{T}_n \mathbf{T}_{n-1} \ldots \mathbf{T}_2 \mathbf{T}_1$.

You will prove this result for two transformations in Activity 2.6.

📺 **TECHNOLOGY**

If you have access to geometrical software, you could investigate this using several different matrices for **T** and **S**.

ACTIVITY 2.6

The transformations T and S are represented by the matrices $\mathbf{T} = \begin{pmatrix} a & b \\ c & d \end{pmatrix}$ and $\mathbf{S} = \begin{pmatrix} p & q \\ r & s \end{pmatrix}$.

T is applied to the point P with position vector $\mathbf{p} = \begin{pmatrix} x \\ y \end{pmatrix}$. The image of P is P′.

S is then applied to the point P′. The image of P′ is P″. This is illustrated in Figure 2.31.

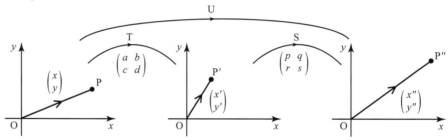

Figure 2.31

Discussion point

→ How can you use the idea of successive transformations to explain the associativity of matrix multiplication (**AB**)**C** = **A**(**BC**)?

(i) Find the position vector $\begin{pmatrix} x' \\ y' \end{pmatrix}$ of P′ by calculating the matrix product $\mathbf{T} \begin{pmatrix} x \\ y \end{pmatrix}$.

(ii) Find the position vector $\begin{pmatrix} x'' \\ y'' \end{pmatrix}$ of P″ by calculating the matrix product $\mathbf{S} \begin{pmatrix} x' \\ y' \end{pmatrix}$.

(iii) Find the matrix product $\mathbf{U} = \mathbf{ST}$ and show that $\mathbf{U} \begin{pmatrix} x \\ y \end{pmatrix}$ is the same as $\begin{pmatrix} x'' \\ y'' \end{pmatrix}$.

Proving results in trigonometry

If you carry out a rotation about the origin through angle θ, followed by a rotation about the origin through angle ϕ, then this is equivalent to a single rotation about the origin through angle $\theta + \phi$. Using matrices to represent these transformations allows you to prove the formulae for $\sin(\theta + \phi)$ and $\cos(\theta + \phi)$ given on page 168. This is done in Activity 2.7.

ACTIVITY 2.7

(i) Write down the matrix **A** representing a rotation about the origin through angle θ, and the matrix **B** representing a rotation about the origin through angle ϕ.

(ii) Find the matrix **BA**, representing a rotation about the origin through angle θ, followed by a rotation about the origin through angle ϕ.

(iii) Write down the matrix **C** representing a rotation about the origin through angle $\theta + \phi$.

(iv) By equating **C** to **BA**, write down expressions for $\sin(\theta + \phi)$ and $\cos(\theta + \phi)$.

(v) Explain why **BA** = **AB** in this case.

Example 2.10

(i) Write down the matrix **A** which represents an anticlockwise rotation of 135° about the origin.

(ii) Write down the matrices **B** and **C** which represent rotations of 45° and 90° respectively about the origin. Find the matrix **BC** and verify that **A** = **BC**.

(iii) Calculate the matrix **B**³ and comment on your answer.

Solution

(i) $\mathbf{A} = \begin{pmatrix} -\dfrac{1}{\sqrt{2}} & -\dfrac{1}{\sqrt{2}} \\ \dfrac{1}{\sqrt{2}} & -\dfrac{1}{\sqrt{2}} \end{pmatrix}$

(ii) $\mathbf{B} = \begin{pmatrix} \dfrac{1}{\sqrt{2}} & -\dfrac{1}{\sqrt{2}} \\ \dfrac{1}{\sqrt{2}} & \dfrac{1}{\sqrt{2}} \end{pmatrix}, \mathbf{C} = \begin{pmatrix} 0 & -1 \\ 1 & 0 \end{pmatrix}$

$\mathbf{BC} = \begin{pmatrix} \dfrac{1}{\sqrt{2}} & -\dfrac{1}{\sqrt{2}} \\ \dfrac{1}{\sqrt{2}} & \dfrac{1}{\sqrt{2}} \end{pmatrix} \begin{pmatrix} 0 & -1 \\ 1 & 0 \end{pmatrix} = \begin{pmatrix} -\dfrac{1}{\sqrt{2}} & -\dfrac{1}{\sqrt{2}} \\ \dfrac{1}{\sqrt{2}} & -\dfrac{1}{\sqrt{2}} \end{pmatrix} = \mathbf{A}$

(iii) $\mathbf{B}^3 = \begin{pmatrix} \dfrac{1}{\sqrt{2}} & -\dfrac{1}{\sqrt{2}} \\ \dfrac{1}{\sqrt{2}} & \dfrac{1}{\sqrt{2}} \end{pmatrix} \begin{pmatrix} \dfrac{1}{\sqrt{2}} & -\dfrac{1}{\sqrt{2}} \\ \dfrac{1}{\sqrt{2}} & \dfrac{1}{\sqrt{2}} \end{pmatrix} \begin{pmatrix} \dfrac{1}{\sqrt{2}} & -\dfrac{1}{\sqrt{2}} \\ \dfrac{1}{\sqrt{2}} & \dfrac{1}{\sqrt{2}} \end{pmatrix} = \begin{pmatrix} -\dfrac{1}{\sqrt{2}} & -\dfrac{1}{\sqrt{2}} \\ \dfrac{1}{\sqrt{2}} & -\dfrac{1}{\sqrt{2}} \end{pmatrix}.$

This verifies that three successive anticlockwise rotations of 45° about the origin is equivalent to a single anticlockwise rotation of 135° about the origin.

① $\mathbf{A} = \begin{pmatrix} 3 & 0 \\ 0 & 3 \end{pmatrix}$, $\mathbf{B} = \begin{pmatrix} 0 & -1 \\ 1 & 0 \end{pmatrix}$, $\mathbf{C} = \begin{pmatrix} 1 & 0 \\ 0 & -1 \end{pmatrix}$ and $\mathbf{D} = \begin{pmatrix} 0 & 1 \\ 1 & 0 \end{pmatrix}$.

(i) Describe the transformations that are represented by matrices **A**, **B**, **C** and **D**.

(ii) Find the following matrix products and describe the single transformation represented in each case:

(a) **BC**   (b) **CB**   (c) **DC**   (d) $\mathbf{A}^2$ (e) **BCB**   (f) $\mathbf{DC}^2\mathbf{D}$

(iii) Write down two other matrix products, using the matrices **A**, **B**, **C** and **D**, which would produce the same single transformation as $\mathbf{DC}^2\mathbf{D}$.

② The matrix **X** represents a reflection in the x-axis.

The matrix **Y** represents a reflection in the y-axis.

(i) Write down the matrices **X** and **Y**.

(ii) Find the matrix **XY** and describe the transformation it represents.

(iii) Find the matrix **YX**.

(iv) Explain geometrically why $\mathbf{XY} = \mathbf{YX}$ in this case.

③ The matrix **P** represents a rotation of 180° about the origin.

The matrix **Q** represents a reflection in the line $y = x$.

(i) Write down the matrices **P** and **Q**.

(ii) Find the matrix **PQ** and describe the transformation it represents.

(iii) Find the matrix **QP**.

(iv) Explain geometrically why $\mathbf{PQ} = \mathbf{QP}$ in this case.

④ Write down matrices which represent the following transformations in three dimensions.

(i) A reflection in the plane $z = 0$.

(ii) A rotation of 90° anticlockwise about the x-axis.

(iii) A reflection in the plane $x = 0$.

(iv) A rotation of 90° clockwise about the y-axis.

(v) A stretch, scale factor 3, in the y-direction.

(vi) A rotation of 60° anticlockwise about the z-axis.

⑤ The transformations R and S are represented by the matrices

$$\mathbf{R} = \begin{pmatrix} 2 & -1 \\ 1 & 3 \end{pmatrix} \text{ and } \mathbf{S} = \begin{pmatrix} 3 & 0 \\ -2 & 4 \end{pmatrix}.$$

(i) Find the matrix which represents the transformation RS.

(ii) Find the image of the point $(3, -2)$ under the transformation RS.

⑥ The transformation represented by $\mathbf{C} = \begin{pmatrix} 0 & 3 \\ -1 & 0 \end{pmatrix}$ is equivalent to a single transformation B followed by a single transformation A. Give geometrical descriptions of a pair of possible transformations B and A and state the matrices that represent them.

Comment on the order in which the transformations are performed.

⑦ Figure 2.32 shows the image of the unit square OABC under the combined transformation with matrix **PQ**.

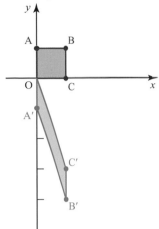

Figure 2.32

(i)   Write down the matrix **PQ**.

Matrix **P** represents a reflection.

(ii)   State the matrices **P** and **Q** and define fully the two transformations represented by these matrices. When describing matrix **Q** you should refer to the image of the point B.

⑧ Find the matrix **X** which represents a rotation of 135° about the origin followed by a reflection in the y-axis.

Explain why matrix **X** cannot represent a rotation about the origin.

⑨ Describe fully the transformations represented by the following matrices.

(i)
$$\begin{pmatrix} 1 & 0 & 0 \\ 0 & 1 & 0 \\ 0 & 0 & 2.5 \end{pmatrix}$$

(ii)
$$\begin{pmatrix} \sqrt{\dfrac{3}{2}} & 0.5 & 0 \\ -0.5 & \sqrt{\dfrac{3}{2}} & 0 \\ 0 & 0 & 1 \end{pmatrix}$$

⑩ (i)   Write down the matrix **P** which represents a stretch of scale factor 2 parallel to the y-axis.

(ii)   The matrix $\mathbf{Q} = \begin{pmatrix} 5 & 0 \\ 0 & -1 \end{pmatrix}$. Write down the two single transformations whose composition is represented by the matrix **Q**.

(iii)   Find the matrix **PQ**. Write a list of the three transformations which are represented by the matrix **PQ**. In how many different orders could the three transformations occur?

(iv)   Find the matrix **R** for which the matrix product **RPQ** would transform an object to its original position.

⑪ There are two basic types of four-terminal electrical networks, as shown in Figure 2.33.

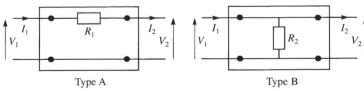

Type A   Type B

Figure 2.33

In Type A the output voltage V_2 and current I_2 are related to the input voltage V_1 and current I_1 by the simultaneous equations:

$$V_2 = V_1 - I_1 R_1$$

$$I_2 = I_1$$

The simultaneous equations can be written as $\begin{pmatrix} V_2 \\ I_2 \end{pmatrix} = A \begin{pmatrix} V_1 \\ I_1 \end{pmatrix}$.

(i)   Find the matrix **A**.

In Type B the corresponding simultaneous equations are:

$$V_2 = V_1$$

$$I_2 = I_1 - \frac{V_1}{R_2}$$

(ii)   Write down the matrix **B** which represents the effect of a Type B network.

(iii)   Find the matrix which represents the effect of Type A followed by Type B.

(iv)   Is the effect of Type B followed by Type A the same as the effect of Type A followed by Type B?

⑫   The matrix **B** represents a rotation of 45° anticlockwise about the origin.

$$\mathbf{B} = \begin{pmatrix} \dfrac{1}{\sqrt{2}} & -\dfrac{1}{\sqrt{2}} \\ \dfrac{1}{\sqrt{2}} & \dfrac{1}{\sqrt{2}} \end{pmatrix}, \mathbf{D} = \begin{pmatrix} a & -b \\ b & a \end{pmatrix} \text{ where } a \text{ and } b \text{ are positive real numbers}$$

Given that $\mathbf{D}^2 = \mathbf{B}$, find exact values for a and b. Write down the transformation represented by the matrix **D**. What do the exact values a and b represent?

In questions 13 and 14 you will need to use the matrix which represents a reflection in the line $y = mx$. This can be written as $\dfrac{1}{1 + m^2} \begin{pmatrix} 1 - m^2 & 2m \\ 2m & m^2 - 1 \end{pmatrix}$.

⑬   (i)   Find the matrix **P** which represents reflection in the line $y = \dfrac{1}{\sqrt{3}} x$, and the matrix **Q** which represents reflection in the line $y = \sqrt{3}x$.

(ii)   Use matrix multiplication to find the single transformation equivalent to reflection in the line $y = \dfrac{1}{\sqrt{3}} x$ followed by reflection in the line $y = \sqrt{3}x$.

Describe this transformation fully.

(iii)   Use matrix multiplication to find the single transformation equivalent to reflection in the line $y = \sqrt{3}x$ followed by reflection in the line $y = \dfrac{1}{\sqrt{3}} x$.

Describe this transformation fully.

⑭   The matrix **R** represents a reflection in the line $y = mx$.

Show that $\mathbf{R}^2 = \begin{pmatrix} 1 & 0 \\ 0 & 1 \end{pmatrix}$ and explain geometrically why this is the case.

5 Invariance

Invariant points

> **Discussion points**
>
> → In a reflection, are there any points which map to themselves?
> In a rotation, are there any points which map to themselves?

Points which map to themselves under a transformation are called **invariant points**. The origin is always an invariant point under a transformation that can be represented by a matrix, as the following statement is always true:

$$\begin{pmatrix} a & b \\ c & d \end{pmatrix}\begin{pmatrix} 0 \\ 0 \end{pmatrix} = \begin{pmatrix} 0 \\ 0 \end{pmatrix}$$

More generally, a point (x, y) is invariant if it satisfies the matrix equation:

$$\begin{pmatrix} a & b \\ c & d \end{pmatrix}\begin{pmatrix} x \\ y \end{pmatrix} = \begin{pmatrix} x \\ y \end{pmatrix}$$

For example, the point $(-2, 2)$ is invariant under the transformation represented by the matrix $\begin{pmatrix} 6 & 5 \\ 2 & 3 \end{pmatrix}$: $\begin{pmatrix} 6 & 5 \\ 2 & 3 \end{pmatrix}\begin{pmatrix} -2 \\ 2 \end{pmatrix} = \begin{pmatrix} -2 \\ 2 \end{pmatrix}$

Example 2.11

M is the matrix $\begin{pmatrix} 2 & -1 \\ 1 & 0 \end{pmatrix}$.

(i) Show that $(5, 5)$ is an invariant point under the transformation represented by **M**.

(ii) What can you say about the invariant points under this transformation?

Solution

(i) $\begin{pmatrix} 2 & -1 \\ 1 & 0 \end{pmatrix}\begin{pmatrix} 5 \\ 5 \end{pmatrix} = \begin{pmatrix} 5 \\ 5 \end{pmatrix}$ so $(5, 5)$ is an invariant point under the transformation represented by **M**.

(ii) Suppose the point $\begin{pmatrix} x \\ y \end{pmatrix}$ maps to itself. Then

$$\begin{pmatrix} 2 & -1 \\ 1 & 0 \end{pmatrix}\begin{pmatrix} x \\ y \end{pmatrix} = \begin{pmatrix} x \\ y \end{pmatrix}$$

$$\begin{pmatrix} 2x - y \\ x \end{pmatrix} = \begin{pmatrix} x \\ y \end{pmatrix}$$

> Both equations simplify to $y = x$.

$\Leftrightarrow 2x - y = x$ and $x = y$.

So the invariant points of the transformation are all the points on the line $y = x$.

> These points all have the form (λ, λ). The point $(5,5)$ is just one of the points on this line.

The simultaneous equations in Example 2.11 were equivalent and so all the invariant points were on a straight line. Generally, any matrix equation set up to find the invariant points will lead to two equations of the form $ax + by = 0$, which can also be expressed in the form $y = -\dfrac{ax}{b}$. These equations may be equivalent, in which case this is a line of invariant points. If the two equations are not equivalent, the origin is the only point which satisfies both equations, and so this is the only invariant point.

Invariant lines

The terms **singular** and **non-singular** are discussed further on page 119.

A line AB is known as an **invariant line** under a non-singular transformation if the image of every point on AB is also on AB. It is important to note that it is not necessary for each of the points to map to itself; it can map to itself or to some other point on the line AB.

Sometimes it is easy to spot which lines are invariant. For example, in Figure 2.34 the position of the points A–F and their images A′–F′ show that the transformation is a reflection in the line *l*. So every point on *l* maps onto itself and *l* is a **line of invariant points**.

Look at the lines perpendicular to the mirror line in Figure 2.34, for example the line ABB′A′. Any point on one of these lines maps onto another point on the same line. Such a line is invariant but it is not a line of invariant points.

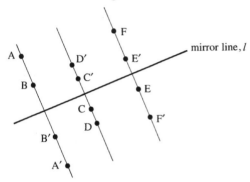

Figure 2.34

Example 2.12

Find the invariant lines of the transformation given by the matrix $\mathbf{M} = \begin{pmatrix} 5 & 1 \\ 2 & 4 \end{pmatrix}$.

Solution

Suppose the invariant line has the form $y = mx + c$.

Let the original point be (x, y) and the image point be (x', y').

$$\begin{pmatrix} x' \\ y' \end{pmatrix} = \begin{pmatrix} 5 & 1 \\ 2 & 4 \end{pmatrix} \begin{pmatrix} x \\ y \end{pmatrix} \Leftrightarrow x' = 5x + y \text{ and } y' = 2x + 4y$$

$$\Leftrightarrow \begin{cases} x' = 5x + mx + c = (5 + m)x + c \\ y' = 2x + 4(mx + c) = (2 + 4m)x + 4c \end{cases}$$

Using $y = mx + c$.

As the line is invariant, (x', y') also lies on the line, so $y' = mx' + c$.

Therefore,

$(2 + 4m)x + 4c = m[(5 + m)x + c] + c$

$\Leftrightarrow 0 = (m^2 + m - 2)x + (m - 3)c$

For the left-hand side to equal zero, both $m^2 + m - 2 = 0$ and $(m - 3)c = 0$.

$(m - 1)(m + 2) = 0 \Leftrightarrow m = 1 \text{ or } m = -2$

and

$(m − 3)c = 0 \Leftrightarrow m = 3$ or $c = 0$ ←

m = 3 is not a viable solution as $m^2 + m − 2 \neq 0$.

So, there are two possible solutions for the invariant line:

$m = 1, c = 0 \Leftrightarrow y = x$

or

$m = −2, c = 0 \Leftrightarrow y = −2x$

Figure 2.35 shows the effect of this transformation, together with its invariant lines.

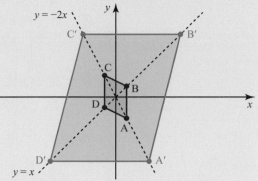

Figure 2.35

Exercise 2.5

① Find the invariant points under the transformations represented by the following matrices.

(i) $\begin{pmatrix} −1 & −1 \\ 2 & 2 \end{pmatrix}$ (ii) $\begin{pmatrix} 3 & 4 \\ 1 & 2 \end{pmatrix}$ (iii) $\begin{pmatrix} 4 & 1 \\ 6 & 3 \end{pmatrix}$ (iv) $\begin{pmatrix} 7 & −4 \\ 3 & −1 \end{pmatrix}$

② What lines, if any, are invariant under the following transformations?

(i)   Enlargement, centre the origin

(ii) Rotation through 180° about the origin

(iii) Rotation through 90° about the origin

(iv) Reflection in the line $y = x$

(v)   Reflection in the line $y = −x$

(vi) Shear, x-axis fixed

③ Figure 2.36 shows the effect on the unit square of a transformation represented by $\mathbf{A} = \begin{pmatrix} 0.6 & 0.8 \\ 0.8 & −0.6 \end{pmatrix}$.

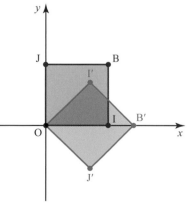

(i)   Find three points which are invariant under this transformation.

(ii) Given that this transformation is a reflection, write down the equation of the mirror line.

(iii) Using your answer to part (ii), write down the equation of an invariant line, other than the mirror line, under this reflection.

Figure 2.36

(iv) Justify your answer to part (iii) algebraically.

④ For the matrix $\mathbf{M} = \begin{pmatrix} 4 & 11 \\ 11 & 4 \end{pmatrix}$

 (i)   show that the origin is the only invariant point

 (ii) find the invariant lines of the transformation represented by $\mathbf{M}$.

⑤ (i)   Find the invariant lines of the transformation given by the matrix
$\begin{pmatrix} 3 & 4 \\ 9 & -2 \end{pmatrix}$.

 (ii) Draw a diagram to show the effect of the transformation on the unit square, and show the invariant lines on your diagram.

⑥ For the matrix $\mathbf{M} = \begin{pmatrix} 0 & 1 \\ -1 & 2 \end{pmatrix}$

 (i)   find the line of invariant points of the transformation given by $\mathbf{M}$

 (ii) find the invariant lines of the transformation

 (iii) draw a diagram to show the effect of the transformation on the unit square.

⑦ The matrix $\begin{pmatrix} \dfrac{1 - m^2}{1 + m^2} & \dfrac{2m}{1 + m^2} \\ \dfrac{2m}{1 + m^2} & \dfrac{m^2 - 1}{1 + m^2} \end{pmatrix}$ represents a reflection in the line $y = mx$.

Prove that the line $y = mx$ is a line of invariant points.

⑧ Show that under the transformation represented by the matrix $\begin{pmatrix} -4 & 2 \\ -15 & 7 \end{pmatrix}$

 (i) $y = 3x$ is an invariant line

 (ii) $y = \frac{5}{2}x$ is a line of invariant points.

⑨ (i)   Write down the matrices for the following transformations.

 A: Rotate 45° anticlockwise about the x-axis

 B: Rotate 45° anticlockwise about the z-axis.

 (ii) Calculate the matrix for the combined transformation BA.

 (iii) Show that the combined transformation BA leaves all points in the

 direction $\begin{pmatrix} 1 \\ \sqrt{2} - 1 \\ 1 \end{pmatrix}$ invariant.

 (iv) Find the image of $\begin{pmatrix} 1 \\ 0 \\ -1 \end{pmatrix}$ under BA.

⑩ The transformation T maps $\begin{pmatrix} x \\ y \end{pmatrix}$ to $\begin{pmatrix} a & b \\ c & d \end{pmatrix}\begin{pmatrix} x \\ y \end{pmatrix}$.

Show that invariant points other than the origin exist if $ad - bc = a + d - 1$.

⑪ T is a translation of the plane by the vector $\begin{pmatrix} a \\ b \end{pmatrix}$. The point (x, y) is mapped to the point (x', y').

(i) Write down equations for x' and y' in terms of x and y.

(ii) Verify that $\begin{pmatrix} x' \\ y' \\ z' \end{pmatrix} = \begin{pmatrix} 1 & 0 & a \\ 0 & 1 & b \\ 0 & 0 & 1 \end{pmatrix} \begin{pmatrix} x \\ y \\ 1 \end{pmatrix}$ produces the same

equations as those obtained in part (i).

The point (X, Y) is the image of the point (x, y) under the combined transformation TM given by

$$\begin{pmatrix} X \\ Y \\ 1 \end{pmatrix} = \begin{pmatrix} -0.6 & 0.8 & a \\ 0.8 & 0.6 & b \\ 0 & 0 & 1 \end{pmatrix} \begin{pmatrix} x \\ y \\ 1 \end{pmatrix}$$

(iii) (a) Show that if $a = -4$ and $b = 2$ then $(0, 5)$ is an invariant point of TM.

(b) Show that if $a = 2$ and $b = 1$ then TM has no invariant point.

(c) Find a relationship between a and b that must be satisfied if TM is to have any invariant points.

LEARNING OUTCOMES

When you have completed this chapter you should be able to:

➤ understand what is meant by the terms order of a matrix, rectangular matrix, square matrix, identity matrix, zero (or null) matrix, transpose of a matrix and equal matrices

➤ add and subtract matrices of the same order

➤ multiply a matrix by a scalar

➤ know when two matrices are conformable for multiplication, and be able to multiply conformable matrices

➤ use a calculator to carry out matrix calculations

➤ know that matrix multiplication is associative but not commutative

➤ find the matrix associated with a linear transformation in two dimensions:
  ○ reflections in the coordinate axes and the lines $y = \pm x$
  ○ rotations about the origin
  ○ enlargements centre the origin
  ○ stretches parallel to the coordinate axes
  ○ shears with a coordinate axis invariant

➤ find the matrix associated with a linear transformation in three dimensions:
  ○ reflection in $x = 0$, $y = 0$ or $z = 0$ as a plane of reflection
  ○ rotations about the x, y or z axes as axis of rotation

➤ understand successive transformations in two dimensions and the connection with matrix multiplication

➤ find any lines of invariant points

➤ find any invariant lines for a linear transformation.

KEY POINTS

1 A matrix is a rectangular array of numbers or letters.

2 The shape of a matrix is described by its order. A matrix with r rows and c columns has order $r \times c$.

3 A matrix with the same number of rows and columns is called a square matrix.

4 The matrix $\mathbf{0} = \begin{pmatrix} 0 & 0 \\ 0 & 0 \end{pmatrix}$ is known as the 2×2 zero matrix. Zero matrices can be of any order.

5 A matrix of the form $\mathbf{I} = \begin{pmatrix} 1 & 0 \\ 0 & 1 \end{pmatrix}$ is known as the 2×2 identity matrix. All identity matrices are square, with 1s on the leading diagonal and zeros elsewhere.

6 Matrices can be added or subtracted if they have the same order.

7 Two matrices $\mathbf{A}$ and $\mathbf{B}$ can be multiplied to give matrix $\mathbf{AB}$ if their orders are of the form $p \times q$ and $q \times r$ respectively. The resulting matrix will have the order $p \times r$.

8 Matrix multiplication

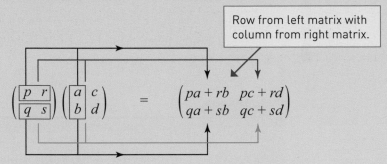

Row from left matrix with column from right matrix.

Figure 2.36

9 Matrix addition and multiplication are associative:
$$\mathbf{A} + (\mathbf{B} + \mathbf{C}) = (\mathbf{A} + \mathbf{B}) + \mathbf{C}$$
$$\mathbf{A}(\mathbf{BC}) = (\mathbf{AB})\mathbf{C}$$

10 Matrix addition is commutative but matrix multiplication is generally not commutative:
$$\mathbf{A} + \mathbf{B} = \mathbf{B} + \mathbf{A}$$
$$\mathbf{AB} \neq \mathbf{BA}$$

11 The matrix $\mathbf{M} = \begin{pmatrix} a & b \\ c & d \end{pmatrix}$ represents the transformation which maps the point with position vector $\begin{pmatrix} x \\ y \end{pmatrix}$ to the point with position vector $\begin{pmatrix} ax + by \\ cx + dy \end{pmatrix}$.

12 A list of the matrices representing common transformations, including rotations, reflections, enlargements, stretches and shears, is given on page 22 .

13 Under the transformation represented by **M**, the image of **i** = $\begin{pmatrix} 1 \\ 0 \end{pmatrix}$ is the first column of **M** and the image of **j** = $\begin{pmatrix} 0 \\ 1 \end{pmatrix}$ is the second column of **M**.

Similarly, in three dimensions the images of the unit vectors **i** = $\begin{pmatrix} 1 \\ 0 \\ 0 \end{pmatrix}$, **j** = $\begin{pmatrix} 0 \\ 1 \\ 0 \end{pmatrix}$ and **k** = $\begin{pmatrix} 0 \\ 0 \\ 1 \end{pmatrix}$ are the first, second and third columns of the transformation matrix.

14 The composite of the transformation represented by M followed by that represented by N is represented by the matrix product **NM**.

15 If (x, y) is an invariant point under a transformation represented by the matrix **M**, then **M** $\begin{pmatrix} x \\ y \end{pmatrix} = \begin{pmatrix} x \\ y \end{pmatrix}$.

16 A line AB is known as an invariant line under a non-singular transformation if the image of every point on AB is also on AB. This may mean that one point on AB maps onto a different point of AB.

17 If every point on AB maps onto itself then AB is known as a line of invariant points.

FUTURE USES

- Work on matrices is developed further in Chapter 6 'Matrices and their inverses'.

3

Roots of polynomials

A **polynomial** is an expression like $4x^3 + x^2 - 4x - 1$. Its terms are all non-negative integer powers of a variable (in this case x) like x^2, or multiples of them like $4x^3$. There are no square roots, reciprocals, etc.

The **order** (or degree) of a polynomial is the highest power of the variable. So the order of $4x^3 + x^2 - 4x - 1$ is 3; this is why it is called a **cubic**.

You often need to solve polynomial equations, and it is usually helpful to think about the associated graph.

The following diagrams show the graphs of two cubic polynomial functions. The first example (in Figure 3.1) has three real roots (where the graph of the polynomial crosses the x-axis). The second example (in Figure 3.2) has only one real root. It can be shown that in this case there are also two **complex** roots.

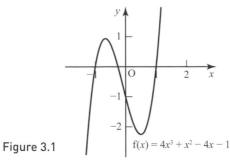

Figure 3.1 $f(x) = 4x^3 + x^2 - 4x - 1$

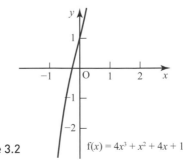

Figure 3.2 $f(x) = 4x^3 + x^2 + 4x + 1$

In general a polynomial equation of order *n* has *n* roots. However, some of these may be complex rather than real numbers and sometimes they coincide so that two or more distinct roots become one repeated root.

Discussion points

➜ How would you solve the polynomial equation $4x^3 + x^2 - 4x - 1 = 0$?

➜ What about $4x^3 + x^2 + 4x + 1 = 0$?

1 Polynomials

The following two statements are true for all polynomials:

- A polynomial equation of order *n* has at most *n* real roots.
- The graph of a polynomial function of order *n* has at most *n* − 1 turning points.

Here are some examples that illustrate these results.

Order 1 (a linear equation)

Example: $2x - 7 = 0$

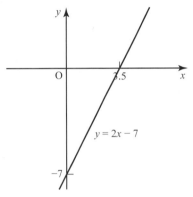

Figure 3.3 The graph is a straight line with no turning points. There is one real root at $x = 3.5$.

Order 3 (a cubic equation)

Example: $x^3 - 1 = 0$

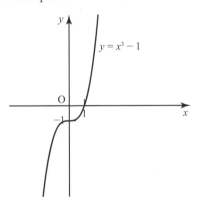

Figure 3.5 The two turning points of this curve coincide to give a point of inflection at $(0, -1)$. There is one real root at $x = 1$ and two complex roots at $x = \dfrac{-1 \pm \sqrt{3}i}{2}$.

Order 2 (a quadratic equation)

Example: $x^2 - 4x + 4 = 0$

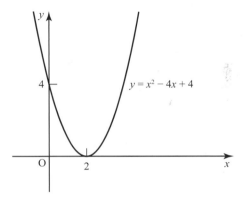

Figure 3.4 The curve has one turning point. There is one repeated root at $x = 2$.

Order 4 (a quartic equation)

Example: $x^4 - 3x^2 - 4 = 0$

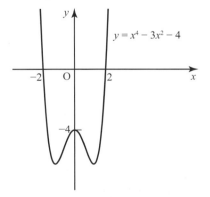

Figure 3.6 This curve has three turning points. There are two real roots at $x = -2$ and $x = 2$ and two complex roots at $x = \pm i$.

There are similar examples for higher order polynomials.

You will learn how to find the complex roots of polynomial equations later in this chapter.

The rest of this chapter explores some properties of polynomials, and ways to use these properties to avoid the difficulties of actually finding the roots of polynomials directly.

It is important that you recognise that the roots of polynomials may be complex. For this reason, in the work that follows, z is used as the variable (or unknown) instead of x to emphasise that the results apply regardless of whether the roots are complex or real.

Quadratic equations

TECHNOLOGY

You could use the equation solver on a calculator.

Discussion point

→ What is the connection between the sums and products of the roots, and the coefficients in the original equation?

ACTIVITY 3.1

Solve each of the following quadratic equations (by factorising or otherwise). Also write down the *sum* and *product* of the two roots.
What do you notice?

Equation	Two roots	Sum of roots	Product of roots
(i) $z^2 - 3z + 2 = 0$			
(ii) $z^2 + z - 6 = 0$			
(iii) $z^2 - 6z + 8 = 0$			
(iv) $z^2 - 3z - 10 = 0$			
(v) $2z^2 - 3z + 1 = 0$			
(vi) $z^2 - 4z + 5 = 0$			

The roots of polynomial equations are usually denoted by Greek letters such as α and β. ← α (alpha) and β (beta) are the first two letters of the Greek alphabet.

 Always be careful to distinguish between:
a – the coefficient of z^2 and
α – one of the roots of the quadratic.

If you know the roots are α and β, you can write the equation

$$az^2 + bz + c = 0$$

in factorised form as

$$a(z - \alpha)(z - \beta) = 0.$$ ← Assuming $a \neq 0$

This gives the identity,

$$az^2 + bz + c \equiv a(z - \alpha)(z - \beta).$$

$$az^2 + bz + c \equiv a\left(z^2 - \alpha z - \beta z + \alpha\beta\right)$$

$$\equiv az^2 - a(\alpha + \beta)z + a\alpha\beta$$ ← Multiplying out

9781471886478

Discussion point

→ What happens if you try to find the values of α and β by solving the equations

$\alpha + \beta = -\dfrac{b}{a}$ and

$\alpha\beta = \dfrac{c}{a}$ as a pair of simultaneous equations?

$b = -a(\alpha + \beta) \Rightarrow \alpha + \beta = -\dfrac{b}{a}$ ← Equating coefficients of z

$c = a\alpha\beta \Rightarrow \alpha\beta = \dfrac{c}{a}$ ← Equating constant terms

So the sum of the roots is

$$\alpha + \beta = -\frac{b}{a}$$

and the product of the roots is

$$\alpha\beta = \frac{c}{a}.$$

From these results you can obtain information about the roots without actually solving the equation.

ACTIVITY 3.2

The quadratic formula gives the roots of the quadratic equation $az^2 + bz + c = 0$ as

$$\alpha = \frac{-b + \sqrt{b^2 - 4ac}}{2a}, \qquad \beta = \frac{-b - \sqrt{b^2 - 4ac}}{2a}.$$

You should see that α and β could be either way round.

Use these expressions to prove that $\alpha + \beta = -\dfrac{b}{a}$ and $\alpha\beta = \dfrac{c}{a}$.

Example 3.1

Find a quadratic equation with roots 5 and −3.

Solution

The sum of the roots is $5 + (-3) = 2$ $\qquad \Rightarrow -\dfrac{b}{a} = 2$

The product of the roots is $5 \times (-3) = -15$ $\qquad \Rightarrow \dfrac{c}{a} = -15$

Taking a to be 1 gives ←

$b = -2$ and $c = -15$

You could choose any value for a but choosing 1 in this case gives the simplest form of the equation.

A quadratic equation with roots 5 and −3 is $z^2 - 2z - 15 = 0$.

Forming new equations

You can find new equations with roots that are related to the roots of the original equation. It is possible to use formulae for $\alpha + \beta$ and $\alpha\beta$, but it is often quicker to use a substitution method. The following example shows you how.

Example 3.2

The roots of the equation $2z^2 + 3z + 5 = 0$ are α and β.

(i) Find the values of $\alpha + \beta$ and $\alpha\beta$.

(ii) Find a quadratic equation with roots 2α and 2β.

Solution

(i) $\alpha + \beta = -\dfrac{3}{2}$ and

$\alpha\beta = \dfrac{5}{2}$

> These lines come from looking at the original quadratic, and quoting the facts $\alpha + \beta = -\dfrac{b}{a}$ and $\alpha\beta = \dfrac{c}{a}$.
> It might be confusing to introduce a, b and c here, since you need different values for them later in the question.

(ii) **Method 1**

This method involves a new variable, $w = 2z$.

$\Rightarrow z = \dfrac{w}{2}$

> So that $y = 2\alpha$ when $z = \alpha$, and $y = 2\beta$ when $z = \beta$.

α and β are the roots of $2z^2 + 3z + 5 = 0$

$\Leftrightarrow 2\alpha$ and 2β are the roots of $2\left(\dfrac{w}{2}\right)^2 + 3\left(\dfrac{w}{2}\right) + 5 = 0$

> Substitute for z

$\Leftrightarrow 2\dfrac{w^2}{4} + 3\dfrac{w}{2} + 5 = 0$

$\Leftrightarrow w^2 + 3w + 10 = 0$

So a quadratic equation with the required roots is $w^2 + 3w + 10 = 0$

Method 2

The sum of the new roots $= 2\alpha + 2\beta$

$= 2(\alpha + \beta)$

$= 2 \times -\dfrac{3}{2}$

$= -3$

The product of the new roots $= 2\alpha \times 2\beta$

$= 4\alpha\beta$

$= 4 \times \dfrac{5}{2}$

$= 10$

Let a, b and c be the coefficients in the new quadratic equation, then

$-\dfrac{b}{a} = -3$ and $\dfrac{c}{a} = 10$.

Taking $a = 1$ gives $b = 3$ and $c = 10$.

So a quadratic equation with the required roots is $z^2 + 3z + 10 = 0$.

Example 3.3	The roots of the equation $3z^2 - 4z - 1 = 0$ are α and β.

Find the quadratic equation with roots $\alpha + 1$ and $\beta + 1$.

Solution

Method 1

Let $w = z + 1$. Then $z = w - 1$.

α and β are the roots of $3z^2 - 4z - 1 = 0$

$\Leftrightarrow \quad \alpha + 1$ and $\beta + 1$ are the roots of $3(w - 1)^2 - 4(w - 1) - 1 = 0$

$\Leftrightarrow \quad 3(w^2 - 2w + 1) - 4(w - 1) - 1 = 0$

$\Leftrightarrow \quad 3w^2 - 6w + 3 - 4w + 4 - 1 = 0$

$\Leftrightarrow \quad 3w^2 - 10w + 2 = 0$

So a quadratic equation with the required roots is $3w^2 - 10w + 2 = 0$

Method 2

$$\alpha + \beta = \frac{4}{3} \text{ and}$$

$$\alpha\beta = -\frac{1}{3}$$

The sum of the new roots $= \alpha + 1 + \beta + 1$

$$= \alpha + \beta + 2$$

$$= \frac{4}{3} + 2$$

$$= \frac{10}{3}$$

The product of the new roots $= (\alpha + 1)(\beta + 1)$

$$= \alpha\beta + (\alpha + \beta) + 1$$

$$= -\frac{1}{3} + \frac{4}{3} + 1$$

So $-\dfrac{b}{a} = \dfrac{10}{3}$ and $\dfrac{c}{a} = 2$. $= 2$

> Choosing $a = 1$ would give a value for b which is not an integer. It is easier here to use $a = 3$.

Choose $a = 3$, then $b = -10$ and $c = 6$. ⟵

So a quadratic equation with the required roots is $3z^2 - 10z + 6 = 0$.

Ⓣ **ACTIVITY 3.3**

Solve the quadratic equations from the previous two examples (perhaps using the equation solver on your calculator, or a computer algebra system):

$2z^2 + 3z + 5 = 0$ $z^2 + 3z + 10 = 0$

$3z^2 - 4z - 1 = 0$ $3z^2 - 10z + 6 = 0$

Verify that the relationships between the roots are correct.

Exercise 3.1

① Write down the sum and product of the roots of each of these quadratic equations.

(i) $2z^2 + 7z + 6 = 0$ (ii) $5z^2 - z - 1 = 0$

(iii) $7z^2 + 2 = 0$ (iv) $5z^2 + 24z = 0$

(v) $z(z + 8) = 4 - 3z$ (vi) $3z^2 + 8z - 6 = 0$

② Write down quadratic equations (in expanded form, with integer coefficients) with the following roots:

(i) $7, 3$ (ii) $4, -1$

(iii) $-5, -4.5$ (iv) $5, 0$

(v) 3 (repeated)   (vi) $3 - 2i, 3 + 2i$

③ The roots of $2z^2 + 5z - 9 = 0$ are α and β.

Find quadratic equations with these roots.

(i) 3α and 3β (ii) $-\alpha$ and $-\beta$

(iii) $\alpha - 2$ and $\beta - 2$ (iv) $1 - 2\alpha$ and $1 - 2\beta$

④ Using the fact that $\alpha + \beta = -\dfrac{b}{a}$, and $\alpha\beta = \dfrac{c}{a}$, what can you say about the roots, α and β, of $az^2 + bz + c = 0$ in the following cases:

(i) a, b, c are all positive and $b^2 - 4ac > 0$

(ii) $b = 0$

(iii) $c = 0$

(iv) a and c have opposite signs

⑤ One root of $az^2 + bz + c = 0$ is twice the other. Prove that $2b^2 = 9ac$.

⑥ The roots of $az^2 + bz + c = 0$ are, α and β. Find quadratic equations with the following roots:

(i) $k\alpha$ and $k\beta$

(ii) $k + \alpha$ and $k + \beta$

> You may wish to introduce different letters (say p, q and r instead of a, b and c) for the coefficients of your target equation.

⑦ (i)   A quadratic equation with *real* coefficients $ax^2 + bx + c = 0$ has complex roots z_1 and z_2. Explain how the relationships between roots and coefficients show that z_1 and z_2 must be complex conjugates.

(ii)   Find a quadratic equation with *complex* coefficients which has roots $2 + 3i$ and $3 - i$.

2 Cubic equations

There are corresponding properties for the roots of higher order polynomials.

To see how to generalise the properties you can begin with the cubics in a similar manner to the discussion of the quadratics. As before, it is conventional to use Greek letters to represent the three roots: α, β and γ (gamma, the third letter of the Greek alphabet).

You can write the general cubic as
$$az^3 + bz^2 + cz + d = 0$$
or in factorised form as
$$a(z - \alpha)(z - \beta)(z - \gamma) = 0.$$

This gives the identity
$$az^3 + bz^2 + cz + d \equiv a(z - \alpha)(z - \beta)(z - \gamma).$$

> Check this for yourself.

Multiplying out the right-hand side gives
$$az^3 + bz^2 + cz + d \equiv az^3 - a(\alpha + \beta + \gamma)z^2 + a(\alpha\beta + \beta\gamma + \gamma\alpha)z - a\alpha\beta\gamma.$$

Comparing coefficients of z^2:

$$b = -a(\alpha + \beta + \gamma) \Rightarrow \alpha + \beta + \gamma = -\frac{b}{a} \qquad \text{Sum of the roots:} \quad \sum \alpha$$

Comparing coefficients of z:

$$c = a(\alpha\beta + \beta\gamma + \gamma\alpha) \Rightarrow \alpha\beta + \beta\gamma + \gamma\alpha = \frac{c}{a} \quad \substack{\text{Sum of products of} \\ \text{pairs of roots:}} \quad \sum \alpha\beta$$

Comparing constant terms:

$$d = -a\alpha\beta\gamma \Rightarrow \alpha\beta\gamma = -\frac{d}{a} \qquad \substack{\text{Product of the three} \\ \text{roots:}} \qquad \alpha\beta\gamma$$

 Note

Notation

It often becomes tedious writing out the sums of various combinations of roots, so shorthand notation is often used:

$\sum \alpha = \alpha + \beta + \gamma$ the sum of individual roots (however many there are)

$\sum \alpha\beta = \alpha\beta + \beta\gamma + \gamma\alpha$ the sum of the products of pairs of roots

$\sum \alpha\beta\gamma = \alpha\beta\gamma$ the sum of the products of triples of roots (in this case only one)

Provided you know the degree of the equation (e.g. cubic, quartic, etc,) it will be quite clear what this means. Functions like these are called symmetric functions of the roots, since exchanging any two of α, β, γ will not change the value of the function.

Using this notation you can shorten tediously long expressions. For example, for a cubic with roots α, β and γ,

$$\alpha^2\beta + \alpha\beta^2 + \beta^2\gamma + \beta\gamma^2 + \gamma^2\alpha + \gamma\alpha^2 = \sum \alpha^2\beta.$$

This becomes particularly useful when you deal with quartics in the next section.

Example 3.4

The roots of the equation $2z^3 - 9z^2 - 27z + 54 = 0$ form a geometric progression (i.e. they may be written as $\frac{a}{r}$, a, ar).

Solve the equation.

> This makes the working easier than using a, ar, ar^2.

Solution

$$\alpha\beta\gamma = -\frac{d}{a} \qquad \Rightarrow \frac{a}{r} \times a \times ar = -\frac{54}{2}$$

$$\Rightarrow a^3 = -27$$

$$\Rightarrow a = -3$$

$$\Sigma \alpha = -\frac{b}{a} \qquad \Rightarrow \frac{a}{r} + a + ar = \frac{9}{2}$$

$$\Rightarrow -3\left(\frac{1}{r} + 1 + r\right) = \frac{9}{2}$$

$$\Rightarrow 2\left(\frac{1}{r} + 1 + r\right) = -3$$

$$\Rightarrow 2 + 2r + 2r^2 = -3r$$

$$\Rightarrow 2r^2 + 5r + 2) = 0$$

$$\Rightarrow (2r + 1)(r + 2) = 0$$

$$\Rightarrow r = -2 \text{ or } r = -\frac{1}{2}$$

Either value of r gives three roots: $\frac{3}{2}, -3, 6$.

The substitution method can be used for cubic and other equations to form new equations with roots related to the roots of the original equation.

Example 3.5

The roots of the cubic equation $2z^3 + 5z^2 - 3z - 2 = 0$ are α, β, γ.

Find the cubic equation with roots $2\alpha + 1, 2\beta + 1, 2\gamma + 1$.

Solution

This method involves a new variable $w = 2z + 1$. You write z in terms of w, and substitute into the original equation:

> This is a transformation of z in the same way as the new roots are a transformation of the original z roots.

$$z = \frac{w-1}{2} \quad \alpha, \beta, \gamma \text{ are the roots of } 2z^3 + 5z^2 - 3z - 2 = 0$$

$$\Leftrightarrow \quad 2\alpha + 1, 2\beta + 1, 2\gamma + 1 \text{ are the roots of}$$

$$2\left(\frac{w-1}{2}\right)^3 + 5\left(\frac{w-1}{2}\right)^2 - 3\left(\frac{w-1}{2}\right) - 2 = 0$$

$$\Leftrightarrow \frac{2}{8}(w-1)^3 + \frac{5}{4}(w-1)^2 - \frac{3}{2}(w-1) - 2 = 0$$

$$\Leftrightarrow (w-1)^3 + 5(w-1)^2 - 6(w-1) - 8 = 0$$

$$\Leftrightarrow w^3 - 3w^2 + 3w - 1 + 5w^2 - 10w + 5 - 6w + 6 - 8 = 0$$

$$\Leftrightarrow w^3 + 2w^2 - 13w + 2 = 0$$

TECHNOLOGY

Use graphing software to draw the graphs of $y = 2x^3 + 5x^2 - 3x - 2$ and $y = x^3 + 2x^2 - 13x + 2$. How do these graphs relate to Example 3.5? What transformations map the first graph on to the second one?

① The roots of the cubic equation $2z^3 + 3z^2 - z + 7 = 0$ are α, β, γ.
Find the following:

(i) $\sum \alpha$ (ii) $\sum \alpha\beta$

(iii) $\sum \alpha\beta\gamma$

② Find cubic equations (with integer coefficients) with the following roots:

(i) $1, 2, 4$ (ii) $2, -2, 3$

(iii) $0, -2, -1.5$ (iv) 2 (repeated), 2.5

(v) $-2, -3, 5$ (vi) $1, 2 + i, 2 - i$

③ The roots of each of these equations are in arithmetic progression (i.e. they may be written as $a - d, a, a + d$).
Solve each equation.

(i) $z^3 - 15z^2 + 66z - 80 = 0$ (ii) $9z^3 - 18z^2 - 4z + 8 = 0$

(iii) $z^3 - 6z^2 + 16 = 0$ (iv) $54z^3 - 189z^2 + 207z - 70 = 0$

④ The roots of the equation $z^3 + z^2 + 2z - 3 = 0$ are α, β, γ.

(i) The substitution $w = z + 3$ is made. Write z in terms of w.

(ii) Substitute your answer to part (i) for z in the equation
$z^3 + z^2 + 2z - 3 = 0$

(iii) Give your answer to part (ii) as a cubic equation in w with integer coefficients.

(iv) Write down the roots of your equation in part (iii), in terms of α, β and γ.

⑤ The roots of the equation $z^3 - 2z^2 + z - 3 = 0$ are α, β, γ. Use the substitution $w = 2z$ to find a cubic equation in w with roots $2\alpha, 2\beta, 2\gamma$.

⑥ The roots of the equation $2z^3 + 4z^2 - 3z + 1 = 0$ are α, β, γ.
Find cubic equations with these roots:

(i) $2 - \alpha, 2 - \beta, 2 - \gamma$ (ii) $3\alpha - 2, 3\beta - 2, 3\gamma - 2$

⑦ The roots of the equation $2z^3 - 12z^2 + kz - 15 = 0$ are in arithmetic progression.
Solve the equation and find k.

⑧ Solve $32z^3 - 14z + 3 = 0$ given that one root is twice the other.

⑨ The equation $z^3 + pz^2 + 2pz + q = 0$ has roots $\alpha, 2\alpha, 4\alpha$.
Find all possible values of p, q, α.

⑩ The roots of $z^3 + pz^2 + qz + r = 0$ are $\alpha, -\alpha, \beta$, and $r \neq 0$.
Show that $r = pq$, and find all three roots in terms of p and q.

⑪ The cubic equation $8x^3 + px^2 + qx + r = 0$ has roots $\alpha, \dfrac{1}{2\alpha}$ and β.

(i) Express p, q and r in terms of α and β.

(ii) Show that $2r^2 - pr + 4q = 16$.

(iii) Given that $p = 6$ and $q = -23$, find the two possible values of r and, in each case, solve the equation $8x^3 + 6x^2 - 23x + r = 0$.

⑫ Show that one root of $az^3 + bz^2 + cz + d = 0$ is the reciprocal of another root if and only if $a^2 - d^2 = ac - dc$.

Verify that this condition is satisfied for the equation

$21z^3 - 16z^2 + 78z - 27 = 0$ and hence solve the equation.

⑬ Find a formula connecting a, b, c and d which is a necessary and sufficient condition for the roots of the equation $az^3 + bz^2 + cz + d = 0$ to be in geometric progression.

Show that this condition is satisfied for the equation

$8z^3 - 52z^2 + 78z - 27 = 0$ and hence solve the equation.

3 Quartic equations

Quartic equations have four roots, denoted by the first four Greek letters: α, β, γ and δ (delta).

Discussion point

→ By looking back at the two formulae for quadratics and the three formulae for cubics, predict the *four* formulae that relate the roots α, β, γ and δ to the coefficients a, b, c and d of the quartic equation $ax^4 + bx^3 + cx^2 + dx + e = 0$.

→ You may wish to check/derive these results yourself before looking at the derivation on the next page.

Historical note

The formulae used to relate the coefficients of polynomials with sums and products of their roots are called **Vieta's Formulae** after François Viète (a Frenchman who commonly used a Latin version of his name: Franciscus Vieta). He was a lawyer by trade but made important progress (while doing mathematics in his spare time) on algebraic notation and helped pave the way for the more logical system of notation you use today.

Derivation of formulae

As before, the quartic equation

$$az^4 + bz^3 + cz^2 + dz + e = 0$$

can be written is factorised form as

$$a(z - \alpha)(z - \beta)(z - \gamma)(z - \delta) = 0.$$

This gives the identity

$$az^4 + bz^3 + cz^2 + dz + e \equiv a(z - \alpha)(z - \beta)(z - \gamma)(z - \delta).$$

Multiplying out the right-hand side gives

$$az^4 + bz^3 + cz^2 + dz + e \equiv az^4 - a(\alpha + \beta + \gamma + \delta)z^3$$
$$+ a(\alpha\beta + \alpha\gamma + \alpha\delta + \beta\gamma + \beta\delta + \gamma\alpha)z^2 - a(\alpha\beta\gamma + \beta\gamma\delta$$
$$+ \gamma\delta\alpha + \delta\alpha\beta)z + a\alpha\beta\gamma\delta.$$

Equating coefficients shows that

$$\sum \alpha = \alpha + \beta + \gamma + \delta = -\frac{b}{a}$$ The sum of the individual roots.

$$\sum \alpha\beta = \alpha\beta + \alpha\gamma + \alpha\delta + \beta\gamma + \beta\delta + \gamma\delta = \frac{c}{a}$$ The sum of the products of roots in pairs.

$$\sum \alpha\beta\gamma = \alpha\beta\gamma + \beta\gamma\delta + \gamma\delta\alpha + \delta\alpha\beta = -\frac{d}{a}$$ The sum of the products of roots in threes.

$$\alpha\beta\gamma\delta = \frac{e}{a}$$ The product of the roots.

Check this for yourself.

Example 3.6

The roots of the quartic equation $4z^4 + pz^3 + qz^2 - z + 3 = 0$ are $\alpha, -\alpha, \alpha + \lambda, \alpha - \lambda$ where α and λ are real numbers.

(i)   Express p and q in terms of α and λ.

(ii) Show that $\alpha = -\frac{1}{2}$, and find the values of p and q.

(iii) Give the roots of the quartic equation.

Solution

(i) $\sum \alpha = \alpha - \alpha + \alpha + \lambda + \alpha - \lambda = -\frac{p}{4}$

$\Rightarrow 2\alpha = -\frac{p}{4}$

$\Rightarrow p = -8\alpha$

Use the sum of the individual roots to find an expression for p.

$\sum \alpha\beta = -\alpha^2 + \alpha(\alpha + \lambda) + \alpha(\alpha - \lambda) - \alpha(\alpha + \lambda) - \alpha(\alpha - \lambda)$
$$+ (\alpha + \lambda)(\alpha - \lambda) = \frac{q}{4}$$

$\Rightarrow -\lambda^2 = \frac{q}{4}$

$\Rightarrow q = -4\lambda^2$

Use the sum of the product of the roots in pairs to find an expression for q.

(ii)
$\sum \alpha\beta\gamma = -\alpha^2(\alpha + \lambda) - \alpha(\alpha + \lambda)(\alpha - \lambda) + \alpha(\alpha + \lambda)(\alpha - \lambda) - \alpha^2(\alpha - \lambda) = \frac{1}{4}$

$\Rightarrow -2\alpha^3 = \frac{1}{4}$

$\Rightarrow \alpha = -\frac{1}{2}$

$p = -8\alpha = -8 \times -\frac{1}{2} = 4$

Use the sum of the product of the roots in threes to find α (λ cancels out) and hence find p, using your answer to part (i).

$$\alpha\beta\gamma\delta = -\alpha^2(\alpha + \lambda)(\alpha - \lambda) = \frac{3}{4}$$

Use the sum of the product of the roots and the value for α to find λ, and hence find q, using your answer to part (i).

$$\Rightarrow -\alpha^2(\alpha^2 - \lambda^2) = \frac{3}{4}$$

$$\Rightarrow -\frac{1}{4}\left(\frac{1}{4} - \lambda^2\right) = \frac{3}{4}$$

$$\Rightarrow \frac{1}{4} - \lambda^2 = -3$$

$$\Rightarrow \lambda^2 = \frac{13}{4}$$

$$q = -4\lambda^2 = -4 \times \frac{13}{4} = -13$$

Substitute the values for α and λ to give the roots.

(iii) The roots of the equation are $\frac{1}{2}, -\frac{1}{2}, -\frac{1}{2} + \frac{1}{2}\sqrt{13}, -\frac{1}{2} - \frac{1}{2}\sqrt{13}$.

Exercise 3.3

① The roots of $2z^4 + 3z^3 + 6z^2 - 5z + 4 = 0$ are α, β, γ and δ.

Write down the following:

(i) $\sum\alpha$

(ii) $\sum\alpha\beta$

(iii) $\sum\alpha\beta\gamma$

(iv) $\sum\alpha\beta\gamma\delta$

② Find quartic equations (with integer coefficients) with the roots.

(i) $1, -1, 2, 4$

(ii) $0, 1.5, -2.5, -4$

(iii) 1.5 (repeated), -3 (repeated)

(iv) $1, -3, 1 + i, 1 - i$.

③ The roots of the quartic equation $2z^4 + 4z^3 - 3z^2 - z + 6 = 0$ are α, β, γ and δ.

Find quartic equations with these roots:

(i) $2\alpha, 2\beta, 2\gamma, 2\delta$

(ii) $\alpha - 1, \beta - 1, \gamma - 1, \delta - 1$.

④ The roots of the quartic equation $x^4 + 4x^3 - 8x + 4 = 0$ are α, β, γ and δ.

(i) Find a quartic equation with roots $\alpha + 1, \beta + 1, \gamma + 1$ and $\delta + 1$.

(ii) Solve the equation found in part (i), and hence find the values of α, β, γ and δ.

⑤ The quartic equation $x^4 + px^3 - 12x + q = 0$, where p and q are real, has roots $\alpha, 3\alpha, \beta, -\beta$.

(i) By considering the coefficients of x^2 and x, find α and β, where $\beta > 0$.

(ii) Show that $p = 4$ and find the value of q.

(iii) By making the substitution $y = x - k$, for a suitable value of k, find a **cubic** equation in y, with integer coefficients, which has roots $-2\alpha, \beta - 3\alpha, -\beta - 3\alpha$.

⑥ (i) Make conjectures about the five properties of the roots $\alpha, \beta, \gamma, \delta$ and ε (epsilon) of the general quintic $ax^5 + bx^4 + cx^3 + dx^2 + ex + f = 0$.

(ii) Prove your conjectures.

4 Solving polynomial equations with complex roots

When solving polynomial equations with real coefficients, it is important to remember that any **complex roots occur in conjugate pairs**. In other words, if $x + y\mathrm{i}$ is a root, so is $x - y\mathrm{i}$.

> ### Discussion point
>
> → Explain how the relationships between the roots and the coefficients of a polynomial equation with real coefficients show that any complex roots must occur in conjugate pairs.

When there is a possibility of complex roots, it is common to express the polynomial in terms of z.

Example 3.7

The equation $z^3 + 7z^2 + 17z + 15 = 0$ has one integer root.

(i) Factorise $f(z) = z^3 + 7z^2 + 17z + 15$.

(ii) Solve $z^3 + 7z^2 + 17z + 15 = 0$.

(iii) Sketch the graph of $y = x^3 + 7x^2 + 17x + 15$.

Solution

(i) $f(1) = 1^3 + 7 \times 1^2 + 17 \times 1 + 15 = 40$ ← If there is an integer root, it must be a factor of 15. So try $z = \pm1, \pm3$, etc.

$f(-1) = (-1)^3 + 7 \times (-1)^2 + 17 \times (-1) + 15 = 4$

$f(3) = 3^3 + 7 \times 3^2 + 17 \times 3 + 15 = 156$

$f(-3) = (-3)^3 + 7 \times (-3)^2 + 17 \times (-3) + 15 = 0$ ← $f(-3) = 0$ so using the factor theorem, $(z + 3)$ is a factor.

Note

For question 6, you should try the algebra by hand, thinking about keeping good presentation habits for long algebraic expansions. You may want to check any long expansions using CAS (computer algebra software). You then might also like to consider whether a 'proof' is still valid if it relies on a computer system to prove it – look up the history of *The Four Colour Theorem* to explore this idea further.

Prior knowledge

You need to know how to use the factor theorem to solve polynomial equations (covered in AS Mathematics Chapter 7).

So one root is $z = -3$, and $(z + 3)$ is a factor of $f(z)$.

Using algebraic division or by inspection, $f(z)$ can be written in the form:

$f(z) = (z + 3)(z^2 + 4z + 5)$ ← Check this for yourself

Now solve the quadratic equation $z^2 + 4z + 5 = 0$:

using the quadratic formula.

$$z = \frac{-4 \pm \sqrt{4^2 - (4 \times 1 \times 5)}}{2} = \frac{-4 \pm \sqrt{-4}}{2} = \frac{-4 \pm 2i}{2} = -2 \pm i$$

So, fully factorised $f(z) = (z + 3)(z - (-2 + i))(z - (-2 - i))$

(ii) The roots are $z = -3$, $z = -2 \pm i$ ←

Note that there is one conjugate pair of complex roots and one real root.

(iii) Figure 3.7 shows the graph of the curve $y = f(x)$.

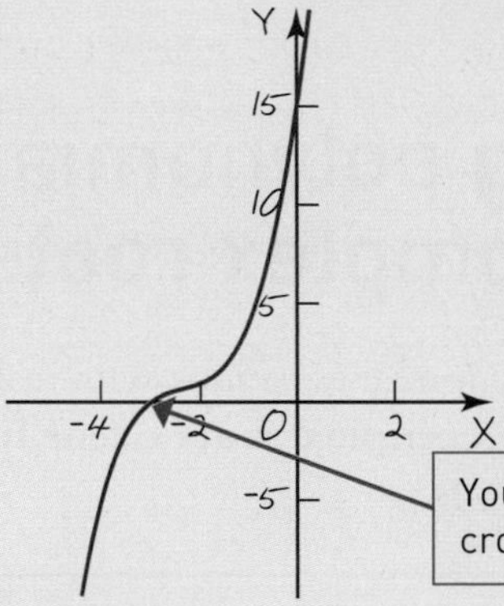

You can see that the graph crosses the x-axis just once.

Figure 3.7

Sometimes you can use the relationships between roots and coefficients of polynomial equations to help you to find roots. In Example 3.8, two solution methods are shown.

Example 3.8

Given that $z = 1 + 2i$ is a root of $4z^3 - 11z^2 + 26z - 15 = 0$, find the other roots.

Solution 1

As complex roots occur in conjugate pairs, the conjugate $z = 1 - 2i$ is also a root.

The next step is to find a quadratic equation $az^2 + bz + c = 0$ with roots $1 + 2i$ and $1 - 2i$.

$$-\frac{b}{a} = (1 + 2i) + (1 - 2i) = 2$$

$$\frac{c}{a} = (1 + 2i)(1 - 2i) = 1 + 4 = 5$$

Taking $a = 1$ gives $b = -2$ and $c = 5$

So the quadratic equation is $z^2 - 2z + 5 = 0$

$4z^3 - 11z^2 + 26z - 15 = (z^2 - 2z + 5)(4z - 3)$

The other roots are $z = 1 - 2i$ and $z = \frac{3}{4}$.

Solution 2

As complex roots occur in conjugate pairs, the conjugate $z = 1 - 2i$ is also a root.

The sum of the three roots is $\dfrac{11}{4}$ ← $\boxed{\alpha + \beta + \gamma = -\dfrac{b}{a}}$

$1 + 2i + 1 - 2i + \gamma = \dfrac{11}{4}$

$\gamma = \dfrac{11}{4} - 2$

$\quad = \dfrac{3}{4}$

The other roots are $z = 1 - 2i$ and $z = \dfrac{3}{4}$.

Notice that Solution 2 is more efficient than Solution 1 in this case. You should look out for situations like this where using the relationships between roots and coefficients can be helpful.

Example 3.9

(i)   Solve $z^4 - 3z^2 - 4 = 0$.

(ii) Sketch the curve $y = x^4 - 3x^2 - 4$.

(iii) Show the roots of $z^4 - 3z^2 - 4 = 0$ on an Argand diagram.

Solution

(i) $z^4 - 3z^2 - 4 = 0$
$(z^2 - 4)(z^2 + 1) = 0$ ← $\boxed{\begin{array}{l} z^4 - 3z^2 - 4 \\ \text{is a quadratic} \\ \text{in } z^2 \text{ and can} \\ \text{be factorised.} \end{array}}$
$(z - 2)(z + 2)(z + i)(z - i) = 0$

The solution is $z = 2, -2, i, -i$.

(ii)

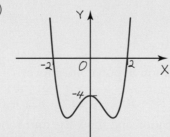

Figure 3.8

(iii)

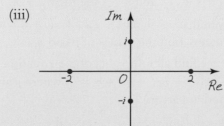

Figure 3.9

Exercise 3.4

① $4 - 5i$ is one root of a quadratic equation with real coefficients.

Write down the second root of the equation and hence find the equation.

② Verify that $2 + i$ is a root of $z^3 - z^2 - 7z + 15 = 0$, and find the other roots.

③ One root of $z^3 - 15z^2 + 76z - 140 = 0$ is an integer.

Solve the equation and show all three roots on an Argand diagram.

④ The equation $z^3 - 2z^2 - 6z + 27 = 0$ has a real integer root in the range $-6 \leq z \leq 0$.

(i) Find the real root of the equation.

(ii) Hence solve the equation and find the exact value of all three roots.

⑤ Given that 4 is a root of the equation $z^3 - z^2 - 3z - k = 0$, find the value of k and hence find the exact value of the other two roots of the equation.

⑥ Given that $1 - i$ is a root of $z^3 + pz^2 + qz + 12 = 0$, find the real numbers p and q, and state the other roots.

⑦ The three roots of a cubic equation are shown on the Argand diagram in Figure 3.10.

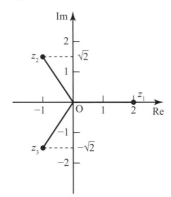

Figure 3.10

Find the equation in polynomial form.

⑧ One root of $z^4 - 10z^3 + 42z^2 - 82z + 65 = 0$ is $3 + 2i$.

Solve the equation and show the four roots on an Argand diagram.

⑨ You are given the complex number $w = 1 - i$.

(i) Express w^2, w^3 and w^4 in the form $a + bi$.

(ii) Given that $w^4 + 3w^3 + pw^2 + qw + 8 = 0$, where p and q are real numbers, find the values of p and q.

(iii) Hence find all four roots of the equation
$z^4 + 3z^3 + pz^2 + qz + 8 = 0$, where p and q are the real numbers found in part (ii).

⑩ (i) Solve the equation $z^4 - 81 = 0$

(ii) Hence show the four fourth roots of 81 on an Argand diagram.

⑪ (i) Given that $\alpha = -1 + 2i$, express α^2 and α^3 in the form $a + bi$.
        Hence show that α is a root of the cubic equation
        $z^3 + 7z^2 + 15z + 25 = 0$

  (ii) Find the other two roots of this cubic equation.

  (iii) Illustrate the three roots of the cubic equation on an Argand diagram.

⑫ For each of these statements about polynomial equations with real coefficients, say whether the statement is TRUE or FALSE, and give an explanation.

  (A) A cubic equation can have three complex roots.

  (B) Some equations of order 6 have no real roots.

  (C) A cubic equation can have a single root repeated three times.

  (D) A quartic equation can have a repeated complex root.

⑬ Given that $z = -2 + i$ is a root of the equation
   $z^4 + az^3 + bz^2 + 10z + 25 = 0$, find the values of a and b, and solve the equation.

⑭ The equation $z^4 - 8z^3 + 20z^2 - 72z + 99 = 0$ has a purely imaginary root.

   Solve the equation.

⑮ In this question, α is the complex number $-1 + 3i$.

  (i) Find α^2 and α^3.

  It is given that λ and μ are real numbers such that

  $\lambda\alpha^3 + 8\alpha^2 + 34\alpha + \mu = 0$

  (ii) Show that $\lambda = 3$, and find the value of μ.

  (iii) Solve the equation $\lambda z^3 + 8z^2 + 34z + \mu = 0$, where λ and μ are as in part (ii).

  (iv) Illustrate the three roots on an Argand diagram.

⑯ Three of the roots of the quintic equation $az^5 + bz^4 + cz^3 + dz^2 + ez + f = 0$ are $3, -4i$ and $3 - i$.

   Find the values of the coefficients of the equation.

LEARNING OUTCOMES

When you have completed this chapter you should be able to:

➤ know the relationships between the roots and coefficients of quadratic, cubic and quartic equations

➤ form new equations whose roots are related to the roots of a given equation by a linear transformation

➤ understand that complex roots of polynomial equations with real coefficients occur in conjugate pairs

➤ solve cubic and quartic equations with complex roots, given sufficient information.

KEY POINTS

1 If α and β are the roots of the quadratic equation $az^2 + bz + c = 0$, then
$$\alpha + \beta = -\frac{b}{a} \text{ and } \alpha\beta = \frac{c}{a}.$$

2 If α, β and γ are the roots of the cubic equation $az^3 + bz^2 + cz + d = 0$, then

$$\Sigma\alpha = \alpha + \beta + \gamma = -\frac{b}{a},$$

$$\Sigma\alpha\beta = \alpha\beta + \beta\gamma + \gamma\alpha = \frac{c}{a} \text{ and,}$$

$$\alpha\beta\gamma = -\frac{d}{a}.$$

3 If α, β, γ and δ are the roots of the quartic equation
$az^4 + bz^3 + cz^2 + dz + e = 0$, then
$$\Sigma\alpha = \alpha + \beta + \gamma + \delta = -\frac{b}{a},$$

$$\Sigma\alpha\beta = \alpha\beta + \alpha\gamma + \alpha\delta + \beta\gamma + \beta\delta + \gamma\delta = \frac{c}{a},$$

$$\Sigma\alpha\beta\gamma = \alpha\beta\gamma + \beta\gamma\delta + \gamma\delta\alpha + \delta\alpha\beta = -\frac{d}{a} \text{ and}$$

$$\alpha\beta\gamma\delta = \frac{e}{a}.$$

4 All of these formulae may be summarised using the shorthand sigma notation for elementary symmetric functions as follows:

$$\Sigma\alpha = -\frac{b}{a}$$

$$\Sigma\alpha\beta = \frac{c}{a}$$

$$\Sigma\alpha\beta\gamma = -\frac{d}{a}$$

$$\Sigma\alpha\beta\gamma\delta = \frac{e}{a}$$

using the convention that polynomials of degree n are labelled

$az^n + bz^{n-1} + \dots = 0$ and have roots α, β, γ, …

5 A polynomial equation of degree n has n roots, taking into account complex roots and repeated roots. In the case of polynomial equations with real coefficients, complex roots always occur in conjugate pairs.

Induction

1 Proof by induction

The oldest person to have ever lived, with documentary evidence, is believed to be a French woman called Jeanne Calment who died aged 122, in 1997.

Emily is an old woman who claims to have broken the record. A reporter asked her, 'How do you know you're 122 years old?'

She replied, 'Because I was 121 last year.'

The sort of argument that Emily was trying to use is called inductive reasoning. If all the elements are present it can be used in proof by induction. This is the subject of this chapter. It is a very beautiful form of proof but it is also very delicate; if you miss out any of the steps in the argument, as Emily did, you invalidate your whole proof.

> **Discussion point**
> → Is this a valid argument?

ACTIVITY 4.1

Work out the first four matrices in this sequence:

$$\begin{pmatrix} 1 & 1 \\ 0 & 1 \end{pmatrix}^1 = \begin{pmatrix} 1 & 1 \\ 0 & 1 \end{pmatrix}$$

$$\begin{pmatrix} 1 & 1 \\ 0 & 1 \end{pmatrix}^2 =$$

$$\begin{pmatrix} 1 & 1 \\ 0 & 1 \end{pmatrix}^3 =$$

$$\begin{pmatrix} 1 & 1 \\ 0 & 1 \end{pmatrix}^4 =$$

Activity 4.1 illustrates one common way of solving problems in mathematics. Looking at a number of particular cases may show a pattern, which can be used to form a **conjecture** (i.e. a theory about a possible general result).

Conjectures are often written algebraically.

The conjecture can then be tested in further particular cases.

In this case, the nth matrix in the sequence can be written as

$$\begin{pmatrix} 1 & 1 \\ 0 & 1 \end{pmatrix}^n$$

and the activity shows that the conjecture

$$\begin{pmatrix} 1 & 1 \\ 0 & 1 \end{pmatrix}^n = \begin{pmatrix} 1 & n \\ 0 & 1 \end{pmatrix}$$

is true for $n = 1, 2, 3$ and 4.

If you find a **counter-example** at any point (a case where the conjecture is not true) then the conjecture is definitely disproved. If, on the other hand, the further cases agree with the conjecture then you may feel that you are on the right lines, but you can never be mathematically certain that trying another particular case might not reveal a counter-example: the conjecture is supported by more evidence but not proved.

The ultimate goal is to prove this conjecture is true for *all* positive integers. But it is often not possible to prove such conjectures by deduction from known results. A different approach is needed: **mathematical induction**.

In Activity 4.1 you established that the conjecture is true for particular cases of n ($n = 1, 2, 3$ and 4).

Now, assume that the conjecture is true for a particular integer, $n = k$ say, so that

$$\begin{pmatrix} 1 & 1 \\ 0 & 1 \end{pmatrix}^k = \begin{pmatrix} 1 & k \\ 0 & 1 \end{pmatrix}$$

and use this assumption to check what happens for the next integer, $n = k + 1$.

If the conjecture is true then you should get

$$\begin{pmatrix} 1 & 1 \\ 0 & 1 \end{pmatrix}^{k+1} = \begin{pmatrix} 1 & k+1 \\ 0 & 1 \end{pmatrix}$$

This is your target result. It is what you need to establish.

Look at the left-hand side. You can see that it can be written as

$$\begin{pmatrix} 1 & 1 \\ 0 & 1 \end{pmatrix}^{k} \times \begin{pmatrix} 1 & 1 \\ 0 & 1 \end{pmatrix}$$

and the first matrix is part of the assumption.

$$\begin{pmatrix} 1 & 1 \\ 0 & 1 \end{pmatrix}^{k} \times \begin{pmatrix} 1 & 1 \\ 0 & 1 \end{pmatrix} = \begin{pmatrix} 1 & k \\ 0 & 1 \end{pmatrix} \times \begin{pmatrix} 1 & 1 \\ 0 & 1 \end{pmatrix}$$ using the assumption

$$= \begin{pmatrix} 1 \times 1 & 1 \times 1 + k \times 1 \\ 0 & 1 \times 1 \end{pmatrix}$$ multiplying the matrices

$$= \begin{pmatrix} 1 & k+1 \\ 0 & 1 \end{pmatrix}$$ which is the target result.

These steps show that *if* the conjecture is true for $n = k$, *then* it is true for $n = k + 1$.

Since you have already proved it is true for $n = 1$, you can deduce that it is therefore true for $n = 2$ (by taking $k = 1$).

You can continue in this way (e.g. take $n = 2$ and deduce it is true for $n = 3$) as far as you want to go. Since you can reach *any* positive integer n you have now proved the conjecture is true for *every positive integer*.

This method of **proof by mathematical induction** (often shortened to **proof by induction**) is a bit like the process of climbing a ladder:

If you can

1 get on the ladder (the bottom rung), and

2 get from one rung to the next, then you can climb as far up the ladder as you like.

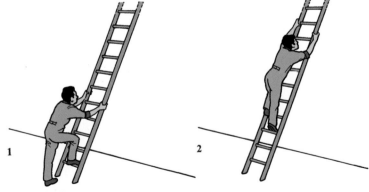

Figure 4.2

The corresponding steps in the previous proof are

1 showing the conjecture is true for $n = 1$, and
2 showing that *if* it is true for a particular value ($n = k$ say), *then* it is true for the next one ($n = k + 1$).

(Notice the *if… then…* structure to this step.)

You should conclude any argument by mathematical induction with a statement of what you have shown.

Steps in mathematical induction

To prove something by mathematical induction you need to state a conjecture to begin with. Then there are five elements needed to try to prove the conjecture is true.

- Proving that it is true for a starting value (e.g. $n = 1$).

- Finding the target expression:
  using the result for $n = k$ to find the equivalent result for $n = k + 1$.

This can be done before or after finding the target expression, but you may find it easier to find the target expression first so that you know what you are working towards.

To find the target expression you replace k with $k + 1$ in the result for $n = k$.

- Proving that:
  if it is true for $n = k$, *then* it is true for $n = k + 1$.

- Arguing that since it is true for $n = 1$, it is also true for $n = 1 + 1 = 2$, and so for $n = 2 + 1 = 3$ and for all subsequent values of n.

This ensures the argument is properly rounded off. You will often use the word 'therefore'.

- Concluding the argument by writing down the result and stating that it has been proved.

So far, you used mathematical induction to prove results about powers of matrices. The method of proof by mathematical induction can be used in many different contexts. The following examples show you how it can be used to prove results about divisibility, matrices, inequalities and factorials.

Example 4.1

Prove that $12^n + 2 \times 5^{n-1}$ is divisible by 7.

Solution

For $n = 1$, $12^1 + 2 \times 5^0 = 12 + 2 = 14$, so the result is true for $n = 1$.

Assume that the result is true for $n = k$, so that $12^k + 2 \times 5^{k-1}$ is divisible by 7.

$12^k + 2 \times 5^{k-1} = 7m$.

> Target statement: $12^{k+1} + 2 \times 5^k$ is divisible by 7.

$12^k = 7m - 2 \times 5^{k-1}$

$12^{k+1} + 2 \times 5^k = 12 \times 12^k + 2 \times 5^k$

> Use $12^{k+1} = 12 \times 12^k$.

$\quad = 12 \times (7m - 2 \times 5^{k-1}) + 2 \times 5^k$

$\quad = 84m - 24 \times 5^{k-1} + 2 \times 5 \times 5^{k-1}$

$\quad = 84m - 14 \times 5^{k-1}$

$\quad = 7[12m - 2 \times 5^{k-1}]$

Now the expression in the square bracket is obviously an integer, so the whole expression is a multiple of 7.

If the result is true for $n = k$, then it is true for $n = k + 1$.

Since it is true for $n = 1$, it is true for all positive integer values of n.

Therefore $12^n + 2 \times 5^{n-1}$ is divisible by 7.

⑦ Prove that $11^n + 3 \times 4^{n-1}$ is divisible by 7 for all positive integers n.

⑧ Prove that $5^{2n+2} - 24n - 25$ is divisible by 576 for all positive integers n.

⑨ Let $\mathbf{M}$ and $\mathbf{I}$ be the matrices $\begin{pmatrix} 1 & 0 \\ 0 & 2 \end{pmatrix}$ and $\begin{pmatrix} 1 & 0 \\ 0 & 1 \end{pmatrix}$ respectively.

   (i) Prove that $\mathbf{M}^2 = 3\mathbf{M} - 2\mathbf{I}$.

   (ii) Prove that for all positive integers n,

     $\mathbf{M}^n = (2^n - 1)\mathbf{M} - 2(2^{n-1} - 1)\mathbf{I}$.

⑩ (i) Prove that, if n is a positive integer greater than or equal to 7, $n! > 3^n$.

   (ii) Find the smallest positive integer n_0 for which $n! > 4^n$ for all positive integers n greater than or equal to n_0.

⑪ Prove that, if m is a given positive integer, $\dfrac{(m+n)!}{m!} > n^m$ for all positive integers n.

⑫ Prove that

   (i) $13^n - 1$ is divisible by 12 for all positive integer n,

   (ii) $r^n - 1$ is divisible by $r - 1$ for all positive integer n,

   (iii) $r^n - s^n$ is divisible by $r - s$ for all positive integer n.

⑬ You are given the matrix $\mathbf{M} = \begin{pmatrix} -1 & 2 \\ 3 & 1 \end{pmatrix}$.

   (i) Calculate $\mathbf{M}^2$, $\mathbf{M}^3$ and $\mathbf{M}^4$.

   (ii) Write down separate conjectures for formulae for $\mathbf{M}^n$, for even n (i.e. $\mathbf{M}^{2m}$) and for odd n (i.e. $\mathbf{M}^{2m+1}$)

   (iii) Prove each conjecture by induction, and hence write down what $\mathbf{M}^n$ is for any $n \geq 1$.

⑭ Prove that for all positive integer $n \geq r$, $\dfrac{r^{n+1}}{(n+1)!} < \dfrac{r^n}{n!}$.

⑮ $\mathbf{A}$ and $\mathbf{B}$ are 2×2 matrices and $\mathbf{I}$ is the 2×2 identity matrix.

   (i) If $\mathbf{AB} = \mathbf{I} + \mathbf{BA}$, prove that for a given r and any integer n in the range $0 \leq n \leq r$,

     $\mathbf{AB}^r = n\mathbf{B}^{n-1} + \mathbf{B}^n\mathbf{AB}^{r-n}$.

   (ii) Hence prove that, if $\mathbf{AB} = \mathbf{I} + \mathbf{BA}$,

     $\mathbf{AB}^r - \mathbf{B}^r\mathbf{A} = r\mathbf{B}^{r-1}$.

LEARNING OUTCOMES

When you have completed this chapter, you should be able to use proof by induction to prove:

➤ statements about matrices

➤ statements about divisibility of expressions

➤ statements involving powers, exponentials and factorials.

KEY POINTS

1 To prove by mathematical induction that a statement involving an integer n is true for all $n \geq n_0$, you need to:

- prove that the result is true for an initial value of n, typically $n_0 = 1$

- prove that: *if* it is true for $n = k$ *then* it is true for $n = k + 1$

- state that as it is true for the initial value, and as if it is true for $n = k$ then it is also true for $n = k + 1$, it must be true for all n greater than or equal to the initial value

- conclude the argument with a precise statement about what has been proved.

2 You will often find it useful to find the target expression: use the result for $n = k$ to find the equivalent result for $n = k + 1$.

FUTURE USES

In the A level Mathematics and Further Mathematics textbooks you will see how induction can be used to prove other types of results, such as formulae for the sum of a series.

For questions 1 to 4 you must show non-calculator methods in your answer.

① (i) The complex number w is given by $w = 1 + 2i$. On a single Argand diagram plot the points which represent the four complex numbers w, w^2, $w - w^*$ and $\dfrac{1}{w} + \dfrac{1}{w^*}$. [5 marks]

(ii) Which two of the numbers w, w^2, $w - w^*$ and $\dfrac{1}{w} + \dfrac{1}{w^*}$ have the same imaginary part? [1 mark]

② You are given that one of the roots of the cubic equation $z^3 - 9z^2 + 28z - 30 = 0$ is an integer and that another is $3 + i$.

Solve the cubic equation. [4 marks]

③ Ezra is investigating whether the formula for solving quadratic equations works if the coefficients of the quadratic are not real numbers. Here is the beginning of his working for one particular quadratic equation.

$$(2+i)z^2 + 6z + (2-i) = 0$$

$$z = \frac{-b \pm \sqrt{b^2 - 4ac}}{2}$$

$$= \frac{-6 \pm \sqrt{36 - 4(2 + i)(2 - i)}}{2(2 + i)}$$

$$= \ldots$$

Finish off Ezra's working. Show that both of the answers given by this method are of the form $\lambda(2-i)$, where λ is real, stating the value of λ in each case. [4 marks]

④ The cubic equation $x^3 + 3x^2 - 6x - 8 = 0$ has roots α, β, γ.

(i) Find a cubic equation with roots $\alpha + 1$, $\beta + 1$, $\gamma + 1$. [4 marks]

(ii) Solve the equation you found as your answer to part (i). [3 marks]

(iii) Solve the equation $x^3 + 3x^2 - 6x - 8$. [2 marks]

PS ⑤ The three numbers a, b and c satisfy the equations

$a + b + c = -4$

$ab + bc + ca = -4$

$abc = 16$

(i) Write down a cubic equation whose roots are a, b and c. [3 marks]

(ii) Solve this cubic to find the possible values of a, b and c. [5 marks]

PS ⑥ You are given that the quadratic equation $az^2 + bz + c = 0$ has roots δ and $\delta + 1$.

By considering the sum and product of its roots, or otherwise, prove that $b^2 - 4ac = a^2$. [5 marks]

⑦ The matrix $\mathbf{R}$ is given by $\mathbf{R} = \begin{pmatrix} -\frac{3}{5} & \frac{4}{5} \\ \frac{4}{5} & \frac{3}{5} \end{pmatrix}$. The transformation corresponding to $\mathbf{R}$ is denoted R. The unit square OIPJ has coordinates $O(0, 0), I(1, 0), P(1, 1), J(0, 1)$.

(i) Plot, on the same diagram, the unit square and its image O'I'P'J' under R. [2 marks]

(ii) Find the equation of the line of invariant points for R. [3 marks]

(iii) Verify that the line which is perpendicular to this line of invariant points, and which passes through the origin, is an invariant line. [3 marks]

(iv) Mark on your diagram in part (i) two points on the unit square which are invariant under R. [2 marks]

MP ⑧ Prove by induction that $3^{2n} - 5^n$ is divisible by 4 for all positive integer n. [5 marks]

MP ⑨ Let $\mathbf{M}$ be the matrix $\begin{pmatrix} 0 & 1 \\ 2 & 0 \end{pmatrix}$.

(i) Evaluate $\mathbf{M}^2$. [1 mark]

(ii) Use the method of induction to prove that
$$\begin{pmatrix} 0 & 1 \\ 2 & 0 \end{pmatrix}^{2n-1} = \begin{pmatrix} 0 & 2^{(n-1)/2} \\ 2^{(n+1)/2} & 0 \end{pmatrix}.$$
[5 marks]

(iii) Write down a formula for $\mathbf{M}^{2n}$. [2 marks]

Complex numbers and geometry

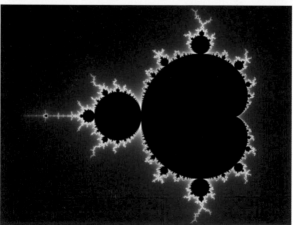

Figure 5.1 The Mandlebrot set

Discussion point

→ Figure 5.1 is an Argand diagram showing the Mandlebrot set. The black area shows all the complex numbers that satisfy a particular rule. Find out about the rule which defines whether or not a particular complex number is in the Mandlebrot set.

1 The modulus and argument of a complex number

Figure 5.2 shows the point representing $z = x + y\mathrm{i}$ on an Argand diagram.

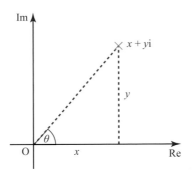

Figure 5.2

> Using Pythagoras' theorem.

The distance of this point from the origin is $\sqrt{x^2 + y^2}$.

This distance is called the modulus of z, and is denoted by $|z|$.

So, for the complex number $z = x + y\mathrm{i}$, $|z| = \sqrt{x^2 + y^2}$.

Notice that since $zz^* = (x + \mathrm{i}y)(x - \mathrm{i}y) = x^2 + y^2$, then $|z|^2 = zz^*$.

Example 5.1

Represent each of the following complex numbers on an Argand diagram. Find the modulus of each complex number, giving exact answers in their simplest form.

$$z_1 = -5 + \mathrm{i} \qquad z_2 = 6 \qquad z_3 = -5 - 5\mathrm{i} \qquad z_4 = -4\mathrm{i}$$

Solution

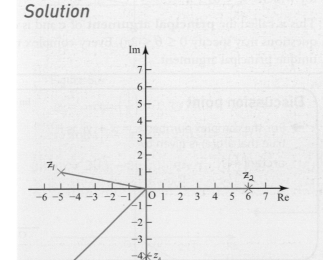

Figure 5.3

$$\theta = \arctan\left(\frac{2}{2\sqrt{3}}\right) = \frac{\pi}{6}$$

As it is measured in a clockwise direction,

$$\arg(z_2) = -\frac{\pi}{6}.$$

(iii) $z_3 = -5 - 5i$

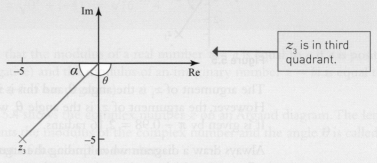

Figure 5.8

$$\alpha = \arctan\left(\frac{5}{5}\right) = \frac{\pi}{4}$$

So, $\theta = \pi - \frac{\pi}{4} = \frac{3\pi}{4}$

Since it is measured in a clockwise direction,

$$\arg(z_3) = -\frac{3\pi}{4}.$$

(iv) $z_4 = -4i$

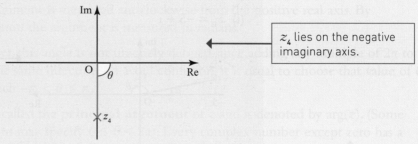

Figure 5.9

On the negative imaginary axis, the argument is $-\frac{\pi}{2}$

$$\arg(z_4) = -\frac{\pi}{2}.$$

The modulus-argument form of a complex number

In Figure 5.10, you can see the relationship between the components of a complex number and its modulus and argument.

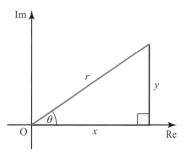

Figure 5.10

Using trigonometry, you can see that $\sin\theta = \dfrac{y}{r}$ and so $y = r\sin\theta$.

Similarly, $\cos\theta = \dfrac{x}{r}$ so $x = r\cos\theta$.

Therefore, the complex number $z = x + y\mathrm{i}$ can be written

$$z = r\cos\theta + r\sin\theta\mathrm{i}$$

or

$$z = r\left(\cos\theta + \mathrm{i}\sin\theta\right).$$

> The modulus–argument form of a complex number is sometimes called the **polar form**, as the modulus of a complex number is its distance from the origin, which is also called the **pole**.

This is called the **modulus-argument form** of the complex number and is sometimes written as $[r, \theta]$, or as r cis θ. Note that r can never be negative.

You may have noticed in the earlier calculations that values of sin, cos and tan for some angles are exact and can be expressed in surds. You will see these values in the following activity – they are worth memorising as this will help make some calculations quicker.

ACTIVITY 5.1

Copy and complete this table. Use the diagrams in Figure 5.11 to help you.

Give your answers as exact values (involving surds where appropriate), rather than as decimals.

	$\dfrac{\pi}{6}$	$\dfrac{\pi}{4}$	$\dfrac{\pi}{3}$
sin			
cos			
tan			

Table 5.1

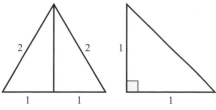

Figure 5.11

> **T**
> **ACTIVITY 5.2**
>
> Most calculators can convert complex numbers given in the form (x, y) to the form $[r, \theta]$ (called *rectangular to polar*, and often shown as R → P) and from $[r, \theta]$ to (x, y) (*polar to rectangular*, P → R).
>
> Find out how to use these facilities on your calculator.
>
> Does your calculator always give the correct θ, or do you sometimes have to add or subtract 2π?

Example 5.3

Write the following complex numbers in modulus–argument form.

(i) $z_1 = \sqrt{3} + 3i$ 　　　　(ii) $z_2 = -3 + \sqrt{3}i$

(iii) $z_3 = \sqrt{3} - 3i$ 　　　　(iv) $z_4 = -3 - \sqrt{3}i$

Solution

Figure 5.12 shows the four complex numbers z_1, z_2, z_3 and z_4.

For each complex number, the modulus is $\sqrt{\left(\sqrt{3}\right)^2 + 3^2} = 2\sqrt{3}$

$$\alpha_1 = \arctan\left(\frac{3}{\sqrt{3}}\right) = \frac{\pi}{3}$$

$$\Rightarrow \arg(z_1) = \frac{\pi}{3}, \text{ so } z_1 = 2\sqrt{3}\left(\cos\frac{\pi}{3} + i\sin\frac{\pi}{3}\right)$$

By symmetry, $\arg(z_3) = -\frac{\pi}{3}$, so $z_3 = 2\sqrt{3}\left(\cos\left(-\frac{\pi}{3}\right) + i\sin\left(-\frac{\pi}{3}\right)\right)$

$$\alpha_2 = \arctan\left(\frac{\sqrt{3}}{3}\right) = \frac{\pi}{6}$$

$$\Rightarrow \arg(z_2) = \pi - \frac{\pi}{6} = \frac{5\pi}{6}, \text{ so } z_2 = 2\sqrt{3}\left(\cos\frac{5\pi}{6} + i\sin\frac{5\pi}{6}\right)$$

By symmetry, $\arg(z_4) = -\frac{5\pi}{6}$, so $z_4 = 2\sqrt{3}\left(\cos\left(-\frac{5\pi}{6}\right) + i\sin\left(-\frac{5\pi}{6}\right)\right)$

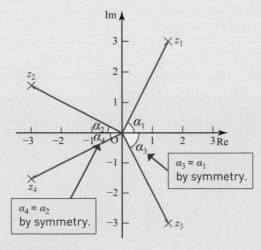

Figure 5.12

① The Argand diagram in Figure 5.13 shows three complex numbers.

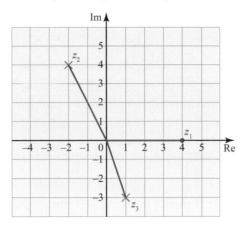

Figure 5.13

Write each of the numbers z_1, z_2 and z_3 in the form:

(i) $a + b$i

(ii) $r(\cos\theta + i\sin\theta)$, giving answers exactly or to 3 significant figures where appropriate.

② Write the following complex numbers in the form $[r, \theta]$, giving your answer exactly or to 3 significant figures where appropriate.

   (i) $3 + 2$i   (ii) $-5 + 2$i   (iii) $-3 - 2$i   (iv) $2 - 5$i

③ Find the modulus and argument of each of the complex numbers on this Argand diagram.

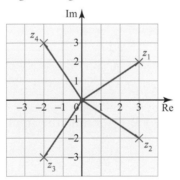

Figure 5.14

Describe the transformations that map z_1 onto each of the other points on the diagram.

④ Write each of the following complex numbers in the form $x + y$i, giving surds in your answer where appropriate.

   (i) $4\left(\cos\left(-\dfrac{\pi}{2}\right) + i\sin\left(-\dfrac{\pi}{2}\right)\right)$

   (ii) $7\left(\cos\dfrac{3\pi}{4} + i\sin\dfrac{3\pi}{4}\right)$

   (iii) $\left[3, \dfrac{5\pi}{6}\right]$

   (iv) $\left[5, -\dfrac{\pi}{6}\right]$

⑤ For each complex number, find the modulus and argument, and hence write the complex number in $[r, \theta]$ form.

Give θ in radians as a multiple of π.

(i)   1   (ii) −2   (iii) 3i   (iv) −4i

⑥ For each of the complex numbers below, find the modulus and argument, and hence write the complex number in modulus-argument form.

Give the argument in radians as a multiple of π.

(i) $1 + i$ (ii) $-1 + i$ (iii) $-1 - i$ (iv) $1 - i$

⑦ Given that $z_1 = 3\left(\cos\frac{\pi}{3} + i\sin\frac{\pi}{3}\right)$ and $z_2 = 4\left(\cos\frac{\pi}{3} + i\sin\frac{\pi}{3}\right)$ calculate

$z_1 + z_2$ and $2z_1 - z_2$, giving your answers in the form $r\,\mathrm{cis}\,\theta$.

⑧ For each complex number, find the modulus and principal argument, and hence write the complex number in modulus-argument form.

Give the argument in radians as a multiple of π.

(i) $6\sqrt{3} + 6i$ (ii) $3 - 4i$ (iii) $-12 + 5i$

(iv) $4 + 7i$ (v) $-58 - 93i$

⑨ Express each of these complex numbers in the form $r(\cos\theta + i\sin\theta)$ giving the argument in radians, either as a multiple of π or correct to 3 significant figures.

(i) $\dfrac{2}{3 - i}$ (ii) $\dfrac{3 - 2i}{3 - i}$ (iii) $\dfrac{-2 - 5i}{3 - i}$

⑩ Represent each of the following complex numbers on a separate Argand diagram and write it in the form $x + yi$, giving surds in your answer where appropriate.

(i) $|z| = 2$, $\arg(z) = \dfrac{\pi}{2}$ (ii) $|z| = 3$, $\arg(z) = \dfrac{\pi}{3}$

(iii) $|z| = 7$, $\arg(z) = \dfrac{5\pi}{6}$ (iv) $|z| = 1$, $\arg(z) = -\dfrac{\pi}{4}$

(v) $|z| = 5$, $\arg(z) = -\dfrac{2\pi}{3}$ (vi) $|z| = 6$, $\arg(z) = -2$

⑪ Given that $\arg(5 + 2i) = \alpha$, find the argument of each of the following in terms of α.

(i) $-5 - 2i$ (ii) $5 - 2i$ (iii) $-5 + 2i$

(iv) $2 + 5i$ (v) $-2 + 5i$

⑫ The complex number z has modulus 1 and argument $\dfrac{\pi}{3}$. Find $1 + z$ in the form $r\,\mathrm{cis}\,\theta$. [Hint: sketch the position of z and 1 on an Argand diagram.]

⑬ The complex numbers z and w are given in modulus-argument form as:

$z = 4\left(\cos\frac{\pi}{10} + i\sin\frac{\pi}{10}\right)$ and $w = 4\left(\cos\frac{13\pi}{30} + i\sin\frac{13\pi}{30}\right)$. Find, in the form

$r(\cos\theta + i\sin\theta)$, simplified expressions for $z + w$ and $z - w$.

⑭ The complex number z has modulus 6 and argument $\dfrac{\pi}{10}$. Use the sine and cosine rules to find $z + 5i$ in the form $r\,\mathrm{cis}\,\theta$. Give the values of r and θ correct to 3 significant figures.

⑮ The complex numbers z_1 and z_2 are shown on the Argand diagram in Figure 5.15.

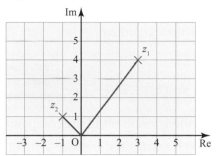

Figure 5.15

(i) Find the modulus and argument of each of the two numbers.

(ii) (a) Find $z_1 z_2$ and $\dfrac{z_1}{z_2}$.

   (b) Find the modulus and argument of each of $z_1 z_2$ and $\dfrac{z_1}{z_2}$.

(iii) What rules can you deduce about the modulus and argument of the two complex numbers and the answers to part (ii)(b)?

2 Multiplying and dividing complex numbers in modulus-argument form

Prior knowledge

You need to be familiar with the compound angle formulae. These are covered in the A Level Mathematics book, and a brief introduction is given on page 168 of this book.

ACTIVITY 5.3

What is the geometrical effect of multiplying one complex number by another? To explore this question, start with the numbers $z_1 = 2 + 3i$ and $z_2 = iz_1$.

(i) Plot the points representing z_1 and z_2 on the same Argand diagram, and describe the geometrical transformation that maps the vector representing z_1 to the vector representing z_2.

(ii) Repeat part (i) with $z_1 = 2 + 3i$ and $z_2 = 2iz_1$.

(iii) Repeat part (i) with $z_1 = 2 + 3i$ and $z_2 = (1 + i)z_1$.

You will have seen in Activity 5.3 that multiplying one complex number by another involves a combination of an enlargement and a rotation.

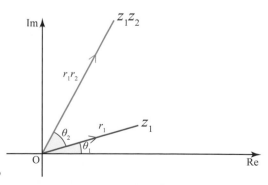

Figure 5.16

You obtain the vector z_1z_2 by enlarging the vector representing z_1 by the scale factor $|z_2|$, and rotate it anticlockwise through an angle of $\arg(z_2)$.

So to multiply complex numbers in modulus-argument form, you *multiply* their moduli and *add* their arguments.

$$|z_1z_2| = |z_1||z_2|$$

$$\arg(z_1z_2) = \arg(z_1) + \arg(z_2)$$

> You may need to add or subtract 2π to give the principal argument.

> See page 168 for more about compound angle formulae.

You can prove these results using the compound angle formulae.

$$z_1z_2 = r_1(\cos\theta_1 + i\sin\theta_1) \times r_2(\cos\theta_2 + i\sin\theta_2)$$

$$= r_1r_2(\cos\theta_1\cos\theta_2 + i\cos\theta_1\sin\theta_2 + i\sin\theta_1\cos\theta_2 - \sin\theta_1\sin\theta_2)$$

$$= r_1r_2[(\cos\theta_1\cos\theta_2 - \sin\theta_1\sin\theta_2) + i(\cos\theta_1\sin\theta_2 + \sin\theta_1\cos\theta_2)]$$

$$= r_1r_2[(\cos(\theta_1 + \theta_2) + i\sin(\theta_1 + \theta_2)]$$

> The identity $\cos(\theta_1 + \theta_2)$.

> The identity $\sin(\theta_1 + \theta_2)$.

So, $|z_1z_2| = r_1r_2$ and $\arg(z_1z_2) = \theta_1 + \theta_2$.

Dividing complex numbers works in a similar way. You obtain the vector $\dfrac{z_1}{z_2}$ by enlarging the vector representing z_1 by the scale factor $\dfrac{1}{|z_2|}$, and rotate it *clockwise* through an angle of $\arg(z_2)$.

So, to divide complex numbers in modulus-argument form, you *divide* their moduli and *subtract* their arguments.

> This is equivalent to rotating it anticlockwise through an angle of $-\arg(z_2)$.

$$\left|\frac{z_1}{z_2}\right| = \frac{|z_1|}{|z_2|}$$

$$\arg\left(\frac{z_1}{z_2}\right) = \arg(z_1) - \arg(z_2)$$

> You may need to add or subtract 2π to give the principal argument.

You can prove this easily from the multiplication results by letting $\dfrac{z_1}{z_2} = w$, so that $z_1 = wz_2$.

Then $|z_1| = |w||z_2|$, so $|w| = \dfrac{|z_1|}{|z_2|}$

and $\arg(z_1) = \arg(w) + \arg(z_2)$, so $\arg(w) = \arg(z_1) - \arg(z_2)$.

Example 5.4

The complex numbers w and z are given by $w = 2\left(\cos\dfrac{\pi}{4} + i\sin\dfrac{\pi}{4}\right)$ and $z = 5\left(\cos\dfrac{5\pi}{6} + i\sin\dfrac{5\pi}{6}\right)$.

Find (i) wz and (ii) $\dfrac{w}{z}$ in modulus-argument form. Illustrate each of these on a separate Argand diagram.

Solution

$|w| = 2 \quad \arg(w) = \dfrac{\pi}{4}$

$|z| = 5 \quad \arg(w) = \dfrac{5\pi}{6}$

(i) $|wz| = |w||z| = 2 \times 5 = 10$

$$\arg(w) + \arg(z) = \frac{\pi}{4} + \frac{5\pi}{6} = \frac{13\pi}{12}$$

> This is not in the range $-\pi < \theta \leq \pi$.

so $\arg(wz) = \dfrac{13\pi}{12} - 2\pi = -\dfrac{11}{12}\pi$

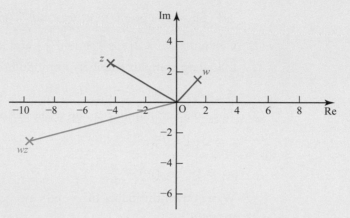

Subtract 2π to obtain the principal argument.

$$wz = 10\left(\cos\left(-\dfrac{11\pi}{12}\right) + i\sin\left(-\dfrac{11\pi}{12}\right)\right)$$

Figure 5.17

(ii) $\left|w/z\right| = \dfrac{|w|}{|z|} = \dfrac{2}{5}$

$$\arg(w) - \arg(z) = \dfrac{\pi}{4} - \dfrac{5\pi}{6} = -\dfrac{7\pi}{12}$$

$$w/z = \dfrac{2}{5}\left(\cos\left(-\dfrac{7\pi}{12}\right) + i\sin\left(-\dfrac{7\pi}{12}\right)\right)$$

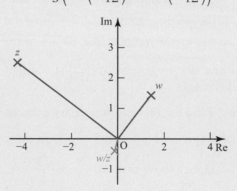

Figure 5.18

Exercise 5.2

① The complex numbers w and z shown in the Argand diagram are $w = 1 + i$ and $z = 1 - \sqrt{3}i$.

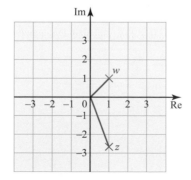

Figure 5.19

(i) Find the modulus and argument of each of the complex numbers w and z.

(ii) Hence write down the modulus and argument of

  (a) wz

  (b) $\dfrac{w}{z}$

(iii) Show the points w, z, wz and $\dfrac{w}{z}$ on a copy of the Argand diagram.

② Given that $z = 2\left(\cos\dfrac{\pi}{4} + i\sin\dfrac{\pi}{4}\right)$ and $w = 3\left(\cos\dfrac{\pi}{3} + i\sin\dfrac{\pi}{3}\right)$, find the following complex numbers in modulus-argument form

  (i) wz (ii) $\dfrac{w}{z}$ (iii) $\dfrac{z}{w}$ (iv) $\dfrac{1}{z}$

③ The complex numbers z and w are defined as follows:

  $z = -3 + 3\sqrt{3}i$

  $|w| = 18$, $\arg(w) - \dfrac{\pi}{6}$

  Write down the values of

  (i) $\arg(z)$ (ii) $|z|$ (iii) $\arg(zw)$ (iv) $|zw|$.

④ Given that $z = 6\left(\cos\dfrac{\pi}{6} + i\sin\dfrac{\pi}{6}\right)$ and $w = 2\left(\cos\left(-\dfrac{\pi}{4}\right) + i\sin\left(-\dfrac{\pi}{4}\right)\right)$, find the following complex numbers in modulus-argument form:

  (i) w^2 (ii) z^5 (iii) $w^3 z^4$

  (iv) $5iz$ (v) $(1 + i)w$

⑤ Find the multiplication scale factor and the angle of rotation which maps

  (i) the vector representing $2 + 3i$ to the vector representing $5 - 2i$

  (ii) the vector representing $-4 + i$ to the vector representing $3i$.

⑥ Prove that, in general, $\arg\left(\dfrac{1}{z}\right) = -\arg(z)$. What are the exceptions to this rule?

⑦ (i) Find the real and imaginary parts of $\dfrac{-1 + i}{1 + \sqrt{3}i}$.

  (ii) Express $-1 + i$ and $1 + \sqrt{3}i$ in modulus-argument form.

  (iii) Hence show that $\cos\dfrac{5\pi}{12} = \dfrac{\sqrt{3} - 1}{2\sqrt{2}}$, and find an exact expression for $\sin\dfrac{5\pi}{12}$.

⑧ Prove that for three complex numbers $w = r_1(\cos\theta_1 + i\sin\theta_1)$, $z = r_2(\cos\theta_2 + i\sin\theta_2)$ and $p = r_3(\cos\theta_3 + i\sin\theta_3)$, $|wzp| = |w||z||p|$ and $\arg(wzp) = \arg(w) + \arg(z) + \arg(p)$ ($\pm 2n\pi$, if necessary, to give the principal argument).

3 Loci in the Argand diagram

A locus is the set of locations that a point can occupy when constrained by a given rule. The plural of locus is loci.

Loci involving $\mathrm{Re}(z)$ or $\mathrm{Im}(z)$

Example 5.5

Describe the locus of z if $\mathrm{Re}(z + 4i) = 3$.

Solution

If $z = x + yi$ then $z + 4i = x + (y + 4)i$

$\Rightarrow \quad \mathrm{Re}(z + 4i) = x$

$\Rightarrow \quad x = 3.$

The locus is the line with equation $x = 3$, a line parallel to the imaginary axis through the point $(3, 0)$.

Loci of the form $|z - a| = r$

Figure 5.20 shows the positions for two general complex numbers $z_1 = x_1 + y_1 i$ and $z_2 = x_2 + y_2 i$.

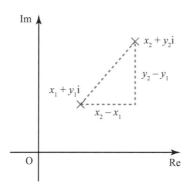

Figure 5.20

You saw earlier that the complex number $z_2 - z_1$ can be represented by the vector from the point representing z_1 to the point representing z_2 (see Figure 5.20). Using Pythagoras' theorem, you can see that the distance between z_1 and z_2 is given by $\sqrt{(x_2 - x_1)^2 + (y_2 - y_1)^2}$ so $|z_1 - z_2|$ is the distance between the points z_1 and z_2. This is the key to solving many questions about sets of points in an Argand diagram, as shown in the following example.

Example 5.6

Draw Argand diagrams showing the following sets of points z for which

(i) $\quad |z| = 5$

(ii) $\quad |z - 3| = 5$

(iii) $|z - 4\mathrm{i}| = 5$

(iv) $|z - 3 - 4\mathrm{i}| = 5$

Solution

(i) $|z| = 5$

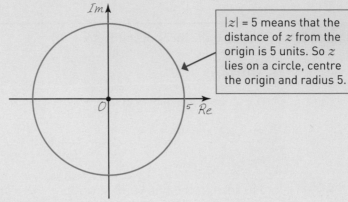

> $|z| = 5$ means that the distance of z from the origin is 5 units. So z lies on a circle, centre the origin and radius 5.

Figure 5.21

(ii) $|z - 3| = 5$

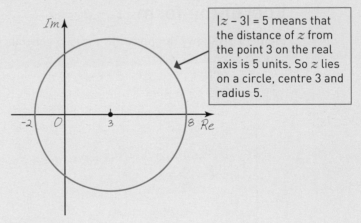

> $|z - 3| = 5$ means that the distance of z from the point 3 on the real axis is 5 units. So z lies on a circle, centre 3 and radius 5.

Figure 5.22

(iii) $|z - 4\mathrm{i}| = 5$

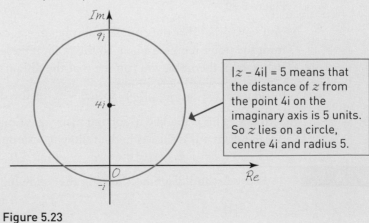

> $|z - 4\mathrm{i}| = 5$ means that the distance of z from the point 4i on the imaginary axis is 5 units. So z lies on a circle, centre 4i and radius 5.

Figure 5.23

(iv) $|z - 3 - 4i| = 5$

$|z - 3 - 4i|$ can be written as $|z - (3 + 4i)|$.

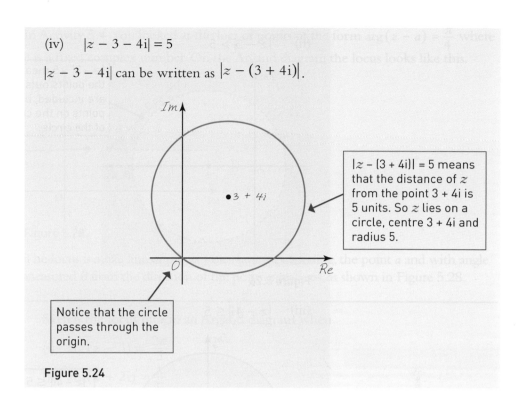

$|z - (3 + 4i)| = 5$ means that the distance of z from the point $3 + 4i$ is 5 units. So z lies on a circle, centre $3 + 4i$ and radius 5.

Notice that the circle passes through the origin.

Figure 5.24

Generally, a locus in an Argand diagram of the form $|z - a| = r$ is a circle, centre a and radius r.

In the example above, each locus is the set of points on the circumference of the circle. It is possible to define a region in the Argand diagram in a similar way.

Example 5.7

Draw Argand diagrams showing the following sets of points z for which

(i) $|z| < 5$

(ii) $|z - 3| > 5$

(iii) $|z - 4i| \leq 5$

Solution

(i) $|z| < 5$

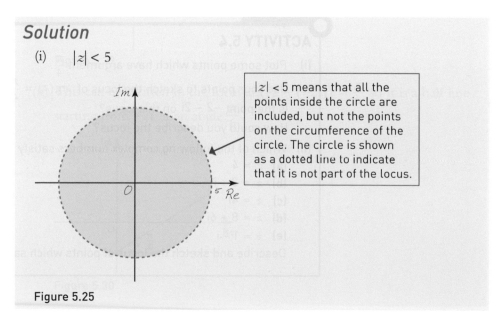

$|z| < 5$ means that all the points inside the circle are included, but not the points on the circumference of the circle. The circle is shown as a dotted line to indicate that it is not part of the locus.

Figure 5.25

(ii)

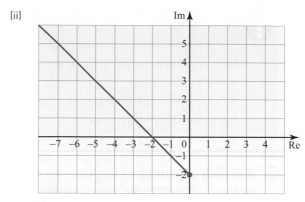

Figure 5.39

(iii)

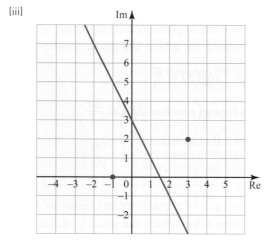

Figure 5.40

⑤ Write down, in terms of z, an algebraic description of the regions that are represented in each of these Argand diagrams.

(i)

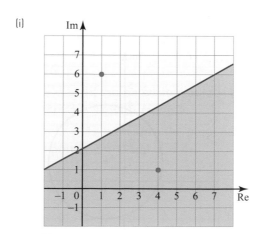

Figure 5.41

(ii)

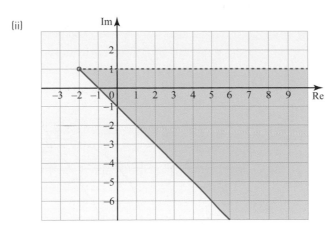

Figure 5.42

(iii)

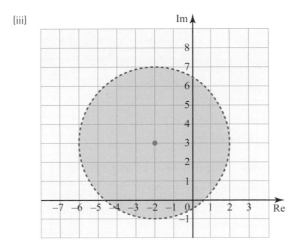

Figure 5.43

⑥ Draw an Argand diagram showing the set of points z for which $|z - 12 + 5i| \leq 7$. Use the diagram to prove that, for these z, $6 \leq |z| \leq 20$.

⑦ For each of parts (i) to (iii), draw an Argand diagram showing the set of points z for which the given condition is true.

(i) $\arg(z - 3 + i) \leq -\dfrac{\pi}{6}$

(ii) $0 \leq \arg(z - 3i) \leq \dfrac{3\pi}{4}$

(iii) $-\dfrac{\pi}{4} < \arg(z + 5 - 3i) < \dfrac{\pi}{3}$

⑧ On an Argand diagram shade in the regions represented by the following inequalities.

(i) $|z - 3| \leq 2$

(ii) $|z - 6i| > |z + 2i|$

(iii) $2 \leq |z - 3 - 4i| \leq 4$

(iv) $|z + 3 + 6i| \leq |z - 2 - 7i|$.

⑨ Shade on an Argand diagram the region satisfied by the inequalities $\{z : |z - 1 + i| \leq 1\} \cap \{z : -\dfrac{\pi}{3} < \arg(z) < 0\}$.

⑩

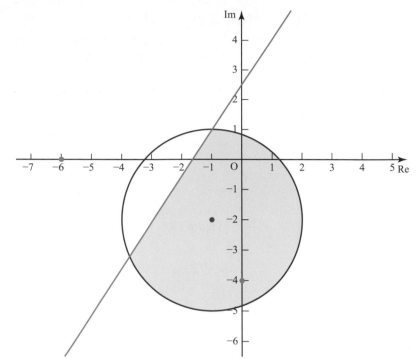

Figure 5.44

(i) For this Argand diagram, write down in terms of z

    (a) an algebraic description of the set of points on the circle

    (b) an algebraic description of the set of points on the straight line.

(ii) Using inequalities, express in terms of z the shaded region on the Argand diagram.

⑪ Sketch on the same Argand diagram

    (i) the locus of points for which $|z - 2 + 2i| = 3$

    (ii) the locus of points for which $\arg(z - 2 + 2i) = -\dfrac{\pi}{4}$

    (iii) the locus of points for which $\arg(z - 2 + 2i) = \dfrac{\pi}{2}$.

    Shade the region defined by

$$\{z : |z - 2 + 2i| \leq 3\} \cap \{z : \arg(z - 2 + 2i) \geq -\tfrac{\pi}{4}\} \cap \{z : \arg(z - 2 + 2i) \leq \tfrac{\pi}{2}\}.$$

⑫ You are given the complex number $w = -\sqrt{3} + 3i$.

    (i) Find $\arg(w)$ and $|w - 2i|$.

    (ii) On an Argand diagram, shade the region representing complex numbers z which satisfy both of these inequalities:

$$|z - 2i| \leq 2 \text{ and } \frac{\pi}{2} \leq \arg z \leq \frac{2\pi}{3}$$

    Indicate the point on your diagram which corresponds to w.

⑬ Sketch a diagram that represents the regions represented by

$$|z - 2 - 2i| \leq 2 \text{ and } 0 \leq \arg(z - 2i) \leq \frac{\pi}{4}.$$

⑭ By using an Argand diagram, determine if it is possible to find values of z for which $|z - 2 + i| \geq 10$ and $|z + 4 + 2i| \leq 2$ simultaneously.

⑮ What are the greatest and least values of $|z + 3 - 2i|$ if $|z - 5 + 4i| \leq 3$?

⑯ You are given that $|z - 3| = 2|z - 3 + 9i|$.

    (i)   Show, using algebra with $z = x + y$i, that the locus of z is a circle and state the centre and radius of the circle.

    (ii) Sketch the locus of the circle on an Argand diagram.

⑰ You are given that $w_1 = 3 + 2i$ and $w_2 = -3 + 2i$. By considering arguments, find the locus of z if:

    (i) $\dfrac{z - w_1}{z - w_2}$ is real   (ii) $\dfrac{z - w_1}{z - w_2}$ is purely imaginary.

LEARNING OUTCOMES

When you have completed this chapter you should be able to:

➤ find the modulus of a complex number

➤ find the principal argument of a complex number in radians

➤ express a complex number in modulus-argument form

➤ multiply and divide complex numbers in modulus-argument form

➤ represent multiplication and division of two complex numbers on an Argand diagram

➤ represent and interpret sets of complex numbers as loci on an Argand diagram:

    ○ circles of the form $|z - a| = r$

    ○ half-lines of the form $\arg(z - a) = \theta$

    ○ lines of the form $|z - a| = |z - b|$

    ○ lines of the form $\mathrm{Re}(z + a) = k$ or $\mathrm{Im}(z + a) = k$

➤ represent and interpret regions defined by inequalities based on the above

➤ use set notation in the context of loci.

FUTURE USES

■ Work on complex numbers will be developed further in A level Further Mathematics.

■ Complex numbers will be needed for work on differential equations in A level Further Mathematics, in particular in modelling oscillations (simple harmonic motion).

KEY POINTS

1 The modulus of $z = x + y$i is $|z| = \sqrt{x^2 + y^2}$. This is the distance of the point z from the origin on the Argand diagram.

2 The argument of z is the angle θ, measured anticlockwise in radians, between the line connecting the origin and the point z and the positive real axis.

3 The principal argument of z, $\arg(z)$, is the angle θ, measured anticlockwise in radians, for which $-\pi < \theta \leq \pi$, between the line connecting the origin and the point z and the positive real axis.

4 For a complex number z, $zz^* = |z|^2$.

5 The modulus–argument form of z is $z = r(\cos\theta + i\sin\theta)$, where $r = |z|$ and $\theta = \arg(z)$. This is often written as (r, θ)

6 For two complex numbers z_1 and z_2:

$z_1 z_2 = [r_1 r_2, \theta_1 + \theta_2]$ $\arg(z_1 z_2) = \arg(z_1) + \arg(z_2)$

$\dfrac{z_1}{z_2} = \left[\dfrac{r_1}{r_2}, \theta_1 - \theta_2\right]$ $\arg\left(\dfrac{z_1}{z_2}\right) = \arg(z_1) - \arg(z_2)$

$\pm 2n\pi$, if necessary, to give the principal argument

7 The distance between the points z_1 and z_2 in an Argand diagram is $|z_1 - z_2|$.

8 $|z - a| = r$ represents a circle, centre a and radius r.

$|z - a| < r$ represents the interior of the circle, and $|z - a| > r$ represents the exterior of the circle.

9 $\arg(z - a) = \theta$ represents a half line starting at $z = a$ at an angle of θ from the positive real direction.

10 $|z - a| = |z - b|$ represents the perpendicular bisector of the points a and b.

6

Matrices and their inverses

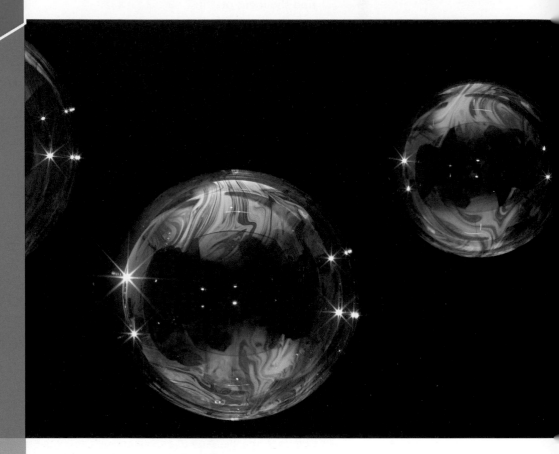

The grand thing is to be able to reason backwards.
Arthur Conan Doyle

Discussion points

➡ What is the same about each of the triangles in the diagram? How many of the yellow triangles are needed to cover the large purple triangle?

Figure 6.1 Sierpinsky triangle.

The diagram in Figure 6.1 is called a Sierpinsky triangle. The pattern can be continued with smaller and smaller triangles.

Prior knowledge

You need to have covered the work on matrices and transformations from Chapter 1.

1 The determinant of a 2 × 2 matrix

Figure 6.2 shows the unit square, labelled OIPJ, and the parallelogram OI′P′J′ formed when OIPJ is transformed using the matrix $\begin{pmatrix} 5 & 4 \\ 1 & 2 \end{pmatrix}$.

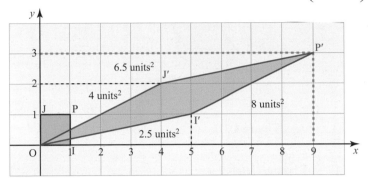

Figure 6.2

What effect does the transformation have on the area of OIPJ?

The area of OIPJ is 1 unit².

To find the area of OI′P′J′, a rectangle has been drawn surrounding it. The area of the rectangle is $9 \times 3 = 27$ units². The part of the rectangle that is not inside OI′P′J′ has been divided up into two triangles and two trapezia and their areas are shown on the diagram.

So, area OI′P′J′ $= 27 - 2.5 - 8 - 6.5 - 4 = 6$ units².

The interesting question is whether you could predict this answer from the numbers in the matrix $\begin{pmatrix} 5 & 4 \\ 1 & 2 \end{pmatrix}$.

You can see that $5 \times 2 - 4 \times 1 = 6$. Is this just a coincidence?

To answer that question you need to transform the unit square by the general 2×2 matrix $\begin{pmatrix} a & b \\ c & d \end{pmatrix}$ and see whether the area of the transformed figure is $(ad - bc)$ units². The answer is, 'Yes', and the proof is left for you to do in the activity below.

Hint

You are advised to use the same method as the example above but replace the numbers by the appropriate letters.

ACTIVITY 6.1

The unit square is transformed by the matrix $\begin{pmatrix} a & b \\ c & d \end{pmatrix}$.

Prove that the resulting shape is a parallelogram with area $(ad - bc)$ units².

It is now evident that the quantity $(ad - bc)$ is the area scale factor associated with the transformation matrix $\mathbf{M} = \begin{pmatrix} a & b \\ c & d \end{pmatrix}$. It is called the **determinant** of the matrix and is written $\det \mathbf{M}$ or $|\mathbf{M}|$ or $\begin{vmatrix} a & b \\ c & d \end{vmatrix}$.

Example 6.1

A shape S has area $8\,\text{cm}^2$. S is mapped to a shape T under the transformation represented by the matrix $\mathbf{M} = \begin{pmatrix} 1 & -2 \\ 3 & 0 \end{pmatrix}$.

Find the area of shape T.

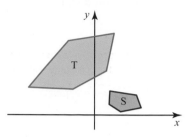

Figure 6.3

> **Note**
>
> In Example 6.1, it does not matter what shape S looks like; for any shape S with area $8\,\text{cm}^2$, the area of the image T under M will always be $48\,\text{cm}^2$.

Solution

$$\det\begin{pmatrix} 1 & -2 \\ 3 & 0 \end{pmatrix} = (1 \times 0) - (-2 \times 3) = 0 + 6 = 6$$

The area scale factor of the transformation is 6 ...

$$\text{Area of T} = 8 \times 6$$
$$= 48\,\text{cm}^2$$

... and so the area of the original shape is multiplied by 6.

Example 6.2

(i) Draw a diagram to show the image of the unit square OIPJ under the transformation represented by the matrix $\mathbf{M} = \begin{pmatrix} 2 & 3 \\ 4 & 1 \end{pmatrix}$.

(ii) Find $|\mathbf{M}|$.

(iii) Use your answer to part (ii) to find the area of the transformed shape.

Solution

(i) $\begin{pmatrix} 2 & 3 \\ 4 & 1 \end{pmatrix}\begin{pmatrix} 0 & 1 & 1 & 0 \\ 0 & 0 & 1 & 1 \end{pmatrix} = \begin{pmatrix} 0 & 2 & 5 & 3 \\ 0 & 4 & 5 & 1 \end{pmatrix}$

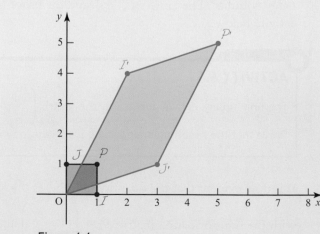

Figure 6.4

(ii) $\begin{vmatrix} 2 & 3 \\ 4 & 1 \end{vmatrix} = (2 \times 1) - (3 \times 4) = 2 - 12 = -10$

(iii) The area of the transformed shape is 10 square units.

Notice that the determinant is negative. Since area cannot be negative, the area of the transformed shape is 10 square units.

The sign of the determinant does have significance. If you move anticlockwise around the original unit square you come to vertices O, I, P, J in that order. However, moving anticlockwise about the image reverses the order of the vertices i.e. O, J', P', I'. This reversal in the **orientation** of the shape results from the negative determinant.

Discussion point

➡ Which of the following transformations reverse the order of the vertices?

(i) rotation

(ii) reflection

(iii) enlargement.

Check your answers by finding the determinants of matrices representing these transformations.

Example 6.3

Given that $\mathbf{P} = \begin{pmatrix} 2 & 1 \\ 0 & 1 \end{pmatrix}$ and $\mathbf{Q} = \begin{pmatrix} 2 & 1 \\ 1 & 2 \end{pmatrix}$, find

(i) $|\mathbf{P}|$

(ii) $|\mathbf{Q}|$

(iii) $|\mathbf{PQ}|$.

What do you notice?

Solution

(i) $|\mathbf{P}| = 2 - 0 = 2$

(ii) $|\mathbf{Q}| = 4 - 1 = 3$

(iii) $\mathbf{PQ} = \begin{pmatrix} 2 & 1 \\ 0 & 1 \end{pmatrix}\begin{pmatrix} 2 & 1 \\ 1 & 2 \end{pmatrix} = \begin{pmatrix} 5 & 4 \\ 1 & 2 \end{pmatrix}$ so $|\mathbf{PQ}| = 10 - 4 = 6$

The determinant of $\mathbf{PQ}$ is given by $|\mathbf{P}| \times |\mathbf{Q}|$.

The example above illustrates the general result that $|\mathbf{MN}| = |\mathbf{M}| \times |\mathbf{N}|$.

Remember that a transformation $\mathbf{MN}$ means 'apply $\mathbf{N}$, then apply $\mathbf{M}$'.

This result makes sense in terms of transformations. In Example 6.3, applying **Q** involves an area scale factor of 3, and applying **P** involves an area scale factor of 2. So applying **Q** followed by **P**, represented by the matrix **PQ**, involves an area scale factor of 6.

The work so far has been restricted to 2 × 2 matrices. All square matrices have determinants; for a 3 × 3 matrix the determinant represents a volume scale factor. However, a non-square matrix does not have a determinant.

Example 6.4

A transformation is represented by the matrix $\mathbf{A} = \begin{pmatrix} -1 & 0 & 0 \\ 0 & 1 & 0 \\ 0 & 0 & 1 \end{pmatrix}$.

(i) Describe the transformation represented by **A**.

(ii) Using a calculator, find the determinant of **A**.

(iii) Decide whether the transformation represented by **A** preserves or reverses the orientation.

Explain how this is connected to your answer to part (ii).

Solution

(i) Matrix **A** represents a reflection in the plane $x = 0$.

(ii) Using a calculator, det **A** = −1.

(iii) Matrix **A** represents a reflection, so the orientation is reversed. This is confirmed by the negative determinant.

> The first column of **A** shows that the unit vector **i** is mapped to −**i**, and the other columns show that the unit vectors **j** and **k** are mapped to themselves.

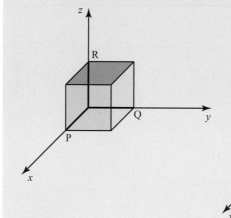
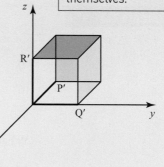

Figure 6.5

Matrices with determinant zero

Figure 6.6 shows the image of the unit square OIPJ under the transformation represented by the matrix $\mathbf{T} = \begin{pmatrix} 6 & 4 \\ 3 & 2 \end{pmatrix}$.

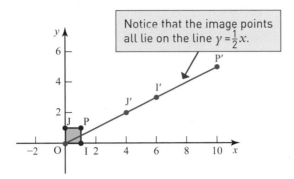

Notice that the image points all lie on the line $y = \frac{1}{2}x$.

Figure 6.6

The determinant of $\mathbf{T} = (6 \times 2) - (4 \times 3) = 12 - 12 = 0$.

This means that the area scale factor of the transformation is zero, so any shape is transformed into a shape with area zero.

In this case, the image of a point (p, q) is given by

$$\begin{pmatrix} 6 & 4 \\ 3 & 2 \end{pmatrix} \begin{pmatrix} p \\ q \end{pmatrix} = \begin{pmatrix} 6p + 4q \\ 3p + 2q \end{pmatrix} = \begin{pmatrix} 2(3p + 2q) \\ 3p + 2q \end{pmatrix}.$$

You can see that for all the possible image points, the y-coordinate is half the x-coordinate, showing that all the image points lie on the line $y = \frac{1}{2}x$.

In this transformation, more than one point maps to the same image point.

For example, $\quad (4, 0) \rightarrow (24, 12)$

$\qquad\qquad (0, 6) \rightarrow (24, 12)$

$\qquad\qquad (1, 4.5) \rightarrow (24, 12).$

Discussion point

➜ What is the effect of a transformation represented by a 3×3 matrix with determinant zero?

Exercise 6.1

① For each of the following matrices:

(a) draw a diagram to show the image of the unit square under the transformation represented by the matrix

(b) find the area of the image in part (a)

(c) find the determinant of the matrix.

(i) $\begin{pmatrix} 3 & -2 \\ 4 & 1 \end{pmatrix}$ (ii) $\begin{pmatrix} 4 & 0 \\ -1 & 4 \end{pmatrix}$ (iii) $\begin{pmatrix} 4 & -8 \\ 1 & -2 \end{pmatrix}$ (iv) $\begin{pmatrix} 5 & -7 \\ -3 & 2 \end{pmatrix}$

② The matrix $\begin{pmatrix} x - 3 & -3 \\ 2 & x - 5 \end{pmatrix}$ has determinant 9.

Find the possible values of x.

③ (i) Write down the matrices **A**, **B**, **C** and **D** which represent:

  A – a reflection in the x-axis

  B – a reflection in the y-axis

  C – a reflection in the line $y = x$

  D – a reflection in the line $y = -x$

(ii) Show that each of the matrices **A**, **B**, **C** and **D** has determinant of -1.

(iii) Draw diagrams for each of the transformations **A**, **B**, **C** and **D** to demonstrate that the images of the vertices labelled anticlockwise on the unit square OIPJ are reversed to a clockwise labelling.

④ A triangle has area $6\,\text{cm}^2$. The triangle is transformed by means of the matrix $\begin{pmatrix} 2 & 3 \\ -3 & 1 \end{pmatrix}$.

Find the area of the image of the triangle.

⑤ The two-way stretch with matrix $\begin{pmatrix} a & 0 \\ 0 & d \end{pmatrix}$ preserves the area (i.e. the area of the image is equal to the area of the original shape).

What is the relationship connecting a and d?

⑥ Figure 6.7 shows the unit square transformed by a shear.

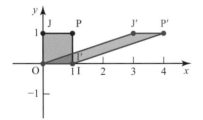

Figure 6.7

(i) Write down the matrix which represents this transformation.

(ii) Show that under this transformation the area of the image is always equal to the area of the object.

⑦ A transformation in three dimensions is represented by the matrix

$$\mathbf{A} = \begin{pmatrix} 2 & 3 & 1 \\ -1 & 1 & 0 \\ 0 & 4 & 2 \end{pmatrix}.$$

A cuboid has volume $5\,\text{cm}^3$. What is the volume of the image of the cuboid under the transformation represented by **A**?

⑧ $\mathbf{M} = \begin{pmatrix} 5 & 3 \\ 4 & 2 \end{pmatrix}$ and $\mathbf{N} = \begin{pmatrix} 3 & 2 \\ -2 & 1 \end{pmatrix}$.

(i) Find the determinants of **M** and **N**.

(ii) Find the matrix **MN** and show that det **MN** = det **M** × det **N**.

⑨ The plane is transformed by the matrix $\mathbf{M} = \begin{pmatrix} 4 & -6 \\ 2 & -3 \end{pmatrix}$.

   (i) Draw a diagram to show the image of the unit square under the transformation represented by $\mathbf{M}$.

   (ii) Describe the effect of the transformation and explain this with reference to the determinant of $\mathbf{M}$.

⑩ The plane is transformed by the matrix $\mathbf{N} = \begin{pmatrix} 5 & -10 \\ -1 & 2 \end{pmatrix}$.

   (i) Find the image of the point (p, q).

   (ii) Hence show that the whole plane is mapped to a straight line and find the equation of this line.

   (iii) Find the determinant of $\mathbf{N}$ and explain its significance.

⑪ A matrix $\mathbf{T}$ maps all points on the line $x + 2y = 1$ to the point $(1, 3)$.

   (i) Find the matrix $\mathbf{T}$ and show that it has determinant zero.

   (ii) Show that $\mathbf{T}$ maps all points on the plane to the line $y = 3x$.

   (iii) Find the coordinates of the point to which all points on the line $x + 2y = 3$ are mapped.

⑫ The plane is transformed using the matrix $\begin{pmatrix} a & b \\ c & d \end{pmatrix}$ where $ad - bc = 0$.

Prove that the general point $\mathrm{P}(x, y)$ maps to P' on the line $cx - ay = 0$.

⑬ The point P is mapped to P' on the line $3y = x$ so that PP' is parallel to the line $y = 3x$.

   (i) Find the equation of the line parallel to $y = 3x$ passing through the point P with coordinates (s, t).

   (ii) Find the coordinates of P', the point where this line meets $3y = x$.

   (iii) Find the matrix of the transformation which maps P to P' and show that the determinant of this matrix is zero.

2 The inverse of a 2 × 2 matrix

The identity matrix

Whenever you multiply a 2 × 2 matrix $\mathbf{M}$ by $\begin{pmatrix} 1 & 0 \\ 0 & 1 \end{pmatrix}$ the product is $\mathbf{M}$. It

makes no difference whether you **pre-multiply**, for example,

$$\begin{pmatrix} 1 & 0 \\ 0 & 1 \end{pmatrix} \begin{pmatrix} 4 & -2 \\ 6 & 3 \end{pmatrix} = \begin{pmatrix} 4 & -2 \\ 6 & 3 \end{pmatrix}$$

or **post-multiply**

$$\begin{pmatrix} 4 & -2 \\ 6 & 3 \end{pmatrix} \begin{pmatrix} 1 & 0 \\ 0 & 1 \end{pmatrix} = \begin{pmatrix} 4 & -2 \\ 6 & 3 \end{pmatrix}.$$

(i) Write down the matrix **P** which represents a reflection in the x-axis.

(ii) Find the matrix **P²**.

(iii) Comment on your answer.

The matrix $\begin{pmatrix} 1 & 0 \\ 0 & 1 \end{pmatrix}$ is known as the 2 × 2 identity matrix.

Identity matrices are often denoted by the letter **I**.

For multiplication of matrices, **I** behaves in the same way as the number 1 when dealing with the multiplication of real numbers.

The transformation represented by the identity matrix maps every points to itself.

Similarly, the 3 × 3 identity matrix is $\begin{pmatrix} 1 & 0 & 0 \\ 0 & 1 & 0 \\ 0 & 0 & 1 \end{pmatrix}$.

Example 6.5

(i) Write down the matrix **A** which represents a rotation of 90° anticlockwise about the origin.

(ii) Write down the matrix **B** which represents a rotation of 90° clockwise about the origin.

(iii) Find the product **AB** and comment on your answer.

Solution

(i) $\mathbf{A} = \begin{pmatrix} 0 & -1 \\ 1 & 0 \end{pmatrix}$

(ii) $\mathbf{B} = \begin{pmatrix} 0 & 1 \\ -1 & 0 \end{pmatrix}$

(iii) $\mathbf{AB} = \begin{pmatrix} 0 & -1 \\ 1 & 0 \end{pmatrix}\begin{pmatrix} 0 & 1 \\ -1 & 0 \end{pmatrix} = \begin{pmatrix} 1 & 0 \\ 0 & 1 \end{pmatrix}$

AB represents a rotation of 90° clockwise followed by a rotation of 90° anticlockwise. The result of this is to return to the starting point.

To undo the effect of a rotation through 90° anticlockwise about the origin, you need to carry out a rotation through 90° clockwise about the origin. These two transformations are inverses of each other.

Similarly, the matrices which represent these transformations are inverses of each other.

In Example 6.5, $\mathbf{B} = \begin{pmatrix} 0 & 1 \\ -1 & 0 \end{pmatrix}$ is the inverse of $\mathbf{A} = \begin{pmatrix} 0 & -1 \\ 1 & 0 \end{pmatrix}$, and vice versa.

Finding the inverse of a matrix

If the product of two square matrices, **M** and **N**, is the identity matrix **I**, then **N** is the inverse of **M**. You can write this as $\mathbf{N} = \mathbf{M}^{-1}$.

Generally, if $\mathbf{M} = \begin{pmatrix} a & b \\ c & d \end{pmatrix}$ you need to find an inverse matrix $\begin{pmatrix} p & q \\ r & s \end{pmatrix}$ such

that $\begin{pmatrix} a & b \\ c & d \end{pmatrix}\begin{pmatrix} p & q \\ r & s \end{pmatrix} = \begin{pmatrix} 1 & 0 \\ 0 & 1 \end{pmatrix}$.

ACTIVITY 6.3

Multiply $\begin{pmatrix} a & b \\ c & d \end{pmatrix}$ by $\begin{pmatrix} d & -b \\ -c & a \end{pmatrix}$.

What do you notice?

Use your result to write down the inverse of the general matrix $\mathbf{M} = \begin{pmatrix} a & b \\ c & d \end{pmatrix}$.
How does the determinant $|\mathbf{M}|$ relate to the matrix $\mathbf{M}^{-1}$?

You should have found in the activity that the inverse of the matrix

$$\mathbf{M} = \begin{pmatrix} a & b \\ c & d \end{pmatrix} \text{ is given by}$$

$$\mathbf{M}^{-1} = \frac{1}{ad - bc} \begin{pmatrix} d & -b \\ -c & a \end{pmatrix}.$$

If the determinant is zero then the inverse matrix does not exist and the matrix is said to be **singular**. If $\det(\mathbf{M}) \neq 0$ the matrix is said to be **non-singular**.

A special case is the zero matrix, which maps all points to the origin.

If a matrix is singular, then it maps all points on the plane to a straight line.

So an infinite number of points are mapped to the same point on the straight line. It is therefore not possible to find the inverse of the transformation, because an inverse matrix would map a point on that straight line to just one other point, not to an infinite number of them.

Example 6.6

$$\mathbf{A} = \begin{pmatrix} 11 & 3 \\ 6 & 2 \end{pmatrix}$$

(i) Find $\mathbf{A}^{-1}$.

(ii) The point P is mapped to the point Q $(5, 2)$ under the transformation represented by $\mathbf{A}$. Find the coordinates of P.

Solution

(i) $\det(\mathbf{A}) = (11 \times 2) - (3 \times 6) = 4$

$$\mathbf{A}^{-1} = \frac{1}{4} \begin{pmatrix} 2 & -3 \\ -6 & 11 \end{pmatrix}$$

(ii) $\mathbf{A}^{-1} \begin{pmatrix} 5 \\ 2 \end{pmatrix} = \frac{1}{4} \begin{pmatrix} 2 & -3 \\ -6 & 11 \end{pmatrix} \begin{pmatrix} 5 \\ 2 \end{pmatrix}$

$$= \frac{1}{4} \begin{pmatrix} 4 \\ -8 \end{pmatrix}$$

$$= \begin{pmatrix} 1 \\ -2 \end{pmatrix} \text{ Therefore the coordinates of P are } (1, -2).$$

$\mathbf{A}$ maps P to Q, so $\mathbf{A}^{-1}$ maps Q to P.

As matrix multiplication is generally non-commutative, it is interesting to find out if $\mathbf{MM}^{-1} = \mathbf{M}^{-1}\mathbf{M}$. The next activity investigates this.

ACTIVITY 6.4

(i) In Example 6.6 you found that the inverse of $\mathbf{A} = \begin{pmatrix} 11 & 3 \\ 6 & 2 \end{pmatrix}$ is

$\mathbf{A}^{-1} = \dfrac{1}{4}\begin{pmatrix} 2 & -3 \\ -6 & 11 \end{pmatrix}$.

Show that $\mathbf{AA}^{-1} = \mathbf{A}^{-1}\mathbf{A} = \mathbf{I}$.

(ii) If the matrix $\mathbf{M} = \begin{pmatrix} a & b \\ c & d \end{pmatrix}$, write down $\mathbf{M}^{-1}$ and show that $\mathbf{MM}^{-1} = \mathbf{M}^{-1}\mathbf{M} = \mathbf{I}$.

The result $\mathbf{MM}^{-1} = \mathbf{M}^{-1}\mathbf{M} = \mathbf{I}$ is important as it means that the identity matrix for pre-multiplication is also the identity matrix for post-multiplication. This is true for all square matrices, not just 2 × 2 matrices.

Discussion point

➡ How would you reverse the effect of a rotation followed by a reflection?

➡ How would you write down the inverse of a matrix product $\mathbf{MN}$ in terms of $\mathbf{M}^{-1}$ and $\mathbf{N}^{-1}$?

The inverse of a product of matrices

Suppose you want to find the inverse of the product $\mathbf{MN}$, where $\mathbf{M}$ and $\mathbf{N}$ are non-singular matrices. This means that you need to find a matrix $\mathbf{X}$ such that $\mathbf{X}(\mathbf{MN}) = \mathbf{I}$.

$\mathbf{X}(\mathbf{MN}) = \mathbf{I} \Rightarrow \mathbf{XMNN}^{-1} = \mathbf{IN}^{-1}$ ⟵ Post multiply by $\mathbf{N}^{-1}$

$\Rightarrow \mathbf{XM} = \mathbf{IN}^{-1}$ ⟵ Using $\mathbf{NN}^{-1} = \mathbf{I}$

$\Rightarrow \mathbf{XMM}^{-1} = \mathbf{N}^{-1}\mathbf{M}^{-1}$ ⟵ Post multiply by $\mathbf{M}^{-1}$

$\Rightarrow \mathbf{X} = \mathbf{N}^{-1}\mathbf{M}^{-1}$ ⟵ Using $\mathbf{MM}^{-1} = \mathbf{I}$

So $(\mathbf{MN})^{-1} = \mathbf{N}^{-1}\mathbf{M}^{-1}$ for matrices $\mathbf{M}$ and $\mathbf{N}$ of the same order. This means that when working backwards, you must reverse the second transformation before reversing the first transformation.

ACTIVITY 6.5

Using the matrices $\mathbf{A} = \begin{pmatrix} 1 & 4 \\ -2 & 3 \end{pmatrix}$ and $\mathbf{B} = \begin{pmatrix} 3 & 1 \\ 2 & 2 \end{pmatrix}$, verify that

$(\mathbf{AB})^{-1} = \mathbf{B}^{-1}\mathbf{A}^{-1}$

① For the matrix $\begin{pmatrix} 5 & -1 \\ -2 & 0 \end{pmatrix}$

(i)   find the image of the point $(3, 5)$

(ii) find the inverse matrix

(iii) find the point which maps to the image $(3, -2)$.

② Determine whether the following matrices are singular or non-singular. For those that are non-singular, find the inverse.

(i) $\begin{pmatrix} 6 & 3 \\ -4 & 2 \end{pmatrix}$ (ii) $\begin{pmatrix} 6 & 3 \\ 4 & 2 \end{pmatrix}$ (iii) $\begin{pmatrix} 11 & 3 \\ 3 & 11 \end{pmatrix}$ (iv) $\begin{pmatrix} 11 & 11 \\ 3 & 3 \end{pmatrix}$

(v) $\begin{pmatrix} 2 & -7 \\ 0 & 0 \end{pmatrix}$ (vi) $\begin{pmatrix} -2a & 4a \\ 4b & -8b \end{pmatrix}$ (vii) $\begin{pmatrix} -2 & 4a \\ 4b & -8 \end{pmatrix}$ (viii) $\begin{pmatrix} 1 & i \\ i & 1 \end{pmatrix}$

③ $\mathbf{M} = \begin{pmatrix} 5 & 6 \\ 2 & 3 \end{pmatrix}$ and $\mathbf{N} = \begin{pmatrix} 8 & 5 \\ -2 & -1 \end{pmatrix}$.

Calculate the following:

(i) $\mathbf{M}^{-1}$ (iii) $\mathbf{MN}$ (v) $(\mathbf{MN})^{-1}$ (vii) $\mathbf{M}^{-1}\mathbf{N}^{-1}$

(ii) $\mathbf{N}^{-1}$ (iv) $\mathbf{NM}$ (vi) $(\mathbf{NM})^{-1}$ (viii) $\mathbf{N}^{-1}\mathbf{M}^{-1}$

④ The diagram shows the unit square OIPJ mapped to the image OI′P′J′ under a transformation represented by a matrix $\mathbf{M}$.

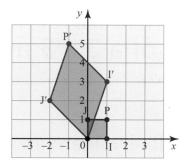

Figure 6.8

(i) Find the inverse of $\mathbf{M}$.

(ii) Use matrix multiplication to show that $\mathbf{M}^{-1}$ maps OI′P′J′ back to OIPJ.

⑤ The matrix $\begin{pmatrix} 1-k & 2 \\ -1 & 4-k \end{pmatrix}$ is singular.

Find the possible values of k.

⑥ Given that $\mathbf{M} = \begin{pmatrix} 2 & 3 \\ -1 & 4 \end{pmatrix}$ and $\mathbf{MN} = \begin{pmatrix} 7 & 2 & -9 & 10 \\ 2 & -1 & -12 & 17 \end{pmatrix}$, find the matrix $\mathbf{N}$.

⑦ Triangle T has vertices at $(1, 0)$, $(0, 1)$ and $(-2, 0)$.

It is transformed to triangle T′ by the matrix $\mathbf{M} = \begin{pmatrix} 3 & 1 \\ 1 & 1 \end{pmatrix}$.

(i) Find the coordinates of the vertices of T′.

Show the triangles T and T′ on a single diagram.

(ii) Find the ratio of the area of T′ to the area of T.

Comment on your answer in relation to the matrix **M**.

(iii) Find **M**$^{-1}$ and verify that this matrix maps the vertices of T′ to the vertices of T.

⑧ **M** = $\begin{pmatrix} a & b \\ c & d \end{pmatrix}$ is a singular matrix.

(i) Show that **M**^{2} = $(a + d)$**M**.

(ii) Find a formula which expresses **M**^{n} in terms of **M**, where n is a positive integer.

Comment on your results.

⑨ Given that **PQR** = **I**, show algebraically that

(i) **Q** = **P**$^{-1}$**R**$^{-1}$

(ii) **Q**$^{-1}$ = **RP**.

Given that **P** = $\begin{pmatrix} 3 & 1 \\ 1 & 2 \end{pmatrix}$ and **R** = $\begin{pmatrix} 12 & -3 \\ 2 & -1 \end{pmatrix}$

(iii) use part (i) to find the matrix **Q**

(iv) calculate the matrix **Q**$^{-1}$

(v) verify that your answer to part (ii) is correct by calculating **RP** and comparing it with your answer to part (iv).

3 Finding the determinant and inverse of a 3 × 3 matrix

> The determinant of a 3 × 3 matrix is sometimes denoted $|a\ b\ c|$.

In this section you will find the determinant and inverse of 3 × 3 matrices using the calculator facility and also using a non-calculator method.

Finding the determinant and inverse of a 3 × 3 matrix using a calculator

ACTIVITY 6.6

Using a calculator, find the determinant and inverse of the matrix

$$\mathbf{A} = \begin{pmatrix} 3 & -2 & 1 \\ 0 & 1 & 2 \\ 4 & 0 & 1 \end{pmatrix}.$$

Still using a calculator, find out which of the following matrices are non-singular and find the inverse in each of these cases.

$$\mathbf{B} = \begin{pmatrix} 5 & 5 & 5 \\ 2 & 2 & 2 \\ 2 & 4 & -3 \end{pmatrix} \quad \mathbf{C} = \begin{pmatrix} 1 & 3 & 2 \\ -1 & 0 & 1 \\ 2 & 1 & 4 \end{pmatrix} \quad \mathbf{D} = \begin{pmatrix} 0 & 3 & -2 \\ 1 & -1 & 2 \\ 3 & 0 & 3 \end{pmatrix}$$

Finding the determinant and inverse of a 3 × 3 matrix without using a calculator

It is also possible to find the determinant and inverse of a 3×3 matrix without using a calculator. This is useful in cases where some of the elements of the matrix are algebraic rather than numerical.

If $\mathbf{M}$ is the 3×3 matrix $\begin{pmatrix} a_1 & b_1 & c_1 \\ a_2 & b_2 & c_2 \\ a_3 & b_3 & c_3 \end{pmatrix}$ then the determinant of $\mathbf{M}$ is defined by

$$\det \mathbf{M} = a_1 \begin{vmatrix} b_2 & c_2 \\ b_3 & c_3 \end{vmatrix} - a_2 \begin{vmatrix} b_1 & c_1 \\ b_3 & c_3 \end{vmatrix} + a_3 \begin{vmatrix} b_1 & c_1 \\ b_2 & c_2 \end{vmatrix},$$

which is sometimes referred to as the **expansion of the determinant by the first column**.

For example, to find the determinant of the matrix $\mathbf{A} = \begin{pmatrix} 3 & -2 & 1 \\ 0 & 1 & 2 \\ 4 & 0 & 1 \end{pmatrix}$ from Activity 6.6:

$$\det \mathbf{A} = 3 \begin{vmatrix} 1 & 2 \\ 0 & 1 \end{vmatrix} - 0 \begin{vmatrix} -2 & 1 \\ 0 & 1 \end{vmatrix} + 4 \begin{vmatrix} -2 & 1 \\ 1 & 2 \end{vmatrix}$$

$$= 3(1 - 0) - 0(-2 - 0) + 4(-4 - 1)$$

$$= 3 - 20$$

$$= -17$$

Notice that you do not really need to calculate $\begin{vmatrix} -2 & 1 \\ 0 & 1 \end{vmatrix}$ as it is going to be multiplied by zero. Keeping an eye open for helpful zeros can reduce the number of calculations needed.

This is the same answer as you will have obtained earlier using your calculator.

The 2×2 determinant $\begin{vmatrix} b_2 & c_2 \\ b_3 & c_3 \end{vmatrix}$ is called the **minor** of the element a_1. It is obtained by deleting the row and column containing:

$$\begin{vmatrix} a_1 & b_1 & c_1 \\ a_2 & b_2 & c_2 \\ a_3 & b_3 & c_3 \end{vmatrix}$$

Other minors are defined in the same way, for example the minor of a_2 is

$$\begin{vmatrix} a_1 & b_1 & c_1 \\ a_2 & b_2 & c_2 \\ a_3 & b_3 & c_3 \end{vmatrix} = \begin{vmatrix} b_1 & c_1 \\ b_3 & c_3 \end{vmatrix}$$

You may have noticed that the signs on the minors alternate as shown:

$$\begin{vmatrix} + & - & + \\ - & + & - \\ + & - & + \end{vmatrix}$$

123

A minor, together with its correct sign, is known as a **cofactor** and is denoted by the corresponding capital letter; for example, the cofactor of a_3 is A_3. This means that the expansion by the first column, say, can be written as

$$a_1 A_1 + a_2 A_2 + a_3 A_3.$$

 Note

As an alternative, you could use the **expansion of the determinant by the second column**:

$$\det \mathbf{M} = -b_1 \begin{vmatrix} a_2 & c_2 \\ a_3 & c_3 \end{vmatrix} + b_2 \begin{vmatrix} a_1 & c_1 \\ a_3 & c_3 \end{vmatrix} - b_3 \begin{vmatrix} a_1 & c_1 \\ a_2 & c_2 \end{vmatrix},$$

or the **expansion of the determinant by the third column**:

$$\det \mathbf{M} = c_1 \begin{vmatrix} a_2 & b_2 \\ a_3 & b_3 \end{vmatrix} - c_2 \begin{vmatrix} a_1 & b_1 \\ a_3 & b_3 \end{vmatrix} + c_3 \begin{vmatrix} a_1 & b_1 \\ a_2 & b_2 \end{vmatrix}.$$

It is fairly easy to show that all three expressions above for **M** simplify to:

$$a_1 b_2 c_3 + a_2 b_3 c_1 + a_3 b_1 c_2 - a_3 b_2 c_1 - a_1 b_3 c_2 - a_2 b_1 c_3$$

Example 6.7

Find the determinant of the matrix $\mathbf{M} = \begin{pmatrix} 3 & 0 & -4 \\ 7 & 2 & -1 \\ -2 & 1 & 3 \end{pmatrix}$

Solution

Expanding by the first column using the expression:

$$\det \mathbf{M} = a_1 \begin{vmatrix} b_2 & c_2 \\ b_3 & c_3 \end{vmatrix} - a_2 \begin{vmatrix} b_1 & c_1 \\ b_3 & c_3 \end{vmatrix} + a_3 \begin{vmatrix} b_1 & c_1 \\ b_2 & c_2 \end{vmatrix}$$

gives:

$$\det \mathbf{M} = 3 \begin{vmatrix} 2 & -1 \\ 1 & 3 \end{vmatrix} - 7 \begin{vmatrix} 0 & -4 \\ 1 & 3 \end{vmatrix} + (-2) \begin{vmatrix} 0 & -4 \\ 2 & -1 \end{vmatrix}$$

$$= 3(6 - (-1)) - 7(0 - (-4)) - 2(0 - (-8))$$

$$= 21 - 28 - 16$$

$$= -23$$

> Notice that expanding by the top row would be quicker here as it has a zero element.

To find the determinant you can also expand by rows. So, for example, expanding by the top row would give:

$$3 \begin{vmatrix} 2 & -1 \\ 1 & 3 \end{vmatrix} - 0 \begin{vmatrix} 7 & -1 \\ -2 & 3 \end{vmatrix} + (-4) \begin{vmatrix} 7 & 2 \\ -2 & 1 \end{vmatrix}$$

which also gives the answer −23.

Earlier you saw that the determinant of a 2×2 matrix represents the area scale factor of the transformation represented by the matrix. In the case of a 3×3 matrix the determinant represents the volume scale factor. For example, the

matrix $\begin{pmatrix} 2 & 0 & 0 \\ 0 & 2 & 0 \\ 0 & 0 & 2 \end{pmatrix}$ has determinant 8; this matrix represents an enlargement

of scale factor 2, centre the origin, so the volume scale factor of the transformation is $2 \times 2 \times 2 = 8$.

Finding the inverse of a 3 x 3 matrix without using a calculator

> Recall that a minor, together with its correct sign, is known as a cofactor and is denoted by the corresponding capital letter; for example the cofactor of a_3 is A_3.

The matrix $\begin{pmatrix} A_1 & A_2 & A_3 \\ B_1 & B_2 & B_3 \\ C_1 & C_2 & C_3 \end{pmatrix}$ is known as the **adjugate** or **adjoint** of **M**,

denoted **adj M**.

adj **M** is formed by

- replacing each element of **M** by its cofactor;

- then transposing the matrix (i.e. changing rows into columns and columns into rows).

The unique inverse of a 3×3 matrix can be calculated as follows:

$$\mathbf{M}^{-1} = \frac{1}{\det \mathbf{M}} \text{ adj } \mathbf{M} = \frac{1}{\det \mathbf{M}} \begin{pmatrix} A_1 & A_2 & A_3 \\ B_1 & B_2 & B_3 \\ C_1 & C_2 & C_3 \end{pmatrix}, \det \mathbf{M} \neq 0$$

The steps involved in the method are shown in the following example.

Example 6.8

Find the inverse of the matrix **M** without using a calculator, where

$$\mathbf{M} = \begin{pmatrix} 2 & 3 & 4 \\ 2 & -5 & 2 \\ -3 & 6 & -3 \end{pmatrix}.$$

Solution

Step 1: Find the determinant Δ and check $\Delta \neq 0$

Expanding by the first column

$$\Delta = 2 \begin{vmatrix} -5 & 2 \\ 6 & -3 \end{vmatrix} - 2 \begin{vmatrix} 3 & 4 \\ 6 & -3 \end{vmatrix} - 3 \begin{vmatrix} 3 & 4 \\ -5 & 2 \end{vmatrix}$$

$$= (2 \times 3) - (2 \times -33) - (3 \times 26) = -6$$

Therefore the inverse matrix exists.

You can evaluate the determinant Δ using these cofactors to check your earlier arithmetic is correct:

2nd column:
$$\Delta = 3B_1 - 5B_2 + 6B_3$$
$$= (3 \times 0) - (5 \times 6)$$
$$+ (6 \times 4)$$
$$= -6$$

3rd column:
$$\Delta = 4C_1 + 2C_2 - 3C_3$$
$$= (4 \times -3) + (2 \times -21)$$
$$-(3 \times -16)$$
$$= -6$$

Step 2: Evaluate the cofactors

$$A_1 = \begin{vmatrix} -5 & 2 \\ 6 & -3 \end{vmatrix} = 3 \qquad A_2 = -\begin{vmatrix} 3 & 4 \\ 6 & -3 \end{vmatrix} = 33 \qquad A_3 = \begin{vmatrix} 3 & 4 \\ -5 & 2 \end{vmatrix} = 26$$

$$B_1 = -\begin{vmatrix} 2 & 2 \\ -3 & -3 \end{vmatrix} = 0 \qquad B_2 = \begin{vmatrix} 2 & 4 \\ -3 & -3 \end{vmatrix} = 6 \qquad B_3 = -\begin{vmatrix} 2 & 4 \\ 2 & 2 \end{vmatrix} = 4$$

$$C_1 = \begin{vmatrix} 2 & -5 \\ -3 & 6 \end{vmatrix} = -3 \qquad C_2 = -\begin{vmatrix} 2 & 3 \\ -3 & 6 \end{vmatrix} = -21 \qquad C_3 = \begin{vmatrix} 2 & 3 \\ 2 & -5 \end{vmatrix} = -16$$

Step 3: Form the matrix of cofactors and transpose it, then multiply by $\frac{1}{\Delta}$

$$\mathbf{M}^{-1} = \frac{1}{-6} \begin{pmatrix} 3 & 0 & -3 \\ 33 & 6 & -21 \\ 26 & 4 & -16 \end{pmatrix}^T$$

Multiply by $\frac{1}{\Delta}$

The capital T indicates the matrix is to be transposed.

Matrix of cofactors.

$$= \frac{1}{-6} \begin{pmatrix} 3 & 33 & 26 \\ 0 & 6 & 4 \\ -3 & -21 & -16 \end{pmatrix}$$

$$= \frac{1}{6} \begin{pmatrix} -3 & -33 & -26 \\ 0 & -6 & -4 \\ 3 & 21 & 16 \end{pmatrix}$$

The final matrix could then be simplified and written as

$$\mathbf{M}^{-1} = \begin{pmatrix} -\dfrac{1}{2} & -\dfrac{11}{2} & -\dfrac{13}{3} \\ 0 & -1 & -\dfrac{2}{3} \\ \dfrac{1}{2} & \dfrac{7}{2} & \dfrac{8}{3} \end{pmatrix}$$

Check:

$$\mathbf{MM}^{-1} = \begin{pmatrix} 2 & 3 & 4 \\ 2 & -5 & 2 \\ -3 & 6 & -3 \end{pmatrix} \frac{1}{6} \begin{pmatrix} -3 & -33 & -26 \\ 0 & -6 & -4 \\ 3 & 21 & 16 \end{pmatrix}$$

$$= \frac{1}{6} \begin{pmatrix} 6 & 0 & 0 \\ 0 & 6 & 0 \\ 0 & 0 & 6 \end{pmatrix} = \begin{pmatrix} 1 & 0 & 0 \\ 0 & 1 & 0 \\ 0 & 0 & 1 \end{pmatrix}$$

This adjugate method for finding the inverse of a 3 × 3 matrix is reasonably straightforward but it is important to check your arithmetic as you go along, as it is very easy to make mistakes. You can use your calculator to check that you have calculated the inverse correctly.

As shown in the example above, you might also multiply the inverse by the original matrix and check that you obtain the 3 × 3 identity matrix.

Exercise 6.3

T

① Using a calculator, find whether the following matrices are singular or non-singular. For those that are non-singular find the inverse.

(i) $\begin{pmatrix} 2 & 4 & 9 \\ -1 & -3 & 0 \\ 4 & -2 & -7 \end{pmatrix}$ (ii) $\begin{pmatrix} 4 & 0 & -1 \\ 2 & -3 & 5 \\ -4 & 6 & -10 \end{pmatrix}$ (iii) $\begin{pmatrix} 1 & 0 & 3 \\ 8 & -2 & -1 \\ 3 & 5 & 11 \end{pmatrix}$

② Evaluate these determinants without using a calculator. Check your answers using your calculator.

(i) (a) $\begin{vmatrix} 1 & 1 & 3 \\ -1 & 0 & 2 \\ 3 & 1 & 4 \end{vmatrix}$ (b) $\begin{vmatrix} 1 & -1 & 3 \\ 1 & 0 & 1 \\ 3 & 2 & 4 \end{vmatrix}$

(ii) (a) $\begin{vmatrix} 1 & -5 & -4 \\ 2 & 3 & 3 \\ -2 & 1 & 0 \end{vmatrix}$ (b) $\begin{vmatrix} 1 & 2 & -2 \\ -5 & 3 & 1 \\ -4 & 3 & 0 \end{vmatrix}$

(iii) (a) $\begin{vmatrix} 2 & 1 & 2 \\ 3 & 5 & 3 \\ 1 & -1 & 1 \end{vmatrix}$ (b) $\begin{vmatrix} 1 & 5 & 0 \\ 1 & 5 & 0 \\ 2 & 1 & -2 \end{vmatrix}$

What do you notice about the determinants?

③ Find the inverses of the following matrices, if they exist, without using a calculator.

(i) $\begin{pmatrix} 1 & 2 & 4 \\ 2 & 4 & 5 \\ 0 & 1 & 2 \end{pmatrix}$ (ii) $\begin{pmatrix} 3 & 2 & 6 \\ 5 & 3 & 11 \\ 7 & 4 & 16 \end{pmatrix}$

(iii) $\begin{pmatrix} 5 & 5 & -5 \\ -9 & 3 & -5 \\ -4 & -6 & 8 \end{pmatrix}$ (iv) $\begin{pmatrix} 6 & 5 & 6 \\ -5 & 2 & -4 \\ -4 & -6 & -5 \end{pmatrix}$

④ Find the inverse of the matrix $\begin{pmatrix} 4 & -5 & 3 \\ 3 & 3 & -4 \\ 5 & 4 & -6 \end{pmatrix}$ and hence solve the simultaneous equations

$4x - 5y + 3z = 3$
$3x + 3y - 4z = 48$
$5x + 4y - 6z = 74$

⑤ Find the inverse of the matrix $\mathbf{M} = \begin{pmatrix} 1 & 3 & -2 \\ k & 0 & 4 \\ 2 & -1 & 4 \end{pmatrix}$ where $k \neq 0$

For what value of k is the matrix $\mathbf{M}$ singular?

⑥ (i) Investigate the relationship between the matrices

$$\mathbf{A} = \begin{pmatrix} 0 & 3 & 1 \\ 2 & 4 & 2 \\ -1 & 3 & 5 \end{pmatrix} \quad \mathbf{B} = \begin{pmatrix} 1 & 0 & 3 \\ 2 & 2 & 4 \\ 5 & -1 & 3 \end{pmatrix} \quad \mathbf{C} = \begin{pmatrix} 3 & 1 & 0 \\ 4 & 2 & 2 \\ 3 & 5 & -1 \end{pmatrix}$$

(ii) Find det A, det B and det C and comment on your answer.

⑦ Show that $x = 1$ is one root of the equation $\begin{vmatrix} 2 & 2 & x \\ 1 & x & 1 \\ x & 1 & 4 \end{vmatrix} = 0$ and find the other roots.

⑧ Find the values of x for which the matrix $\begin{pmatrix} 3 & -1 & 1 \\ 2 & x & 4 \\ x & 1 & 3 \end{pmatrix}$ is singular.

⑨ Given that the matrix $\mathbf{M} = \begin{pmatrix} k & 2 & 1 \\ 0 & -k & 2 \\ 2k & 1 & 3 \end{pmatrix}$ has determinant greater than 5, find the range of possible values for k.

⑩ (i) **P** and **Q** are non-singular matrices. Prove that $(\mathbf{PQ})^{-1} = \mathbf{Q}^{-1}\mathbf{P}^{-1}$

(ii) Find the inverses of the matrices $\mathbf{P} = \begin{pmatrix} 0 & 3 & -1 \\ -2 & 2 & 2 \\ -3 & 0 & 1 \end{pmatrix}$ and $\mathbf{Q} = \begin{pmatrix} 2 & 1 & 2 \\ 1 & 0 & 1 \\ 4 & -3 & 2 \end{pmatrix}$.

Using the result from part (i), find $(\mathbf{PQ})^{-1}$.

⑪ (i) Prove that $\begin{vmatrix} ka_1 & b_1 & c_1 \\ ka_2 & b_2 & c_2 \\ ka_3 & b_3 & c_3 \end{vmatrix} = k \begin{vmatrix} a_1 & b_1 & c_1 \\ a_2 & b_2 & c_2 \\ a_3 & b_3 & c_3 \end{vmatrix}$, where k is a constant.

(ii) Explain in terms of volumes why multiplying all the elements in the first column by a constant multiplies the value of the determinant by k.

(iii) What happens if you multiply a different column by k?

⑫ Given that $\begin{vmatrix} 1 & 2 & 3 \\ 6 & 4 & 5 \\ 7 & 5 & 1 \end{vmatrix} = 43$, write down the values of the determinants:

(i) $\begin{vmatrix} 10 & 2 & 3 \\ 60 & 4 & 5 \\ 70 & 5 & 1 \end{vmatrix}$ (ii) $\begin{vmatrix} 4 & 10 & -21 \\ 24 & 20 & -35 \\ 28 & 25 & -7 \end{vmatrix}$ (iii) $\begin{vmatrix} x & 4 & 3y \\ 6x & 8 & 5y \\ 7x & 10 & y \end{vmatrix}$ (iv) $\begin{vmatrix} x & \frac{1}{x} & 12y \\ 6x & \frac{2}{x} & 20y \\ 7x & \frac{5}{2x} & 4y \end{vmatrix}$

⑬ $\mathbf{A} = \begin{pmatrix} 1 & 7 & 4 \\ 0 & 1 & 2 \\ 0 & 0 & 1 \end{pmatrix}$, $\mathbf{B} = \begin{pmatrix} 1 & 0 & 0 \\ 3 & 1 & 0 \\ -1 & -4 & 1 \end{pmatrix}$ and $\mathbf{C} = \mathbf{AB}$.

(i) Calculate the matrix **C**.

(ii) Work out the matrix product $\mathbf{A} \begin{pmatrix} 1 & a & b \\ 0 & 1 & c \\ 0 & 0 & 1 \end{pmatrix}$.

(iii) Using the answer to part (ii), find $\mathbf{A}^{-1}$.

(iv) Using a calculator, find $\mathbf{B}^{-1}$.

(v) Using your results from parts (iii) and (iv), find $\mathbf{C}^{-1}$.

⑭ The matrix $\mathbf{M} = \begin{pmatrix} k-1 & k-1 & 0 \\ 1 & k+1 & -2 \\ k-1 & k-2 & 1 \end{pmatrix}$ has inverse

$$\mathbf{M}^{-1} = \begin{pmatrix} k & -1 & -2 \\ -\dfrac{5}{2} & k-2 & k-1 \\ -\dfrac{7}{2} & 1 & k \end{pmatrix}.$$

Find the value of k.

4 Using matrices to solve simultaneous equations

There are a number of methods to solve a pair of linear simultaneous equations of the form

$$3x + 2y = 17$$
$$2x - 5y = 24$$

These include elimination, substitution or graphical methods.

An alternative method involves the use of inverse matrices. This method has the advantage that it can more easily be extended to solving a set of n equations in n variables.

Example 6.9

Use a matrix method to solve the simultaneous equations

$$3x + 2y = 17$$
$$2x - 5y = 24$$

Solution

$$\begin{pmatrix} 3 & 2 \\ 2 & -5 \end{pmatrix} \begin{pmatrix} x \\ y \end{pmatrix} = \begin{pmatrix} 17 \\ 24 \end{pmatrix}.$$ ← Write the equations in matrix form.

The inverse of the matrix $\begin{pmatrix} 3 & 2 \\ 2 & -5 \end{pmatrix}$ is $-\dfrac{1}{19} \begin{pmatrix} -5 & -2 \\ -2 & 3 \end{pmatrix}$.

$$-\frac{1}{19} \begin{pmatrix} -5 & -2 \\ -2 & 3 \end{pmatrix} \begin{pmatrix} 3 & 2 \\ 2 & -5 \end{pmatrix} \begin{pmatrix} x \\ y \end{pmatrix} = -\frac{1}{19} \begin{pmatrix} -5 & -2 \\ -2 & 3 \end{pmatrix} \begin{pmatrix} 17 \\ 24 \end{pmatrix}$$

Pre-multiply both sides of the matrix equation by the inverse matrix.

$$\begin{pmatrix} x \\ y \end{pmatrix} = -\frac{1}{19} \begin{pmatrix} -133 \\ 38 \end{pmatrix} = \begin{pmatrix} 7 \\ -2 \end{pmatrix}$$

As $\mathbf{M}^{-1}\mathbf{Mp} = \mathbf{p}$ the left-hand side simplifies to $\begin{pmatrix} x \\ y \end{pmatrix}$.

The solution is $x = 7$, $y = -2$.

Geometrical interpretation in two dimensions

Two equations in two unknowns can be represented in a plane by two straight lines. The number of points of intersection of the lines determines the number of solutions to the equations.

There are three different possibilities.

Case 1

Example 6.7 shows that two simultaneous equations can have a unique solution. Graphically, this is represented by a single point of intersection.

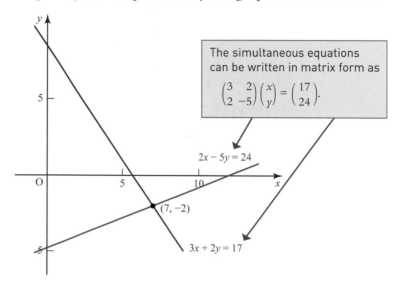

The simultaneous equations can be written in matrix form as

$$\begin{pmatrix} 3 & 2 \\ 2 & -5 \end{pmatrix} \begin{pmatrix} x \\ y \end{pmatrix} = \begin{pmatrix} 17 \\ 24 \end{pmatrix}.$$

$2x - 5y = 24$

$(7, -2)$

$3x + 2y = 17$

Figure 6.9

This is the case where $\det \mathbf{M} \neq 0$ and so the inverse matrix $\mathbf{M}^{-1}$ exists, allowing the equations to be solved.

Case 2

If two lines are parallel they do not have a point of intersection. For example, the lines

$$x + 2y = 10$$
$$x + 2y = 4$$

are parallel.

The equations can be written in matrix form as

$$\begin{pmatrix} 1 & 2 \\ 1 & 2 \end{pmatrix} \begin{pmatrix} x \\ y \end{pmatrix} = \begin{pmatrix} 10 \\ 4 \end{pmatrix}.$$

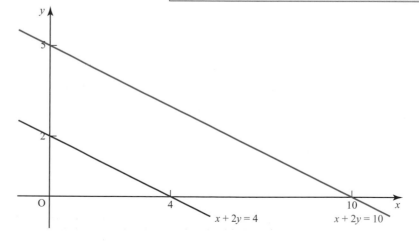

$x + 2y = 4$ $x + 2y = 10$

Figure 6.10

The matrix $\mathbf{M} = \begin{pmatrix} 1 & 2 \\ 1 & 2 \end{pmatrix}$ has determinant zero and hence the inverse matrix does not exist.

Case 3

More than one solution is possible in cases where the lines are **coincident**, i.e. lie on top of each other. For example, the two lines

$$x + 2y = 10$$
$$3x + 6y = 30$$

> The equations can be written in matrix form as
> $$\begin{pmatrix} 1 & 2 \\ 3 & 6 \end{pmatrix}\begin{pmatrix} x \\ y \end{pmatrix} = \begin{pmatrix} 10 \\ 30 \end{pmatrix}.$$

are coincident. You can see this because the equations are multiples of each other.

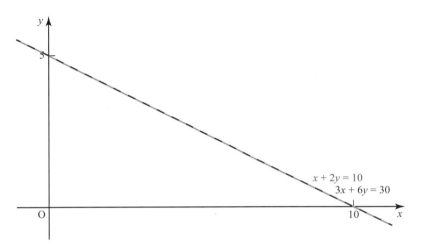

Figure 6.11

In this case the matrix $\mathbf{M}$ is $\begin{pmatrix} 1 & 2 \\ 3 & 6 \end{pmatrix}$ and $\det \mathbf{M} = 0$.

There are infinitely many solutions to these equations.

ACTIVITY 6.7

(i) Write the three simultaneous equations
$$2x - 2y + 3z = 4$$
$$5x + y - z = -6$$
$$3x + 4y - 2z = 1$$
as a matrix equation.

Use a matrix method and your calculator to solve the simultaneous equations.

(ii) Repeat part (i) for the three simultaneous equations
$$2x - 2y + 3z = 4$$
$$5x + y - z = -6$$
$$3x + 3y - 4z = 1$$

What happens in this case?

Try to solve the equations algebraically. Comment on your answer.

① (i) Find the inverse of the matrix $\begin{pmatrix} 3 & -1 \\ 2 & 3 \end{pmatrix}$.

   (ii) Hence use a matrix method to solve the simultaneous equations

$$3x - y = 2$$
$$2x + 3y = 5$$

② Use matrices to solve the following pairs of simultaneous equations.

   (i) $3x + 2y = 4$

        $x - 2y = 4$

   (ii) $3x - 2y = 9$

        $x - 4y = -2$

③ (i) Use a calculator to find the inverse of the matrix $\begin{pmatrix} 3 & 1 & 1 \\ -5 & -2 & 3 \\ 1 & 1 & 1 \end{pmatrix}$.

   (ii) Hence use a matrix method to solve the simultaneous equations

$$3x + y + z = -2$$
$$-5x - 2y + 3z = -1$$
$$x + y + z = 2$$

④ Find the inverse of the matrix $\begin{pmatrix} 1 & i \\ 2i & 3 \end{pmatrix}$.

Hence solve the simultaneous equations

$$x + yi = 2 + 2i$$
$$2xi + 3y = 1 - i$$

⑤ Use a matrix method to solve these simultaneous equations. (You should use a calculator to find the inverse matrix.)

$$x + 5y + z = 0$$
$$2x - 3y - 4z = 7$$
$$3x + 2y - 6z = 4$$

⑥ For each of the following pair of equations, describe the intersections of the pair of straight lines represented by the simultaneous equations.

   (i) $3x + 5y = 18$

        $2x + 4y = 11$

   (ii) $3x + 6y = 18$

        $2x + 4y = 12$

   (iii) $3x + 6y = 18$

        $2x + 4y = 15$

⑦ Find the two values of k for which the equations

$$2x + ky = 3$$
$$kx + 8y = 6$$

do not have a unique solution.

⑧ (i) Find **AB** where $\mathbf{A} = \begin{pmatrix} 5 & -2 & k \\ 3 & -4 & -5 \\ -2 & 3 & 4 \end{pmatrix}$

and $\mathbf{B} = \begin{pmatrix} -1 & 3k+8 & 4k+10 \\ -2 & 2k+20 & 3k+25 \\ 1 & -11 & -14 \end{pmatrix}$.

Hence write down the inverse matrix $\mathbf{A}^{-1}$, stating the condition on the value of k required for the inverse to exist.

(ii) Using the result from part (i) solve the equation

$$\begin{pmatrix} 5 & -2 & k \\ 3 & -4 & -5 \\ -2 & 3 & 4 \end{pmatrix} \begin{pmatrix} x \\ y \\ z \end{pmatrix} = \begin{pmatrix} 28 \\ 0 \\ m \end{pmatrix}$$

when $k = 8$ and $m = 2$.

LEARNING OUTCOMES

When you have completed this chapter you should be able to:

➤ find the determinant of a 2 × 2 matrix and of a 3 × 3 matrix, with and without a calculator

➤ know what is meant by a singular matrix

➤ find the inverse of a non-singular 2 × 2 matrix and of a non-singular 3 × 3 matrix, with and without a calculator

➤ understand that the determinant of a 2 × 2 matrix represents the area scale factor of the corresponding transformation, and understand the significance of the sign of the determinant

➤ know that the determinant of a 3 × 3 matrix represents the volume scale factor of the corresponding transformation, and understand the significance of the sign of the determinant

➤ understand the significance of a zero determinant in terms of transformations

➤ use the product rule for inverse matrices

➤ use matrices to solve a pair of linear simultaneous equations in two unknowns

➤ use matrices to solve three linear simultaneous equations in three unknowns.

KEY POINTS

1 If $\mathbf{M} = \begin{pmatrix} a & b \\ c & d \end{pmatrix}$ then the determinant of $\mathbf{M}$, written $\begin{vmatrix} a & b \\ c & d \end{vmatrix}$ or det $\mathbf{M}$ or $|\mathbf{M}|$, is given by det $\mathbf{M} = ad - bc$

2 The determinant of a 2 × 2 matrix represents the area scale factor of the transformation.
  The determinant of a 3 × 3 matrix represents the volume scale factor of the transformation.

3 When the determinant is negative, the orientation of the image is reversed.

4 det $(\mathbf{AB})$ = det $\mathbf{A}$ det $\mathbf{B}$

5 If $\mathbf{M} = \begin{pmatrix} a & b \\ c & d \end{pmatrix}$ then $\mathbf{M}^{-1} = \dfrac{1}{ad - bc} \begin{pmatrix} d & -b \\ -c & a \end{pmatrix}$

6 $(\mathbf{MN})^{-1} = \mathbf{N}^{-1}\mathbf{M}^{-1}$

7 A matrix is singular if the determinant is zero. If the determinant is non-zero the matrix is said to be non-singular.

8 If the determinant of a matrix is zero, all points are mapped to either a straight line (in two dimensions) or to a plane (three dimensions).

9 If $\mathbf{A}$ is a non-singular matrix, $\mathbf{AA}^{-1} = \mathbf{A}^{-1}\mathbf{A} = \mathbf{I}$.

10 When solving two simultaneous equations in two unknowns, the equations can be written as a matrix equation $\mathbf{M} \begin{pmatrix} x \\ y \end{pmatrix} = \begin{pmatrix} a \\ b \end{pmatrix}$.

  When solving three simultaneous equations in three unknowns, the equations can be written as a matrix equation $\mathbf{M} \begin{pmatrix} x \\ y \\ z \end{pmatrix} = \begin{pmatrix} a \\ b \\ c \end{pmatrix}$.

  In both cases, if det $\mathbf{M} \neq 0$ there is a unique solution to the equations which can be found by pre-multiplying both sides of the equation by the inverse matrix $\mathbf{M}^{-1}$.

7 Vectors and 3D space

> *Why is there space rather than no space? Why is space three-dimensional? Why is space big? We have a lot of room to move around in. How come it's not tiny? We have no consensus about these things. We're still exploring them.*
>
> Leonard Susskind

1 Finding the angle between two vectors

In this section you will learn how to find the angle between two vectors in two dimensions or three dimensions.

Discussion point

→ Are there any right angles in the building shown above?

Prior knowledge

From AS Mathematics Chapter 12, you need to be able to use the language of vectors, including the terms magnitude, direction and position vector. You should also be able to find the distance between two points represented by position vectors and be able to add and subtract vectors and multiply a vector by a scalar.

Example 7.1

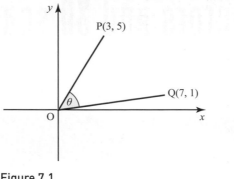

Figure 7.1

Find the angle POQ.

Remember that $\overrightarrow{OP}$ denotes the vector from O to P, and $|\overrightarrow{OP}|$ is the **magnitude** (length) of $\overrightarrow{OP}$.

Solution

Using the cosine rule: $\cos\theta = \dfrac{\left|\overrightarrow{OP}\right|^2 + \left|\overrightarrow{OQ}\right|^2 - \left|\overrightarrow{PQ}\right|^2}{2 \times \left|\overrightarrow{OP}\right| \times \left|\overrightarrow{OQ}\right|}$

$\overrightarrow{OP} = \begin{pmatrix} 3 \\ 5 \end{pmatrix}$ so $\left|\overrightarrow{OP}\right| = \sqrt{3^2 + 5^2} = \sqrt{34}$

$\overrightarrow{OQ} = \begin{pmatrix} 7 \\ 1 \end{pmatrix}$ so $\left|\overrightarrow{OQ}\right| = \sqrt{7^2 + 1^2} = \sqrt{50}$

Using Pythagoras' theorem.

$\overrightarrow{PQ} = \overrightarrow{OQ} - \overrightarrow{OP} = \begin{pmatrix} 7 \\ 1 \end{pmatrix} - \begin{pmatrix} 3 \\ 5 \end{pmatrix} = \begin{pmatrix} 4 \\ -4 \end{pmatrix}$ so $\left|\overrightarrow{PQ}\right| = \sqrt{4^2 + 4^2} = \sqrt{32}$

so $\cos\theta = \dfrac{34 + 50 - 32}{2 \times \sqrt{34} \times \sqrt{50}}$

$\theta = 50.9°$

More generally, to find the angle between $\overrightarrow{OA} = \mathbf{a} = \begin{pmatrix} a_1 \\ a_2 \end{pmatrix}$ and $\overrightarrow{OB} = \mathbf{b} = \begin{pmatrix} b_1 \\ b_2 \end{pmatrix}$ start by applying the cosine rule to the triangle OAB in Figure 7.2.

Discussion point

➡ How else could you find the angle θ?

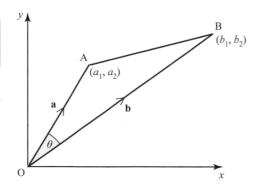

Figure 7.2

$$\cos\theta = \frac{\left|\overrightarrow{OA}\right|^2 + \left|\overrightarrow{OB}\right|^2 - \left|\overrightarrow{AB}\right|^2}{2 \times \left|\overrightarrow{OA}\right| \times \left|\overrightarrow{OB}\right|} \quad \textcircled{1}$$

> $\left|\overrightarrow{OA}\right|, \left|\overrightarrow{OB}\right|$ and $\left|\overrightarrow{AB}\right|$ are the lengths of the vectors $\overrightarrow{OA}$, $\overrightarrow{OB}$ and $\overrightarrow{AB}$.

Also from the diagram:

$$\left|\overrightarrow{OA}\right| = |\mathbf{a}| = \sqrt{a_1^2 + a_2^2} \quad \text{and} \quad \left|\overrightarrow{OB}\right| = |\mathbf{b}| = \sqrt{b_1^2 + b_2^2} \quad \textcircled{2}$$

and

$$\overrightarrow{AB} = \mathbf{b} - \mathbf{a} = \begin{pmatrix} b_1 \\ b_2 \end{pmatrix} - \begin{pmatrix} a_1 \\ a_2 \end{pmatrix} = \begin{pmatrix} b_1 - a_1 \\ b_2 - a_2 \end{pmatrix}$$

so $\left|\overrightarrow{AB}\right| = \sqrt{\left(b_1 - a_1\right)^2 + \left(b_2 - a_2\right)^2} \quad \textcircled{3}$

ACTIVITY 7.1

By substituting ② and ③ into ① show that $\cos\theta = \dfrac{a_1 b_1 + a_2 b_2}{|\mathbf{a}||\mathbf{b}|}$

where $|\mathbf{a}| = \sqrt{a_1^2 + a_2^2}$ and $|\mathbf{b}| = \sqrt{b_1^2 + b_2^2}$.

The activity above showed that for Figure 7.2, $\cos\theta = \dfrac{a_1 b_1 + a_2 b_2}{|\mathbf{a}||\mathbf{b}|}$.

The expression on the numerator, $a_1 b_1 + a_2 b_2$, is called the scalar product of the vectors $\mathbf{a}$ and $\mathbf{b}$, which is written $\mathbf{a}.\mathbf{b}$.

So $\cos\theta = \dfrac{\mathbf{a}.\mathbf{b}}{|\mathbf{a}||\mathbf{b}|}$.

> This is sometimes called the dot product.

This result is sometimes written $\mathbf{a}.\mathbf{b} = |\mathbf{a}||\mathbf{b}|\cos\theta$.

Using the column format, the scalar product can be written as

$$\mathbf{a}.\mathbf{b} = \begin{pmatrix} a_1 \\ a_2 \end{pmatrix}.\begin{pmatrix} b_1 \\ b_2 \end{pmatrix} = a_1 b_1 + a_2 b_2.$$

Note

1 The scalar product, unlike a vector, has size but no direction.

2 The scalar product of two vectors is **commutative**. This is because multiplication of numbers is commutative. For example:

$$\begin{pmatrix} 3 \\ -4 \end{pmatrix}.\begin{pmatrix} 1 \\ 5 \end{pmatrix} = (3 \times 1) + (-4 \times 5) = (1 \times 3) + (5 \times -4) = \begin{pmatrix} 1 \\ 5 \end{pmatrix}.\begin{pmatrix} 3 \\ -4 \end{pmatrix}$$

The scalar product is found in a similar way for vectors in three dimensions:

$$\begin{pmatrix} a_1 \\ a_2 \\ a_3 \end{pmatrix} \cdot \begin{pmatrix} b_1 \\ b_2 \\ b_3 \end{pmatrix} = a_1b_1 + a_2b_2 + a_3b_3$$

This is used in Example 7.2 to find the angle between two vectors in three dimensions.

Example 7.2

The position vectors of three points A, B and C are given by

$$\mathbf{a} = \begin{pmatrix} 2 \\ 5 \\ -1 \end{pmatrix}, \mathbf{b} = \begin{pmatrix} 0 \\ 7 \\ 3 \end{pmatrix} \text{ and } \mathbf{c} = \begin{pmatrix} 8 \\ 0 \\ 3 \end{pmatrix}. \text{ Find the vectors } \overrightarrow{AB} \text{ and } \overrightarrow{CB}$$

and hence calculate the angle ABC.

Solution

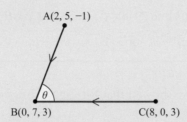

A(2, 5, −1)

B(0, 7, 3) C(8, 0, 3)

θ

Figure 7.3

$$\overrightarrow{AB} = \mathbf{b} - \mathbf{a} = \begin{pmatrix} 0 \\ 7 \\ 3 \end{pmatrix} - \begin{pmatrix} 2 \\ 5 \\ -1 \end{pmatrix} = \begin{pmatrix} -2 \\ 2 \\ 4 \end{pmatrix}$$

$$\overrightarrow{CB} = \mathbf{b} - \mathbf{c} = \begin{pmatrix} 0 \\ 7 \\ 3 \end{pmatrix} - \begin{pmatrix} 8 \\ 0 \\ 3 \end{pmatrix} = \begin{pmatrix} -8 \\ 7 \\ 0 \end{pmatrix}$$

The angle ABC is found using the scalar product of the vectors $\overrightarrow{AB}$ and $\overrightarrow{CB}$.

$$\overrightarrow{AB} \cdot \overrightarrow{CB} = \begin{pmatrix} -2 \\ 2 \\ 4 \end{pmatrix} \cdot \begin{pmatrix} -8 \\ 7 \\ 0 \end{pmatrix} = 16 + 14 + 0 = 30$$

$$\left|\overrightarrow{AB}\right| = \sqrt{(-2)^2 + 2^2 + 4^2} = \sqrt{24} \text{ and } \left|\overrightarrow{CB}\right| = \sqrt{(-8)^2 + 7^2 + 0^2} = \sqrt{113}$$

$$\overrightarrow{AB} \cdot \overrightarrow{CB} = \left|\overrightarrow{AB}\right|\left|\overrightarrow{CB}\right| \cos\theta$$

$$\Rightarrow 30 = \sqrt{24}\sqrt{113} \cos\theta$$

$$\Rightarrow \cos\theta = \frac{30}{\sqrt{24}\sqrt{113}}$$

$$\Rightarrow \theta = 54.8°$$

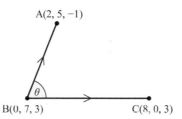

Figure 7.4

Discussion point

➜ For the points A, B and C in Example 7.2, find the scalar product of the vectors $\overrightarrow{BA}$ and $\overrightarrow{BC}$, and comment on your answer.

Notice that $\overrightarrow{AB}$ and $\overrightarrow{CB}$ are both directed towards the point B, and $\overrightarrow{BA}$ and $\overrightarrow{BC}$ are both directed away from the point B (as in Figure 7.4). Using either pair of vectors gives the angle ABC. This angle could be acute or obtuse.

However, if you use vectors $\overrightarrow{AB}$ (directed towards B) and $\overrightarrow{BC}$ (directed away from B), then you will obtain the angle $180° - \theta$ instead.

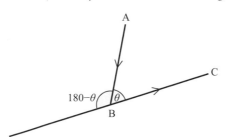

Figure 7.5

Perpendicular vectors

If two vectors are perpendicular, then the angle between them is 90°.

Since $\cos 90° = 0$, it follows that if vectors **a** and **b** are perpendicular then $\mathbf{a.b} = 0$.

Conversely, if the scalar product of two non-zero vectors is zero, they are perpendicular.

Example 7.3

Two points, P and Q, have coordinates $(1, 3, -2)$ and $(4, 2, 5)$.
Show that angle POQ = 90°
(i)   using column vectors
(ii) using $\mathbf{i, j, k}$ notation.

Solution

(i) $\mathbf{p} = \begin{pmatrix} 1 \\ 3 \\ -2 \end{pmatrix}, \mathbf{q} = \begin{pmatrix} 4 \\ 2 \\ 5 \end{pmatrix}$

$\mathbf{p.q} = \begin{pmatrix} 1 \\ 3 \\ -2 \end{pmatrix} . \begin{pmatrix} 4 \\ 2 \\ 5 \end{pmatrix}$

$= (1 \times 4) + (3 \times 2) + (-2 \times 5)$

$= 4 + 6 - 10$

$= 0$

So the angle POQ = 90°.

(ii) $\mathbf{p} = \mathbf{i} + 3\mathbf{j} - 2\mathbf{k}$, $\mathbf{q} = 4\mathbf{i} + 2\mathbf{j} + 5\mathbf{k}$ | Multiply out the brackets. |

$\mathbf{p.q} = (\mathbf{i} + 3\mathbf{j} - 2\mathbf{k}).(4\mathbf{i} + 2\mathbf{j} + 5\mathbf{k})$

$= 4\mathbf{i.i} + 14\mathbf{i.j} - 3\mathbf{i.k} + 6\mathbf{j.j} + 11\mathbf{j.k} - 10\mathbf{k.k}$ | Since $\mathbf{i}$, $\mathbf{j}$ and $\mathbf{k}$ are unit vectors, $\mathbf{i.i} = \mathbf{j.j} = \mathbf{k.k} = 1$. |

$= 4 + 6 - 10$

$= 0$ | Since $\mathbf{i}$, $\mathbf{j}$ and $\mathbf{k}$ are all perpendicular, $\mathbf{i.j} = \mathbf{i.k} = \mathbf{j.k} = 0$. |

So the angle POQ = 90°.

Exercise 7.1

① Find:

(i) $\begin{pmatrix} 2 \\ 3 \end{pmatrix} \cdot \begin{pmatrix} 1 \\ -2 \end{pmatrix}$ (ii) $\begin{pmatrix} 2 \\ 3 \end{pmatrix} \cdot \begin{pmatrix} -1 \\ 2 \end{pmatrix}$

(iii) $\begin{pmatrix} 1 \\ 2 \\ 3 \end{pmatrix} \cdot \begin{pmatrix} 4 \\ 0 \\ -1 \end{pmatrix}$ (iv) $\begin{pmatrix} 1 \\ 2 \\ 3 \end{pmatrix} \cdot \begin{pmatrix} -1 \\ 4 \\ 0 \end{pmatrix}$

② Find the angle between the vectors $\mathbf{p}$ and $\mathbf{q}$ shown in Figure 7.6.

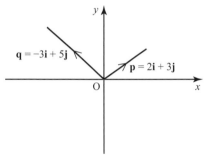

Figure 7.6

③ Find the angle between the vectors:

(i) $\mathbf{a} = 3\mathbf{i} + 2\mathbf{j} - 4\mathbf{k}$ and $\mathbf{b} = -2\mathbf{i} + \mathbf{j} - 3\mathbf{k}$

(ii) $\mathbf{a} = -3\mathbf{i} - 2\mathbf{j} + 4\mathbf{k}$ and $\mathbf{b} = -2\mathbf{i} + \mathbf{j} - 3\mathbf{k}$

(iii) $\mathbf{a} = 3\mathbf{i} + 2\mathbf{j} - 4\mathbf{k}$ and $\mathbf{b} = 2\mathbf{i} - \mathbf{j} + 3\mathbf{k}$

④ Find the angle between the following pairs of vectors and comment on your answers.

(i) $\begin{pmatrix} 3 \\ -2 \\ 5 \end{pmatrix}$ and $\begin{pmatrix} 6 \\ -4 \\ 10 \end{pmatrix}$ (ii) $\begin{pmatrix} 3 \\ -2 \\ 5 \end{pmatrix}$ and $\begin{pmatrix} -9 \\ 6 \\ -15 \end{pmatrix}$

⑤ Show that the three following vectors are mutually perpendicular.

$\begin{pmatrix} 2 \\ 3 \\ 1 \end{pmatrix}, \begin{pmatrix} -1 \\ 0 \\ 2 \end{pmatrix}, \begin{pmatrix} 6 \\ -5 \\ 3 \end{pmatrix}$

⑥ Find the value of α for which the vectors $\begin{pmatrix} 2 \\ 5 \\ -1 \end{pmatrix}$ and $\begin{pmatrix} 4 \\ -5 \\ \alpha \end{pmatrix}$ are perpendicular.

⑦ Given the vectors $\mathbf{c} = \begin{pmatrix} \alpha \\ 5 \\ 3 \end{pmatrix}$ and $\mathbf{d} = \begin{pmatrix} \alpha \\ \alpha \\ 2 \end{pmatrix}$ are perpendicular, find the possible values of α.

⑧ The vector $\begin{pmatrix} s+t \\ s+2t-1 \\ 2s-t-7 \end{pmatrix}$ is perpendicular to both $\begin{pmatrix} 4 \\ 1 \\ -2 \end{pmatrix}$ and $\begin{pmatrix} 1 \\ 2 \\ 3 \end{pmatrix}$.

Find the value of s and the value of t.

⑨ A triangle has vertices at the points A(2, 1, −3), B(4, 0, 6) and C(−1, 2, 1). Using the scalar product, find the three angles of the triangle ABC and check that they add up to 180°.

⑩ The point A has position vector $\mathbf{a} = \begin{pmatrix} 5 \\ 2 \\ 3 \end{pmatrix}$.

Find the angle that the vector $\mathbf{a}$ makes with each of the coordinate axes.

⑪ Show that the triangle with vertices A(5, 4, 4), B(4, −2, 3) and C(−9, 2, −8) is right angled. Hence find the centre and radius of the circle that passes through A, B and C.

⑫ The room illustrated in Figure 7.7 has rectangular walls, floor and ceiling. A string has been stretched in a straight line between the corners A and G.

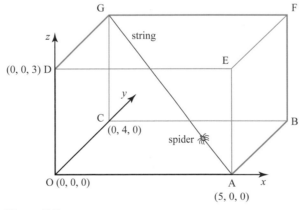

Figure 7.7

The corner O is taken as the origin. A is (5, 0, 0), C is (0, 4, 0) and D is (0, 0, 3), where the lengths are in metres.

A spider walks up the string, starting from A.

(i) Write down the coordinates of G.

(ii) Find the vector $\overrightarrow{AG}$ and the distance the spider walks along the string from A to G.

(iii) Find the angle of elevation of the spider's journey along the string.

⑬ Figure 7.8 shows the design for a barn. Its base and walls are rectangular. All measurements are in metres.

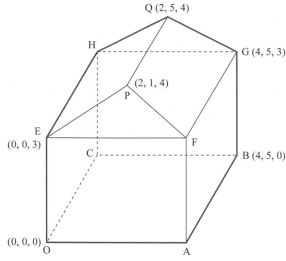

Figure 7.8

(i)   Write down the coordinates of the other vertices of the barn.

(ii) Determine whether the section EPF is vertical and hence state the type of quadrilateral formed by the roof sections PFGQ and PQHE.

(iii) Find the cosine of angle FPE and hence find the exact area of the triangle FPE.

The engineer plans to increase the strength of the barn by installing supporting metal bars along OG and AH.

(iv) Calculate the acute angle between the metal bars.

2 The vector equation of a line

Lines in two dimensions

Before you focus on the equation of a line in three dimensions, Activity 7.2 looks at a new format for the equation of a line in two dimensions. This is called **the vector equation of the line**.

ACTIVITY 7.2

The position vector of a general point is given by $\mathbf{r} = \begin{pmatrix} 2 \\ -1 \end{pmatrix} + \lambda \begin{pmatrix} 2 \\ 4 \end{pmatrix}$, where λ is a parameter that can take any value and A is the point $(2, -1)$.

(i)   Show that $\lambda = 1$ corresponds to the point B with position vector $\begin{pmatrix} 4 \\ 3 \end{pmatrix}$.

(ii) Find the position vectors of the points corresponding to values of λ of $-2, -1,$ $0, \frac{1}{2}, \frac{3}{4}, 2$ and 3.

(iii) Plot the points from parts (i) and (ii) on a sheet of graph paper. Show how the points can be joined to form a straight line.

(iv) What can you say about the position of the point if:
   (a) $0 < \lambda < 1$?
   (b) $\lambda > 1$?
   (c) $\lambda < 0$?

Activity 7.2 should have convinced you that $\mathbf{r} = \begin{pmatrix} 2 \\ -1 \end{pmatrix} + \lambda \begin{pmatrix} 2 \\ 4 \end{pmatrix}$ is the equation

of a straight line passing through the point $(2, -1)$. The vector $\begin{pmatrix} 2 \\ 4 \end{pmatrix}$ determines the direction of the line. You might find it helpful to think of this as shown in Figure 7.9.

Starting from the origin, you can 'step' on to the line at a given point, A. All other points on the line can then be reached by taking 'steps' of different sizes (λ) in the direction of a given vector, called the **direction vector**.

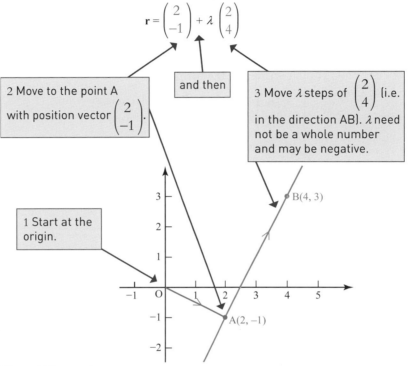

Figure 7.9

You should also have noticed that when:

> $\lambda = 0$ corresponds to the point A
> $\lambda = 1$ corresponds to the point B, one 'step' along the line away from A
> $0 < \lambda < 1$ corresponds to points lying between A and B
> $\lambda > 1$ corresponds to points lying beyond B
> $\lambda < 0$ corresponds to points beyond A, in the opposite direction to B.

The vector equation of a line is not unique. In this case, any vector parallel or in

the opposite direction to $\begin{pmatrix} 2 \\ 4 \end{pmatrix}$ could be used as the direction vector; for example,

$\begin{pmatrix} 1 \\ 2 \end{pmatrix}, \begin{pmatrix} -3 \\ -6 \end{pmatrix}$ or $\begin{pmatrix} 20 \\ 40 \end{pmatrix}$. Similarly, you can 'step' on to the line at any point,

such as B(4, 3).

So the line $\mathbf{r} = \begin{pmatrix} 2 \\ -1 \end{pmatrix} + \lambda \begin{pmatrix} 2 \\ 4 \end{pmatrix}$ could also have equation $\mathbf{r} = \begin{pmatrix} 2 \\ -1 \end{pmatrix} + \lambda \begin{pmatrix} 1 \\ 2 \end{pmatrix}$

or $\mathbf{r} = \begin{pmatrix} 4 \\ 3 \end{pmatrix} + \lambda \begin{pmatrix} 2 \\ 4 \end{pmatrix}$ for example.

In general, the **vector equation of a line** in two dimensions is given by:

$$\mathbf{r} = \mathbf{a} + \lambda\mathbf{d}$$

> In two dimensions the equation of a line usually looks easier in cartesian form than in vector form. However, as you are about to see, the opposite is the case in three dimensions, where the vector form is much easier to work with.

where **a** is the position vector of a point A on the line and **d** is the direction vector of the line. Sometimes a different letter, such as μ or t, is used as the parameter instead of λ.

ACTIVITY 7.3

The vector equation of a line

$$\mathbf{r} = \mathbf{a} + \lambda\mathbf{d}$$

is written in the form

$$\begin{pmatrix} x \\ y \end{pmatrix} = \begin{pmatrix} a_1 \\ a_2 \end{pmatrix} + \lambda\begin{pmatrix} d_1 \\ d_2 \end{pmatrix}.$$

(i)   Write down expressions for x and y in terms of λ.

(ii) Rearrange the two expressions from part (i) to make λ the subject.

(iii) By equating the two expressions from part (ii), show that the vector equation of the line can be written in the form

$$y = mx + c,$$

where m and c are constants.

Activity 7.3 shows that the vector and cartesian equations of a line are equivalent.

Lines in three dimensions

The same form for the vector equation of a line can be used in three dimensions. For example, $\mathbf{r} = \begin{pmatrix} 3 \\ 4 \\ 1 \end{pmatrix} + \lambda\begin{pmatrix} 2 \\ 3 \\ 6 \end{pmatrix}$ represents a line through the

point with position vector $\begin{pmatrix} 3 \\ 4 \\ 1 \end{pmatrix}$ and direction vector $\begin{pmatrix} 2 \\ 3 \\ 6 \end{pmatrix}$.

Writing $\mathbf{r}$ as $\begin{pmatrix} x \\ y \\ z \end{pmatrix}$ gives $\begin{pmatrix} x \\ y \\ z \end{pmatrix} = \begin{pmatrix} 3 \\ 4 \\ 1 \end{pmatrix} + \lambda\begin{pmatrix} 2 \\ 3 \\ 6 \end{pmatrix}$. This equation contains the

three relationships

$$x = 3 + 2\lambda \qquad y = 4 + 3\lambda \qquad z = 1 + 6\lambda.$$

Making λ the subject of each of these gives

$$\lambda = \frac{x - 3}{2} = \frac{y - 4}{3} = \frac{z - 1}{6}$$

> This form is not easy to work with and you will often find that the first step in a problem is to convert the cartesian form into vector form.

This is the **cartesian equation of a line** in three dimensions.

Generally, a line with direction vector $\mathbf{d} = \begin{pmatrix} d_1 \\ d_2 \\ d_3 \end{pmatrix}$ passing through the point A

with position vector $\mathbf{a} = \begin{pmatrix} a_1 \\ a_2 \\ a_3 \end{pmatrix}$ has the cartesian equation

$$\frac{x - a_1}{d_1} = \frac{y - a_2}{d_2} = \frac{z - a_3}{d_3}$$

> The direction vector of the line can be read from the denominators of the three expressions in this equation; the point A can be determined from the three numerators.

Special cases of the cartesian equation of a line

In the equation $\frac{x - a_1}{d_1} = \frac{y - a_2}{d_2} = \frac{z - a_3}{d_3}$ it is possible that one or two of the values of d_i might equal zero. In such cases, the equation of the line needs to be written differently.

For example, the line through $(7, 2, 3)$ in the direction $\begin{pmatrix} 0 \\ 5 \\ 2 \end{pmatrix}$ would have equation

$$\lambda = \frac{x - 7}{0} = \frac{y - 2}{5} = \frac{z - 3}{2}$$

The first fraction involves division by zero, which is undefined. The expression $\frac{x - 7}{0}$ comes from the rearrangement of $x - 7 = 0\lambda$, and so you can write this as $x - 7 = 0$ or $x = 7$.

So the equation of this line would be written as $x = 7$ and $\lambda = \frac{y - 2}{5} = \frac{z - 3}{2}$.

Similarly, the line through the point $(1, 2, 3)$ which is parallel to the vector

$\begin{pmatrix} 1 \\ 0 \\ 0 \end{pmatrix}$ can be written as $\begin{pmatrix} x \\ y \\ z \end{pmatrix} = \begin{pmatrix} 1 \\ 2 \\ 3 \end{pmatrix} + \lambda \begin{pmatrix} 1 \\ 0 \\ 0 \end{pmatrix}$. You can see that this implies

that $y = 2$ and $z = 3$. You can also see that x can take any value, and so the equation of the line can be written as simply $y = 2$ and $z = 3$.

Note that it is impossible for all three of the d_i to equal zero as it is not possible for a line to have a zero direction vector.

Example 7.4

Write the equation of this line in vector form:

$$\frac{x - 4}{3} = \frac{y - 3}{-2} = \frac{z + 6}{4}$$

Solution

$$\lambda = \frac{x - 4}{3} = \frac{y - 3}{-2} = \frac{z + 6}{4}$$

$$\lambda = \frac{x - 4}{3} \Rightarrow x = 3\lambda + 4$$

$$\lambda = \frac{y - 3}{-2} \Rightarrow y = -2\lambda + 3$$

$$\lambda = \frac{z+6}{4} \Rightarrow z = 4\lambda - 6$$

$$\text{so } \mathbf{r} = \begin{pmatrix} x \\ y \\ z \end{pmatrix} = \begin{pmatrix} 3\lambda + 4 \\ -2\lambda + 3 \\ 4\lambda - 6 \end{pmatrix} \Rightarrow \mathbf{r} = \begin{pmatrix} 4 \\ 3 \\ -6 \end{pmatrix} + \lambda \begin{pmatrix} 3 \\ -2 \\ 4 \end{pmatrix}$$

Example 7.5

Find the cartesian form of the equation of the line through the point A $(7, -12, 4)$ in the direction $2\mathbf{i} - 5\mathbf{j} - 3\mathbf{k}$.

Solution

The line has vector form $\mathbf{r} = \mathbf{a} + \lambda\mathbf{d} = \begin{pmatrix} 7 \\ -12 \\ 4 \end{pmatrix} + \lambda \begin{pmatrix} 2 \\ -5 \\ -3 \end{pmatrix}$.

This leads to the equations

$$x = 7 + 2\lambda \qquad y = -12 - 5\lambda \qquad z = 4 - 3\lambda$$

which can be rearranged to give the cartesian equation

$$\lambda = \frac{x-7}{2} = \frac{y+12}{-5} = \frac{z-4}{-3}$$

The intersection of straight lines in two dimensions

You already know how to use simultaneous equations to find the point of intersection of two straight lines given in cartesian form. You can also use vector methods to find the position vector of the point where two lines intersect.

Example 7.6

Find the position vector of the point where the following lines intersect.

$$\mathbf{r} = \begin{pmatrix} 2 \\ 3 \end{pmatrix} + \lambda \begin{pmatrix} 1 \\ 2 \end{pmatrix} \text{ and } \mathbf{r} = \begin{pmatrix} 6 \\ 1 \end{pmatrix} + \mu \begin{pmatrix} 1 \\ -3 \end{pmatrix}$$

> Notice that different letters are used for the parameters in the two equations.

Solution

When the lines intersect, the position vector is the same for each of them.

$$\mathbf{r} = \begin{pmatrix} x \\ y \end{pmatrix} = \begin{pmatrix} 2 \\ 3 \end{pmatrix} + \lambda \begin{pmatrix} 1 \\ 2 \end{pmatrix} = \begin{pmatrix} 6 \\ 1 \end{pmatrix} + \mu \begin{pmatrix} 1 \\ -3 \end{pmatrix}$$

This gives two simultaneous equations for λ and μ.

$$2 + \lambda = 6 + \mu$$
$$3 + 2\lambda = 1 - 3\mu$$

Solving these gives $\lambda = 2$ and $\mu = -2$. Substituting in either equation gives $\mathbf{r} = \begin{pmatrix} 4 \\ 7 \end{pmatrix}$, which is the position vector of the point of intersection.

The intersection of straight lines in three dimensions

Hold a pen and a pencil to represent two distinct straight lines as follows.

- Hold them to represent two parallel lines.
- Hold them to represent two lines intersecting at a unique point.
- Hold them to represent lines which are not parallel and which do not intersect even if you were to extend them.

In three-dimensional space, two or more straight lines that are not parallel and which do not meet are known as **skew lines**. In two dimensions, two distinct lines are either parallel or intersecting, but in three dimensions there are three possibilities. The lines are either parallel, intersecting or skew. This is illustrated in Examples 7.7 and 7.8.

Example 7.7

The lines l_1 and l_2 are represented by the equations

$$l_1 : \frac{x-1}{1} = \frac{y+6}{2} = \frac{z+1}{3} \qquad l_2 : \frac{x-9}{2} = \frac{y-7}{2} = \frac{z-2}{2}$$

(i) Write these lines in vector form.

(ii) Hence find whether the lines meet, and, if so, the coordinates of their point of intersection.

Solution

(i) The equation of l_1 is $\mathbf{r} = \begin{pmatrix} 1 \\ -6 \\ -1 \end{pmatrix} + \lambda \begin{pmatrix} 1 \\ 2 \\ 3 \end{pmatrix}$

The equation of l_2 is $\mathbf{r} = \begin{pmatrix} 9 \\ 7 \\ 2 \end{pmatrix} + \mu \begin{pmatrix} 2 \\ 3 \\ -1 \end{pmatrix}$

(ii) If there is a point $\begin{pmatrix} X \\ Y \\ Z \end{pmatrix}$ that is common to both lines then

$$\begin{pmatrix} X \\ Y \\ Z \end{pmatrix} = \begin{pmatrix} 1 \\ -6 \\ -1 \end{pmatrix} + \lambda \begin{pmatrix} 1 \\ 2 \\ 3 \end{pmatrix} = \begin{pmatrix} 9 \\ 7 \\ 2 \end{pmatrix} + \mu \begin{pmatrix} 2 \\ 3 \\ -1 \end{pmatrix}$$

for some parameters λ and μ.

This gives the three equations:

$$X = \lambda + 1 = 2\mu + 9 \qquad ①$$
$$Y = 2\lambda - 6 = 3\mu + 7 \qquad ②$$
$$Z = 3\lambda - 1 = -\mu + 2 \qquad ③$$

Now solve any two of the three equations simultaneously.

$$\left. \begin{array}{l} \lambda - 2\mu = 8 \\ 2\lambda - 3\mu = 13 \end{array} \right\} \Leftrightarrow \left. \begin{array}{l} 2\lambda - 4\mu = 16 \\ 2\lambda - 3\mu = 13 \end{array} \right\} \Leftrightarrow \mu = -3, \lambda = 2 \quad \boxed{\text{Using ① and ②.}}$$

If these values for λ and μ also satisfy equation ③, then the lines meet.

Using equation ③, when $\lambda = 2$, $Z = 6 - 1 = 5$ and when $\mu = -3$, $Z = 3 + 2 = 5$.

As both values of Z are equal, this proves the lines intersect.

Using either $\lambda = 2$ or $\mu = -3$ in equations ①, ② and ③ gives $X = 3$, $Y = -2$ and $Z = 5$, so the lines meet at the point $(3, -2, 5)$.

Example 7.8

Prove that the lines l_1 and l_2 are skew, where:

$$l_1 : \mathbf{r} = \begin{pmatrix} 1 \\ -6 \\ -1 \end{pmatrix} + \lambda \begin{pmatrix} 1 \\ 2 \\ 3 \end{pmatrix} \qquad l_2 : \mathbf{r} = \begin{pmatrix} 9 \\ 8 \\ 2 \end{pmatrix} + \mu \begin{pmatrix} 2 \\ 3 \\ -1 \end{pmatrix}$$

Solution

If there is a point (X, Y, Z) common to both lines then

$$\begin{pmatrix} X \\ Y \\ Z \end{pmatrix} = \begin{pmatrix} 1 \\ -6 \\ 1 \end{pmatrix} + \lambda \begin{pmatrix} 1 \\ 2 \\ 3 \end{pmatrix} = \begin{pmatrix} 9 \\ 8 \\ 2 \end{pmatrix} + \mu \begin{pmatrix} 2 \\ 3 \\ -1 \end{pmatrix}$$

for some parameters λ and μ.

$$X = \lambda + 1 = 2\mu + 9 \qquad ①$$
$$Y = 2\lambda - 6 = 3\mu + 8 \qquad ②$$
$$Z = 3\lambda - 1 = -\mu + 2 \qquad ③$$

$\boxed{\text{Solve equations ① and ② simultaneously.}}$

$$\left. \begin{array}{l} \lambda - 2\mu = 8 \\ 2\lambda - 3\mu = 14 \end{array} \right\} \Leftrightarrow \left. \begin{array}{l} 2\lambda - 4\mu = 16 \\ 2\lambda - 3\mu = 14 \end{array} \right\} \Leftrightarrow \mu = -2, \lambda = 4$$

When $\lambda = 4$, $Z = 12 - 1 = 11$ and when $\mu = -2$, $Z = 2 + 2 = 4$.

$\boxed{\text{Substitute these values into equation ③.}}$

Therefore the values $\mu = -2$, $\lambda = 4$ do not satisfy the third equation and so the lines do not meet. The only other alternatives are that the lines are parallel or skew.

Look at the direction vectors of the lines $\begin{pmatrix} 1 \\ 2 \\ 3 \end{pmatrix}$ and $\begin{pmatrix} 2 \\ 3 \\ -1 \end{pmatrix}$. Neither of these is a multiple of the other so they are not parallel and hence the two lines are not parallel. So, lines l_1 and l_2 are skew.

Finding the angle between two lines

Figure 7.10 shows two lines in two dimensions, with their equations given in vector form.

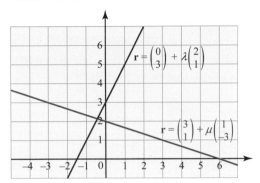

Figure 7.10

The angle between the two lines is the same as the angle between their direction vectors, $\begin{pmatrix} 2 \\ 1 \end{pmatrix}$ and $\begin{pmatrix} 1 \\ -3 \end{pmatrix}$. So you can use the scalar product to find the angle between the two lines.

Example 7.9

Find the acute angle between the lines $\mathbf{r} = \begin{pmatrix} 0 \\ 3 \end{pmatrix} + \lambda \begin{pmatrix} 2 \\ 1 \end{pmatrix}$ and $\mathbf{r} = \begin{pmatrix} 3 \\ 1 \end{pmatrix} + \mu \begin{pmatrix} 1 \\ -3 \end{pmatrix}$.

Solution

$$\begin{pmatrix} 2 \\ 1 \end{pmatrix} . \begin{pmatrix} 1 \\ -3 \end{pmatrix} = (2 \times 1) + (1 \times -3) = 2 - 3 = -1$$

$$\left| \begin{pmatrix} 2 \\ 1 \end{pmatrix} \right| = \sqrt{2^2 + 1^2} = \sqrt{5} \text{ and } \left| \begin{pmatrix} 1 \\ -3 \end{pmatrix} \right| = \sqrt{1^2 + (-3)^2} = \sqrt{10}$$

$$\cos \theta = \frac{-1}{\sqrt{5}\sqrt{10}}$$

$$\theta = 98.1°$$

So the acute angle between the lines is $180° - 98.1° = 81.9°$.

Sometimes this method gives you an obtuse angle. If one of the direction vectors is replaced by its negative, the supplementary angle $(180 - \theta)$ is obtained. Either the acute angle or the supplementary obtuse angle can be called 'an angle between the two lines', but it is usual to be asked for 'the acute angle between the lines'. If your method has produced an obtuse angle, you merely have to remember to subtract your final answer from $180°$.

ACTIVITY 7.4

Find the cartesian forms of the two equations in Example 7.9. How can you find the angle between them without using vectors?

The same method can be used for lines in three dimensions. Even if the lines do not meet, the angle between them is still the angle between their direction vectors.

The lines l and m shown in Figure 7.11 are skew. The angle between them is shown in the diagram below by the angle θ between the lines l and m', where m' is a translation of the line m to a position where it intersects the line l.

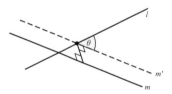

Figure 7.11

Example 7.10

Find the angle between the lines $\mathbf{r} = \begin{pmatrix} 1 \\ 0 \\ 4 \end{pmatrix} + \lambda \begin{pmatrix} 2 \\ -1 \\ -1 \end{pmatrix}$ and

$\mathbf{r} = \begin{pmatrix} 2 \\ -1 \\ 3 \end{pmatrix} + \mu \begin{pmatrix} 3 \\ 0 \\ 1 \end{pmatrix}$.

Solution

The angle between the lines is the angle between their direction vectors $\begin{pmatrix} 2 \\ -1 \\ -1 \end{pmatrix}$ and $\begin{pmatrix} 3 \\ 0 \\ 1 \end{pmatrix}$.

Using $\mathbf{a.b} = |a|\,|b|\cos\theta$

$$\begin{pmatrix} 2 \\ -1 \\ -1 \end{pmatrix} \cdot \begin{pmatrix} 3 \\ 0 \\ 1 \end{pmatrix} = \sqrt{2^2 + (-1)^2 + (-1)^2}\,\sqrt{3^2 + 0^2 + 1^2}\,\cos\theta$$

$$\Rightarrow 6 + 0 - 1 = \sqrt{6}\sqrt{10}\,\cos\theta$$

$$\Rightarrow \theta = \cos^{-1}\left(\frac{5}{\sqrt{6}\sqrt{10}}\right) = 49.8°$$

Exercise 7.2

① Find the equation of the following lines in vector form.

(i) through $(3, 1)$ in the direction $\begin{pmatrix} 5 \\ -2 \end{pmatrix}$

(ii) through $(5, -1)$ in the direction $\begin{pmatrix} 0 \\ 4 \end{pmatrix}$

(iii) through $(-2, 4)$ and $(3, 9)$

(iv) through $(0, 8)$ and $(-2, -3)$

② Find the equation of the following lines in vector form.

(i) through $(2, 4, -1)$ in the direction $\begin{pmatrix} 3 \\ 6 \\ 4 \end{pmatrix}$

(ii) through $(1, 0, -1)$ in the direction $\begin{pmatrix} 1 \\ 0 \\ 0 \end{pmatrix}$

(iii) through $(1, 0, 4)$ and $(6, 3, -2)$

(iv) through $(0, 0, 1)$ and $(2, 1, 4)$

③ Write the equations of the following lines in cartesian form.

(i) $\mathbf{r} = \begin{pmatrix} 2 \\ 4 \\ -1 \end{pmatrix} + t\begin{pmatrix} 3 \\ 6 \\ 4 \end{pmatrix}$ (ii) $\mathbf{r} = \begin{pmatrix} 1 \\ 0 \\ -1 \end{pmatrix} + t\begin{pmatrix} 1 \\ 3 \\ 4 \end{pmatrix}$

(iii) $\mathbf{r} = \begin{pmatrix} 3 \\ 0 \\ 4 \end{pmatrix} + t\begin{pmatrix} 1 \\ 0 \\ 2 \end{pmatrix}$ (iv) $\mathbf{r} = \begin{pmatrix} 0 \\ 4 \\ 1 \end{pmatrix} + t\begin{pmatrix} 2 \\ 0 \\ 4 \end{pmatrix}$

④ Write the equations of the following lines in vector form.

(i) $\dfrac{x - 3}{5} = \dfrac{y + 2}{3} = \dfrac{z - 1}{4}$

(ii) $x = \dfrac{y}{2} = \dfrac{z + 1}{3}$

(iii) $x = y = z$

(iv) $x = 2$ and $y = z$

⑤ Write down the vector and cartesian equations of the line through the point $(3, -5, 2)$ which is parallel to the y-axis.

⑥ Find the position vector of the point of intersection of each of these pairs of lines.

(i) $\mathbf{r} = \begin{pmatrix} 2 \\ 1 \end{pmatrix} + \lambda \begin{pmatrix} 1 \\ 0 \end{pmatrix}$ and $\mathbf{r} = \begin{pmatrix} 3 \\ 0 \end{pmatrix} + \mu \begin{pmatrix} 1 \\ 1 \end{pmatrix}$

(ii) $\mathbf{r} = \begin{pmatrix} 2 \\ -1 \end{pmatrix} + \lambda \begin{pmatrix} 1 \\ 2 \end{pmatrix}$ and $\mathbf{r} = \mu \begin{pmatrix} 1 \\ 1 \end{pmatrix}$

(iii) $\mathbf{r} = \begin{pmatrix} -2 \\ -3 \end{pmatrix} + \lambda \begin{pmatrix} -1 \\ 3 \end{pmatrix}$ and $\mathbf{r} = \begin{pmatrix} 1 \\ 3 \end{pmatrix} + \mu \begin{pmatrix} 2 \\ -1 \end{pmatrix}$

⑦ Decide whether the following pairs of lines intersect or not. If they do intersect, find the point of intersection; if not, state whether the lines are parallel or skew.

(i) $L_1: \dfrac{x-6}{1} = \dfrac{y+4}{-2} = \dfrac{z-2}{5}$ $L_2: \dfrac{x-1}{1} = \dfrac{y-4}{-1} = \dfrac{z+17}{2}$

(ii) $L_1: \dfrac{x}{5} = \dfrac{y+1}{3} = \dfrac{z-4}{-3}$ $L_2: \dfrac{x-2}{4} = \dfrac{y-5}{-3} = \dfrac{z+1}{2}$

(iii) $\mathbf{r}_1 = \begin{pmatrix} 2 \\ 0 \\ 1 \end{pmatrix} + \lambda \begin{pmatrix} 3 \\ 2 \\ 1 \end{pmatrix}$ $\mathbf{r}_2 = \begin{pmatrix} 4 \\ 9 \\ -1 \end{pmatrix} + \mu \begin{pmatrix} -6 \\ -4 \\ -2 \end{pmatrix}$

(iv) $\mathbf{r}_1 = \begin{pmatrix} 9 \\ 3 \\ -4 \end{pmatrix} + \lambda \begin{pmatrix} 1 \\ 2 \\ -3 \end{pmatrix}$ $\mathbf{r}_2 = \begin{pmatrix} 1 \\ -4 \\ 5 \end{pmatrix} + \mu \begin{pmatrix} 1 \\ -1 \\ 2 \end{pmatrix}$

(v) $\mathbf{r}_1 = \begin{pmatrix} 2 \\ 3 \\ 1 \end{pmatrix} + \lambda \begin{pmatrix} 1 \\ 1 \\ -2 \end{pmatrix}$ $\mathbf{r}_2 = \begin{pmatrix} -1 \\ -3 \\ -1 \end{pmatrix} + \mu \begin{pmatrix} 1 \\ 3 \\ 2 \end{pmatrix}$

⑧ Find the acute angle between these pairs of lines.

(i) $\mathbf{r} = \begin{pmatrix} 2 \\ 5 \end{pmatrix} + \lambda \begin{pmatrix} 1 \\ 2 \end{pmatrix}$ and $\mathbf{r} = \begin{pmatrix} 1 \\ 2 \end{pmatrix} + \mu \begin{pmatrix} -1 \\ 3 \end{pmatrix}$

(ii) $\mathbf{r} = \begin{pmatrix} 0 \\ 3 \end{pmatrix} + \lambda \begin{pmatrix} -5 \\ 1 \end{pmatrix}$ and $\mathbf{r} = \begin{pmatrix} 2 \\ -1 \end{pmatrix} + \mu \begin{pmatrix} 1 \\ 1 \end{pmatrix}$

(iii) $\mathbf{r} = \begin{pmatrix} 2 \\ 1 \\ 3 \end{pmatrix} + \lambda \begin{pmatrix} 1 \\ 4 \\ 0 \end{pmatrix}$ and $\mathbf{r} = \begin{pmatrix} 6 \\ 10 \\ 4 \end{pmatrix} + \mu \begin{pmatrix} 2 \\ 1 \\ 1 \end{pmatrix}$

(iv) $\mathbf{r} = \lambda \begin{pmatrix} 4 \\ 1 \\ 4 \end{pmatrix}$ and $\mathbf{r} = \begin{pmatrix} 7 \\ 0 \\ -3 \end{pmatrix} + \mu \begin{pmatrix} 1 \\ 2 \\ -1 \end{pmatrix}$

⑨ To support a tree damaged in a gale, a tree surgeon attaches wire ropes to four of the branches, as shown in Figure 7.12.

Figure 7.12

He joins $(2, 0, 3)$ to $(-1, 2, 6)$ and $(0, 3, 5)$ to $(-2, -2, 4)$.

Do the ropes, assumed to be straight, meet?

⑩ Show that the following lines form a triangle and find the length of its sides.

$$L_1: \frac{x+7}{4} = \frac{y-24}{-7} = \frac{z+4}{4}$$

$$L_2: \frac{x-3}{2} = \frac{y+10}{2} = \frac{z-15}{-1}$$

$$L_3: \frac{x+3}{8} = \frac{y-6}{-3} = \frac{z-6}{2}$$

⑪ Figure 7.13 shows a music stand, consisting of a rectangle $DEFG$ with a vertical support OA.

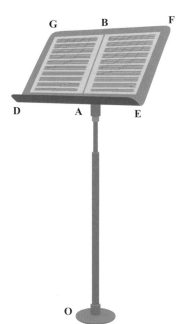

Relative to axes through the origin O, which is on the floor, the coordinates of various points are given, with dimensions in metres, as $A(0, 0, 1)$, $D(-0.25, 0, 1)$ and $F(0.25, 0.15, 1.3)$.

DE and GF are horizontal. A is the midpoint of DE and B is the midpoint of GF.

C is on AB so that $AC = \frac{1}{3} AB$.

Figure 7.13

(i) Write down the vector $\overrightarrow{AD}$ and show that $\overrightarrow{EF}$ is $\begin{pmatrix} 0 \\ 1.15 \\ 0.3 \end{pmatrix}$.

(ii) Calculate the coordinates of C.

(iii) Find the equations of the lines DE and EF in vector form.

⑫ Figure 7.14 illustrates the flight path of a helicopter, H, taking off from an airport. The origin, O, is situated at the base of the airport control tower, the *x*-axis is due east, the *y*-axis due north and the *z*-axis vertical. The units of distance are kilometres. The helicopter takes off from the point G.

The position vector **r** of the helicopter *t* minutes after take-off is given by

$$\mathbf{r} = (1 + t)\mathbf{i} + (0.5 + 2t)\mathbf{j} + 2t\mathbf{k}$$

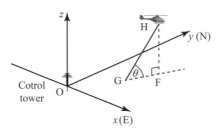

Figure 7.14

(i) Write down the coordinates of G.

(ii) Find the angle the flight path makes with the horizontal (this is shown as angle θ in the diagram).

(iii) Find the bearing of the flight path (i.e. the bearing of the line GF).

The helicopter enters a cloud at a height of 2 km.

(iv) Find the coordinates of the point where the helicopter enters the cloud.

A mountain top is situated at M(5, 4.5, 3).

(v) Find the value of *t* when HM is perpendicular to the flight path GH.

(vi) Find the distance from the helicopter to the mountain top at this time.

⑬ Three of the vertices of a parallelogram are $(0, 0, 0)$, $(1, 5, -3)$ and $(6, 2, 7)$.

(i) Find the coordinates of each of the three possible points that could form the fourth vertex.

(ii) Show by means of a diagram that the parallelogram has the same area regardless of which point is chosen as the fourth vertex.

(iii) Find the area of the parallelogram.

⑭ The line l_1 has equation $\mathbf{r} = \begin{pmatrix} 1 \\ -1 \\ 5 \end{pmatrix} + s \begin{pmatrix} 1 \\ 0 \\ -1 \end{pmatrix}$. The line l_2 has equation

$\mathbf{r} = \begin{pmatrix} 4 \\ -2 \\ 9 \end{pmatrix} + t \begin{pmatrix} 2 \\ 3 \\ -5 \end{pmatrix}$.

(i) Explain why $(1 + s, -1, 5 - s)$ are the coordinates of a general point *A* on l_1, and write down a similar expression for the coordinates of a general point *B* on l_2.

(ii) Write down an expression for the vector $\overrightarrow{AB}$ in terms of *s* and *t*.

(iii) Given that *AB* is perpendicular to both l_1 and l_2, write down two equations satisfied by *s* and *t*.

(iv) Solve these equations and hence find the coordinates of *A* and the coordinates of *B*.

(v) Find the distance *AB* and explain what your answer represents.

3 The vector (cross) product

The **vector product** is a different method for 'multiplying' two vectors. As the name suggests, in this case the result is a vector rather than a scalar. The vector product of **a** and **b** is a vector perpendicular to both **a** and **b** and it is written **a** × **b** (so it is sometimes called the 'cross product'). It is given by

$$\mathbf{a} \times \mathbf{b} = |\mathbf{a}||\mathbf{b}|\sin\theta\,\hat{\mathbf{n}}$$

where θ is the angle between **a** and **b**, and $\hat{\mathbf{n}}$ is a unit vector which is perpendicular to both **a** and **b**.

There are two unit vectors perpendicular to both **a** and **b**, but they point in opposite directions. This is often described as having 'opposite senses'.

The vector $\hat{\mathbf{n}}$ is chosen such that **a**, **b** and $\hat{\mathbf{n}}$ (in that order) form a **right-handed set** of vectors, as shown in Figure 7.15. If you point the thumb of your right hand in the direction of **a**, and your index finger in the direction of **b**, then your second finger coming up from your palm points in the direction **a** × **b** as shown below.

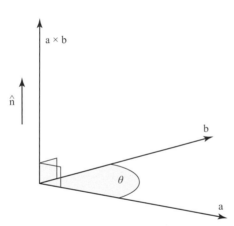 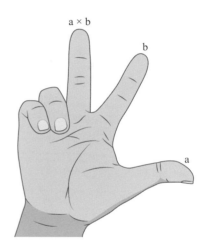

Figure 7.15

In component form, the vector product is expressed as follows:

$$\mathbf{a} \times \mathbf{b} = \begin{pmatrix} a_1 \\ a_2 \\ a_3 \end{pmatrix} \times \begin{pmatrix} b_1 \\ b_2 \\ b_3 \end{pmatrix} = \begin{pmatrix} a_2 b_3 - a_3 b_2 \\ a_3 b_1 - a_1 b_3 \\ a_1 b_2 - a_2 b_1 \end{pmatrix}$$

You will have the opportunity to prove this result in Exercise 7.3.

Notice that the first component of **a** × **b** is the value of the 2 × 2 determinant

$\begin{vmatrix} a_2 & b_2 \\ a_3 & b_3 \end{vmatrix}$, obtained by covering up the top row of $\begin{pmatrix} a_1 \\ a_2 \\ a_3 \end{pmatrix} \times \begin{pmatrix} b_1 \\ b_2 \\ b_3 \end{pmatrix}$. The second component is the negative of the 2 × 2 determinant, obtained by covering up the middle row. The third component is the 2 × 2 determinant, obtained by covering up the bottom row.

This means that the formula for the vector product can be expressed as a determinant:

$$\mathbf{a} \times \mathbf{b} = \begin{vmatrix} \mathbf{i} & a_1 & b_1 \\ \mathbf{j} & a_2 & b_2 \\ \mathbf{k} & a_3 & b_3 \end{vmatrix}$$

Expanding this determinant by the first column gives

$$\mathbf{a} \times \mathbf{b} = \begin{vmatrix} a_2 & b_2 \\ a_3 & b_3 \end{vmatrix} \mathbf{i} - \begin{vmatrix} a_1 & b_1 \\ a_3 & b_3 \end{vmatrix} \mathbf{j} + \begin{vmatrix} a_1 & b_1 \\ a_2 & b_2 \end{vmatrix} \mathbf{k}$$

Note this sign.

Example 7.11

(i) Calculate $\mathbf{a} \times \mathbf{b}$ when $\mathbf{a} = 3\mathbf{i} + 2\mathbf{j} + 5\mathbf{k}$ and $\mathbf{b} = \mathbf{i} - 4\mathbf{j} + 2\mathbf{k}$.

(ii) Hence find $\hat{\mathbf{n}}$, a unit vector which is perpendicular to both $\mathbf{a}$ and $\mathbf{b}$.

Solution

(i) There are two possible methods:

(Method 1)

Using determinants:

$$\mathbf{a} \times \mathbf{b} = \begin{vmatrix} \mathbf{i} & a_1 & b_1 \\ \mathbf{j} & a_2 & b_2 \\ \mathbf{k} & a_3 & b_3 \end{vmatrix}$$

$$\mathbf{a} \times \mathbf{b} = \begin{vmatrix} \mathbf{i} & 3 & 1 \\ \mathbf{j} & 2 & -4 \\ \mathbf{k} & 5 & 2 \end{vmatrix}$$

$$= \mathbf{i} \begin{vmatrix} 2 & -4 \\ 5 & 2 \end{vmatrix} - \mathbf{j} \begin{vmatrix} 3 & 1 \\ 5 & 2 \end{vmatrix} + \mathbf{k} \begin{vmatrix} 3 & 1 \\ 2 & -4 \end{vmatrix}$$

$$= 24\mathbf{i} - \mathbf{j} - 14\mathbf{k}$$

(Method 2)

Using the result

$$\mathbf{a} \times \mathbf{b} = \begin{pmatrix} a_1 \\ a_2 \\ a_3 \end{pmatrix} \times \begin{pmatrix} b_1 \\ b_2 \\ b_3 \end{pmatrix} = \begin{pmatrix} a_2 b_3 - a_3 b_2 \\ a_3 b_1 - a_1 b_3 \\ a_1 b_2 - a_2 b_1 \end{pmatrix}$$

gives

$$\mathbf{a} \times \mathbf{b} = \begin{pmatrix} 3 \\ 2 \\ 5 \end{pmatrix} \times \begin{pmatrix} 1 \\ -4 \\ 2 \end{pmatrix} = \begin{pmatrix} 2 \times 2 - 5 \times (-4) \\ 5 \times 1 - 3 \times 2 \\ 3 \times (-4) - 2 \times 1 \end{pmatrix} = \begin{pmatrix} 24 \\ -1 \\ -14 \end{pmatrix}$$

Discussion point

➜ How can you use the scalar product to check that the answer to Example 7.11 is correct?

So $\mathbf{a} \times \mathbf{b} = \begin{pmatrix} 24 \\ -1 \\ -14 \end{pmatrix}$, which is a vector perpendicular to the vectors $\mathbf{a}$ and $\mathbf{b}$.

$$|\mathbf{a} \times \mathbf{b}| = \sqrt{24^2 + (-1)^2 + (-14)^2} = \sqrt{773}$$

(ii) So a unit vector perpendicular to both $\mathbf{a}$ and $\mathbf{b}$ is $\hat{\mathbf{n}} = \dfrac{1}{\sqrt{773}} \begin{pmatrix} 24 \\ -1 \\ -14 \end{pmatrix}$.

Discussion point

➜ What result would you obtain for the unit vector if you worked out $\mathbf{b} \times \mathbf{a}$ instead of $\mathbf{a} \times \mathbf{b}$? Explain why there are two possible unit vectors.

Properties of the vector product

1 **The vector product is anti-commutative**
   The vector products $\mathbf{a} \times \mathbf{b}$ and $\mathbf{b} \times \mathbf{a}$ have the same magnitude but are in opposite directions, so $\mathbf{a} \times \mathbf{b} = -(\mathbf{b} \times \mathbf{a})$. This is known as the **anti-commutative property**.

2 **The vector product of parallel vectors is zero**
   This is because the angle θ between two parallel vectors is $0°$ or $180°$, so $\sin \theta = 0$. In particular, $\mathbf{i} \times \mathbf{i} = \mathbf{j} \times \mathbf{j} = \mathbf{k} \times \mathbf{k} = \mathbf{0}$.

Note

Investigate whether your calculator will find the vector product of two vectors.

If so, use your calculator to check the vector product calculated in Example 7.11.

3 **The vector product is compatible with scalar multiplication**
   For scalars m and n, $(m\mathbf{a}) \times (n\mathbf{b}) = mn\,(\mathbf{a} \times \mathbf{b})$
   This is because the vector $m\mathbf{a}$ has magnitude $|m|\,|\mathbf{a}|$; and $\mathbf{a}$ and $m\mathbf{a}$ have the same direction if m is positive, but opposite directions if m is negative.

4 **The vector product is distributive over vector addition**
   The result $\mathbf{a} \times (\mathbf{b} + \mathbf{c}) = \mathbf{a} \times \mathbf{b} + \mathbf{a} \times \mathbf{c}$ enables you to change a product into the sum of two simpler products. In doing so, the multiplication is 'distributive' over the two terms of the original sum.

Vector product – geometrical interpretation

For the moment you can take $\mathbf{a}$ to be a vector of length 1 (so that $\mathbf{a}$ is a **unit vector**) in the direction vertically downwards (in the negative z direction). You can write $\hat{\mathbf{a}}$ in place of $\mathbf{a}$ as a reminder that it is a unit vector. Let θ denote the angle between $\hat{\mathbf{a}}$ and $\mathbf{b}$.

The magnitude (length) of the vector $\hat{\mathbf{a}} \times \mathbf{b}$ is then $1 \times (\text{length of } \mathbf{b}) \times \sin\theta$, which is simply the length NB on Figure 7.16.

The direction of $\hat{\mathbf{a}} \times \mathbf{b}$ is perpendicular to both $\hat{\mathbf{a}}$ and $\mathbf{b}$, so it is horizontal and at right angles to $\mathbf{b}$.

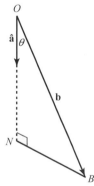

Figure 7.16

Imagine **b** to be represented, in both magnitude and direction, by a thin solid rod. Imagine that the plane $z = 0$ is horizontal on your writing table, and imagine that there is a light source a long way vertically above the table, in line with the z-axis. Then the shadow cast by **b** has length $|\mathbf{b}| \sin\theta = |\hat{\mathbf{a}} \times \mathbf{b}|$, and the direction of $\hat{\mathbf{a}} \times \mathbf{b}$ is at right angles to **b**, on the table. Thus, in Figure 7.17, $\hat{\mathbf{a}} \times \mathbf{b}$ is represented by the line NC, which is the same length as NB and is at right angles to it.

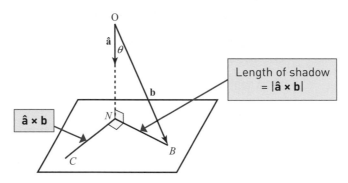

Figure 7.17

So you can picture $\hat{\mathbf{a}} \times \mathbf{b}$ to be the length of the **projection** of **b** onto the plane perpendicular to $\hat{\mathbf{a}}$, rotated through a right angle.

If **a** is not a unit vector, you will have to enlarge the projection by a scale factor of $|\mathbf{a}|$, but its direction remains the same.

Hence: **a** × **b** represents the projection of vector **b** onto a plane perpendicular to **a**, enlarged by scale factor $|\mathbf{a}|$ and rotated through 90°.

You can see that this interpretation leads to a very important result.

Proof that the cross product is distributive; that is, $\hat{\mathbf{a}} \times (\mathbf{b} + \mathbf{c}) = \hat{\mathbf{a}} \times \mathbf{b} + \hat{\mathbf{a}} \times \mathbf{c}$.

Imagine **b**, **c** and **b** + **c** forming a vector triangle (Figure 7.18). The shadows (projections) of **b**, **c** and **b** + **c** are drawn in purple.

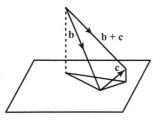

Figure 7.18

Then the projections of **b**, **c** and **b** + **c** onto the horizontal plane (that is, the shadows cast by the rods representing these vectors) also form a vector triangle. And if all three of these projections are rotated through a right angle, the lengths and relative directions of the sides of the triangle remain the same. The resulting vectors are $\hat{\mathbf{a}} \times \mathbf{b}$, $\hat{\mathbf{a}} \times \mathbf{c}$ and $\hat{\mathbf{a}} \times (\mathbf{b} + \mathbf{c})$.

So $\hat{\mathbf{a}} \times \mathbf{b} + \hat{\mathbf{a}} \times \mathbf{c} = \hat{\mathbf{a}} \times (\mathbf{b} + \mathbf{c})$.

And if **a** is not a unit vector? Then, just as before, all the projections are simply enlarged by a scale factor of $|\mathbf{a}|$, and the result is still true.

And if **a** is not vertically downwards? Simply rotate all the diagrams, including the plane of the paper onto which the shadows are cast and the light source, until the z-axis and the light source are in the direction of **a**, and exactly the same results hold true.

Hence, for any three vectors **a**, **b** and **c**, **a** × (**b** + **c**) = **a** × **b** + **a** × **c**.

Coordinate version of the cross product

Using the distributive property, you can now obtain a formula for the cross product of two vectors $\mathbf{a} = a_1\mathbf{i} + a_2\mathbf{j} + a_3\mathbf{k}$ and $\mathbf{b} = b_1\mathbf{i} + b_2\mathbf{j} + b_3\mathbf{k}$ in terms of the individual components.

First note the following: $\mathbf{i} \times \mathbf{i} = \mathbf{j} \times \mathbf{j} = \mathbf{k} \times \mathbf{k} = \mathbf{0}$;

$$\mathbf{i} \times \mathbf{j} = \mathbf{k}, \mathbf{j} \times \mathbf{k} = \mathbf{i} \text{ and } \mathbf{k} \times \mathbf{i} = \mathbf{j}$$

$$\mathbf{j} \times \mathbf{i} = -\mathbf{k}, \mathbf{k} \times \mathbf{j} = -\mathbf{i} \text{ and } \mathbf{i} \times \mathbf{k} = -\mathbf{j}.$$

Multiplying out $(a_1\mathbf{i} + a_2\mathbf{j} + a_3\mathbf{k}) \times (b_1\mathbf{i} + b_2\mathbf{j} + b_3\mathbf{k})$ using the distributive property gives

$$a_1b_1(\mathbf{i} \times \mathbf{i}) + a_1b_2(\mathbf{i} \times \mathbf{j}) + a_1b_3(\mathbf{i} \times \mathbf{k})$$

$$+ \quad a_2b_1(\mathbf{j} \times \mathbf{i}) + a_2b_2(\mathbf{j} \times \mathbf{j}) + a_2b_3(\mathbf{j} \times \mathbf{k})$$

$$+ \quad a_3b_1(\mathbf{k} \times \mathbf{i}) + a_3b_2(\mathbf{k} \times \mathbf{j}) + a_3b_3(\mathbf{k} \times \mathbf{k})$$

$$= (\mathbf{0} + a_1b_2\mathbf{k} - a_1b_3\mathbf{j}) + (-a_2b_1\mathbf{k} + \mathbf{0} + a_2b_3\mathbf{i}) + (a_3b_1\mathbf{j} - a_3b_2\mathbf{i} + \mathbf{0})$$

$$= (a_2b_3 - a_3b_2)\mathbf{i} + (a_3b_1 - a_1b_3)\mathbf{j} + (a_1b_2 - a_2b_1)\mathbf{k}.$$ ← This is the formula given on page 149.

Example 7.12

Evaluate $(3\mathbf{i} + 2\mathbf{j} - \mathbf{k}) \times (2\mathbf{i} - 5\mathbf{j} + 3\mathbf{k})$.

Solution

$(2 \times 3 - (-1) \times (-5))\mathbf{i} + ((-1) \times 2 - 3 \times 3)\mathbf{j} + (3 \times (-5) - 2 \times 2)\mathbf{k}$
$\quad = \mathbf{i} - 11\mathbf{j} - 19\mathbf{k}.$

You may find the formula easier to remember in determinant form:

$$\mathbf{a} \times \mathbf{b} = \begin{vmatrix} \mathbf{i} & a_1 & b_1 \\ \mathbf{j} & a_2 & b_2 \\ \mathbf{k} & a_3 & b_3 \end{vmatrix}.$$

ACTIVITY 7.5

In this activity you might find it helpful to take the edges of a rectangular table to represent the unit vectors $\mathbf{i}$, $\mathbf{j}$ and $\mathbf{k}$ as shown in Figure 7.20.

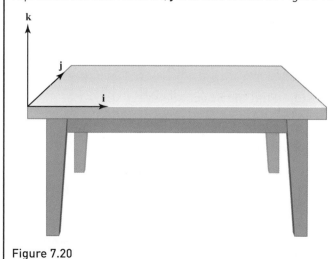

Figure 7.20

You could use pens to represent:

i, the unit vector pointing to the right along the x-axis

j, the unit vector pointing away from you along the y-axis

k, the unit vector pointing upwards along the z-axis.

The vector product of **a** and **b** is defined as

$$\mathbf{a} \times \mathbf{b} = |\mathbf{a}||\mathbf{b}| \sin\theta \hat{\mathbf{n}}$$

where θ is the angle between **a** and **b** and $\hat{\mathbf{n}}$ is a unit vector which is perpendicular to both **a** and **b** such that **a**, **b** and $\hat{\mathbf{n}}$ (in that order) form a right-handed set of vectors.

Using this definition, check the truth of each of the following results.

$$\mathbf{i} \times \mathbf{i} = \mathbf{0} \qquad\qquad \mathbf{i} \times \mathbf{j} = \mathbf{k} \qquad\qquad \mathbf{i} \times \mathbf{k} = -\mathbf{j}$$

Give a further six results for vector products of pairs of **i**, **j** and **k**.

Exercise 7.3

In this exercise you should calculate the vector products by hand. You could check your answers using the vector product facility on a calculator.

① Calculate each of the following vector products.

(i) $\begin{pmatrix} 3 \\ 5 \\ 2 \end{pmatrix} \times \begin{pmatrix} 2 \\ 4 \\ -3 \end{pmatrix}$ (ii) $\begin{pmatrix} 7 \\ -4 \\ -5 \end{pmatrix} \times \begin{pmatrix} -4 \\ 5 \\ -3 \end{pmatrix}$

(iii) $(5\mathbf{i} - 2\mathbf{j} + 4\mathbf{k}) \times (\mathbf{i} + 5\mathbf{j} - 6\mathbf{k})$

(iv) $(3\mathbf{i} - 7\mathbf{k}) \times (2\mathbf{i} + 3\mathbf{j} + 5\mathbf{k})$

② Find a vector perpendicular to each of the following pairs of vectors.

(i) $\mathbf{a} = \begin{pmatrix} 2 \\ 0 \\ 5 \end{pmatrix}, \mathbf{b} = \begin{pmatrix} 3 \\ -1 \\ -2 \end{pmatrix}$ (ii) $\mathbf{a} = \begin{pmatrix} 12 \\ 3 \\ -2 \end{pmatrix}, \mathbf{b} = \begin{pmatrix} 7 \\ 1 \\ 4 \end{pmatrix}$

(iii) $\mathbf{a} = 2\mathbf{i} + 3\mathbf{j} + 4\mathbf{k}, \quad \mathbf{b} = 3\mathbf{i} + 6\mathbf{j} + 7\mathbf{k}$

(iv) $\mathbf{a} = 3\mathbf{i} - 4\mathbf{j} + 6\mathbf{k}, \quad \mathbf{b} = 8\mathbf{i} + 5\mathbf{j} - 3\mathbf{k}$

③ Three points A, B and C have coordinates $(1, 4, -2)$, $(2, 0, 1)$ and $(5, 3, -2)$ respectively.

(i) Find the vectors $\overrightarrow{AB}$ and $\overrightarrow{AC}$.

(ii) Use the vector product to find a vector that is perpendicular to $\overrightarrow{AB}$ and $\overrightarrow{AC}$.

④ Find a unit vector perpendicular to both $\mathbf{a} = \begin{pmatrix} 1 \\ 2 \\ 7 \end{pmatrix}$ and $\mathbf{b} = \begin{pmatrix} 3 \\ -1 \\ 6 \end{pmatrix}$.

⑤ Find the magnitude of $\begin{pmatrix} 3 \\ 1 \\ -4 \end{pmatrix} \times \begin{pmatrix} 1 \\ -1 \\ 1 \end{pmatrix}$.

⑥ Simplify the following.

(i) $4\mathbf{i} \times 2\mathbf{k}$ (ii) $2\mathbf{i} \times (5\mathbf{i} - 2\mathbf{j} - 3\mathbf{k})$

(iii) $(6\mathbf{i} + \mathbf{j} - \mathbf{k}) \times 2\mathbf{k}$ (iv) $(3\mathbf{i} - \mathbf{j} + 2\mathbf{k}) \times (\mathbf{i} - \mathbf{j} - 4\mathbf{k})$

⑦ Prove algebraically that for two vectors $\mathbf{a} = a_1\mathbf{i} + a_2\mathbf{j} + a_3\mathbf{k}$ and $\mathbf{b} = b_1\mathbf{i} + b_2\mathbf{j} + b_3\mathbf{k}$

$$\mathbf{a} \times \mathbf{b} = \begin{pmatrix} a_2b_3 - a_3b_2 \\ a_3b_1 - a_1b_3 \\ a_1b_2 - a_2b_1 \end{pmatrix}$$

⑧ Two points A and B have position vectors $\mathbf{a} = 3\mathbf{i} + 5\mathbf{j} + 2\mathbf{k}$ and $\mathbf{b} = 2\mathbf{i} - \mathbf{j} + 4\mathbf{k}$ respectively.

(i) Find the lengths of each of the sides of the triangle OAB, and hence find the area of the triangle.

(ii) Find $|\mathbf{a} \times \mathbf{b}|$.

(iii) How does the definition $\mathbf{a} \times \mathbf{b} = |\mathbf{a}||\mathbf{b}| \sin\theta\, \hat{\mathbf{n}}$ explain the relationship between your answers to (i) and (ii)?

LEARNING OUTCOMES

When you have completed this chapter you should be able to:

➤ find the scalar product of two vectors

➤ use the scalar product to find the angle between two vectors

➤ know that two vectors are perpendicular if and only if their scalar product is zero

➤ form the equation of a line in 2D or in 3D in vector or cartesian form

➤ find the angle between two lines

➤ know the different ways in which two lines can intersect or not in 3D space

➤ find out whether two lines in three dimensions are parallel, skew or intersect, and find the point of intersection if there is one

➤ use the vector product in component form to find a vector perpendicular to two given vectors

➤ know that $\mathbf{a} \times \mathbf{b} = |\mathbf{a}||\mathbf{b}| \sin\theta\, \hat{\mathbf{n}}$, where $\mathbf{a}$, $\mathbf{b}$ and $\hat{\mathbf{n}}$, in that order, form a right-handed triple.

KEY POINTS

1 In two dimensions, the scalar product

$$\mathbf{a}.\mathbf{b} = \begin{pmatrix} a_1 \\ a_2 \end{pmatrix}.\begin{pmatrix} b_1 \\ b_2 \end{pmatrix} = a_1a_2 + b_1b_2 = |\mathbf{a}||\mathbf{b}|\cos\theta.$$

2 In three dimensions, $\mathbf{a}.\mathbf{b} = \begin{pmatrix} a_1 \\ a_2 \\ a_3 \end{pmatrix}.\begin{pmatrix} b_1 \\ b_2 \\ b_3 \end{pmatrix} = a_1b_1 + a_2b_2 + a_3b_3 = |\mathbf{a}||\mathbf{b}|\cos\theta.$

3 The angle θ between two vectors $\mathbf{a}$ and $\mathbf{b}$ is given by

$$\cos\theta = \frac{\mathbf{a}.\mathbf{b}}{|\mathbf{a}||\mathbf{b}|}$$

where $\mathbf{a}.\mathbf{b} = a_1b_1 + a_2b_2$ (in two dimensions)

$\mathbf{a}.\mathbf{b} = a_1b_1 + a_2b_2 + a_3b_3$ (in three dimensions).

4 The vector equation of a line is given by $\mathbf{r} = \mathbf{a} + \lambda\mathbf{d}$, where $\mathbf{a}$ is the position vector of a point A on the line and $\mathbf{d}$ is the direction vector of the line. Sometimes a different letter, such as μ or t, is used as the parameter instead of λ.

5 The line with direction vector $\mathbf{d} = \begin{pmatrix} d_1 \\ d_2 \\ d_3 \end{pmatrix}$ passing through the point A with

position vector $\mathbf{a} = \begin{pmatrix} a_1 \\ a_2 \\ a_3 \end{pmatrix}$ has the cartesian equation

$$\lambda = \frac{x - a_1}{d_1} = \frac{y - a_2}{d_2} = \frac{z - a_3}{d_3}$$

assuming d_1 d_2 and d_3 are not 0.

6 If two straight lines have equations $\mathbf{r}_1 = \mathbf{a}_1 + \lambda\mathbf{d}_1$ and $\mathbf{r}_2 = \mathbf{a}_2 + \mu\mathbf{d}_2$, the angle between the lines is found by calculating the scalar product $\mathbf{d}_1 . \mathbf{d}_2$.

7 In three dimensions there are three possibilities for the arrangement of the lines. They are either parallel, intersecting or skew.

8 The vector product $\mathbf{a} \times \mathbf{b}$ of $\mathbf{a}$ and $\mathbf{b}$ is a vector perpendicular to both $\mathbf{a}$ and $\mathbf{b}$.
$$\mathbf{a} \times \mathbf{b} = |\mathbf{a}||\mathbf{b}|\sin\theta\hat{\mathbf{n}}$$
where θ is the angle between $\mathbf{a}$ and $\mathbf{b}$ and $\hat{\mathbf{n}}$ is a unit vector which is perpendicular to both $\mathbf{a}$ and $\mathbf{b}$ such that $\mathbf{a}$, $\mathbf{b}$ and $\hat{\mathbf{n}}$ (in that order) form a right-handed set of vectors.

9
$$\mathbf{a} \times \mathbf{b} = \begin{pmatrix} a_1 \\ a_2 \\ a_3 \end{pmatrix} \times \begin{pmatrix} b_1 \\ b_2 \\ b_3 \end{pmatrix} = \begin{pmatrix} a_2b_3 - a_3b_2 \\ a_3b_1 - a_1b_3 \\ a_1b_2 - a_2b_1 \end{pmatrix} = \begin{vmatrix} \mathbf{i} & a_1 & b_1 \\ \mathbf{j} & a_2 & b_2 \\ \mathbf{k} & a_3 & b_3 \end{vmatrix}$$

FUTURE USES

You will learn more about lines in the Year 2 book.

① Prove that the lines with vector equations

$$\mathbf{r} = \begin{pmatrix} -5 \\ 4 \\ 1 \end{pmatrix} + s \begin{pmatrix} 3 \\ 0 \\ -2 \end{pmatrix} \text{ and } \mathbf{r} = \begin{pmatrix} 3 \\ 5 \\ 1 \end{pmatrix} + t \begin{pmatrix} 2 \\ 1 \\ 4 \end{pmatrix}$$

meet, and find the acute angle between them. [6 marks]

② (i) Describe the transformation represented by the matrix

$$\mathbf{A} = \begin{pmatrix} 1 & 0 \\ 0 & -1 \end{pmatrix}.$$ [1 mark]

(ii) Describe the transformation represented by the matrix

$$\mathbf{B} = \begin{pmatrix} -1 & 0 \\ 0 & 1 \end{pmatrix}.$$ [1 mark]

(iii) Determine **BA** and describe the transformation it represents. [2 marks]

(iv) Determine $(\mathbf{BA})^{-1}$. What do you notice? Explain your answer in terms of the transformation represented by **BA**. [3 marks]

MP ③ Let $z_1 = a + b\mathrm{i}$ and $z_2 = c + d\mathrm{i}$.

(i) Find $z_1 z_2$. [2 marks]

(ii) Write down expressions for $|z_1|$ and $|z_2|$. [1 mark]

(iii) Prove that $|z_1 z_2| = |z_1| |z_2|$. [4 marks]

PS ④

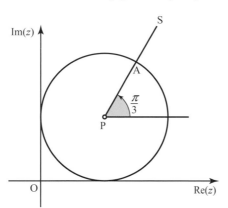

Figure 4.3

On the Argand diagram above, the point P is at $3 + 3\mathrm{i}$.

(i) The circle P is the locus of points satisfying an equation in z. Write down this equation. [2 marks]

(ii) Write down the equation of the locus of points represented by the half-line from P through A. [2 marks]

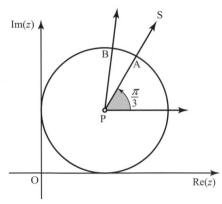

(iii) The sector PAB has area $\dfrac{3\pi}{8}$. Find the equation of the locus of points represented by the half line from P through B. [4 marks]

⑤ (i) Find the inverse of the matrix $\begin{pmatrix} 3 & 2 & -1 \\ 0 & k & 4 \\ 0 & -2 & 2 \end{pmatrix}$ in terms of k. [3 marks]

(ii) Use your answer to solve the simultaneous equations

$3x + 2y - z = 5$

$ky + 4z = -2$

$-2y + 2z = -1$ [3 marks]

PS ⑥ A and B are points with coordinates $(-4, 0, 0)$ and $(3, 2, 5)$ respectively.

(i) Write down a vector equation of the line through A and B. [2 marks]

(ii) The point A is reflected in the plane $x = 0$. Find the coordinates of the image A'. [4 marks]

(iii) Find the area of the triangle ABA'. [4 marks]

PS ⑦ The points P and Q have coordinates $(-2, 4, 5)$ and $(2, 1, 0)$ respectively, and O is the origin.

(i) Show that $\angle POQ = 90°$. [2 marks]

(ii) Find a vector perpendicular to both $\overrightarrow{OP}$ and $\overrightarrow{OQ}$. [2 marks]

(iii) The point R satisfies the following conditions:

$\angle ROP = \angle ROQ = 90°; OR = 6.$

Find the coordinates of each of the two possible positions of R. [3 marks]

⑧ **M** is the matrix $\begin{pmatrix} 4 & 1 \\ 2 & 3 \end{pmatrix}$.

(i) Show that **M** satisfies the equation $\mathbf{M}^2 - 7\mathbf{M} + 10\mathbf{I} = 0$. [4 marks]

(ii) Use this equation to find $\mathbf{M}^{-1}$ in terms of **M** and **I**. [2 marks]

(iii) Use this equation to find $\mathbf{M}^3$ in terms of **M** and **I**. [3 marks]

An introduction to radians

Radians are an alternative way to measure angles. They make it easier to relate the arc length of a sector to its angle. In Figure 1 the arc AB has been drawn so that it is equal to the length of the radius, r. The angle subtended at the centre of the circle is one radian.

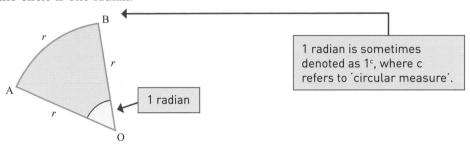

1 radian is sometimes denoted as 1^c, where c refers to 'circular measure'.

Figure 1

Since an angle of 1 radian at the centre of the circle corresponds to an arc length r it follows that an angle of 2 radians corresponds to an arc length of $2r$ and so on. In general, an angle of θ radians corresponds to an arc length of $r\theta$, as shown in Figure 2.

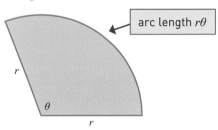

arc length $r\theta$

Figure 2

The circumference of a circle is $2\pi r$, so the angle at the centre of a full circle is 2π radians. This is 360°.

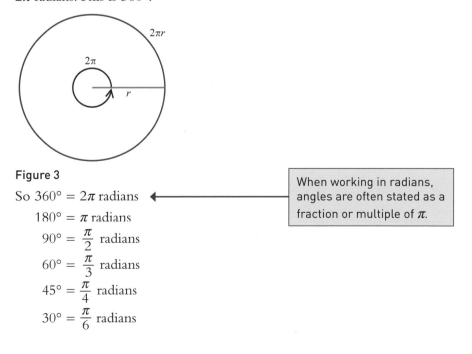

Figure 3

So 360° = 2π radians

180° = π radians

90° = $\dfrac{\pi}{2}$ radians

60° = $\dfrac{\pi}{3}$ radians

45° = $\dfrac{\pi}{4}$ radians

30° = $\dfrac{\pi}{6}$ radians

When working in radians, angles are often stated as a fraction or multiple of π.

$360° = 2\pi^c$ and so 1 radian is equivalent to $360 \div 2\pi = 57.3°$ to one decimal place.

The fact that one radian is just under 60° can be a helpful reference point.

When a multiple of π is used the 'c' symbol is usually omitted, as it is implied that the measure is radians.

To convert degrees into radians you multiply by $\frac{\pi}{180}$, and to convert radians into degrees you multiply by $\frac{180}{\pi}$.

Example

(i) Express in radians, giving your answers as a multiple of π:

(a) 120° (b) 225° (c) 390°

(ii) Express in radians, giving your answers to 3 significant figures:

(a) 34° (b) 450° (c) 1°

(iii) Express in degrees, giving your answers to 3 significant figures where appropriate:

(a) $\frac{5\pi}{12}$ (b) $\frac{\pi}{24}$ (c) 3.4^c

Solution

(i) (a) $60° = \frac{\pi}{3}$ radians so $120° = \frac{2\pi}{3}$ radians

(b) $45° = \frac{\pi}{4}$ radians so $225° = 5 \times 45° = \frac{5\pi}{4}$

(c) $30° = \frac{\pi}{6}$ radians so $390° = 360° + 30° = 2\pi + \frac{\pi}{6} = \frac{13\pi}{6}$

(ii) (a) $34 \times \frac{\pi}{180} = 0.593$ radians

(b) $450 \times \frac{\pi}{180} = 7.85$ radians

(c) $1 \times \frac{\pi}{180} = 0.0175$ radians

(iii) (a) $\frac{5\pi}{12} \times \frac{180}{\pi} = 75°$

(b) $\frac{\pi}{24} \times \frac{180}{\pi} = 7.5°$

(c) $3.4 \times \frac{180}{\pi} = 195°$

! When working in radians with trigonometric functions on your calculator, ensure it is set in 'RAD' or 'R' mode.

① Express the following angles in radians, leaving your answers in terms of π or to 3 significant figures as appropriate.

(i) $60°$ (ii) $45°$ (iii) $150°$ (iv) $200°$

(v) $44.4°$ (vi) $405°$ (vii) $270°$ (viii) $99°$

(ix) $300°$ (x) $720°$ (xi) $15°$ (xii) $3°$

② Express the following angles in degrees, rounding to 3 significant figures where appropriate.

(i) $\dfrac{\pi}{9}$ (ii) $\dfrac{2\pi}{15}$ (iii) 4^c (iv) $\dfrac{5\pi}{3}$

(v) $\dfrac{\pi}{7}$ (vi) $\dfrac{\pi}{20}$ (vii) 1.8^c (viii) $\dfrac{11\pi}{9}$

(ix) $\dfrac{7\pi}{2}$ (x) 5π (xi) $\dfrac{9\pi}{4}$ (xii) $\dfrac{17\pi}{12}$

The identities $\sin(\theta \pm \phi)$ and $\cos(\theta \pm \phi)$

In Chapters 1 and 5 of this book you use the trigonometric identities known as the **addition formulae** or **compound angle formulae**. The proofs of these identities are given in the A level Mathematics textbook.

These identities are:

$$\sin(\theta + \phi) \equiv \sin\theta\cos\phi + \cos\theta\sin\phi$$

$$\sin(\theta - \phi) \equiv \sin\theta\cos\phi - \cos\theta\sin\phi$$

$$\cos(\theta + \phi) \equiv \cos\theta\cos\phi - \sin\theta\sin\phi$$

$$\cos(\theta - \phi) \equiv \cos\theta\cos\phi + \sin\theta\sin\phi$$

Note the change of sign in the formulae for the cosine of the sum or difference of two angles:

$$\cos(\theta + \phi) \equiv \cos\theta\cos\phi - \sin\theta\sin\phi$$

$$\cos(\theta - \phi) \equiv \cos\theta\cos\phi + \sin\theta\sin\phi$$

Although these results are often referred to as 'formulae', they are in fact identities (as indicated by the identity symbol $\equiv$) and they are true for all values of θ and ϕ. However, it is common for the identity symbol to be replaced by an equals sign when the formulae are being used.

These identities will be used:

- in Chapter 1 to look at combinations of two rotations
- in Chapter 5 to look at multiplying two complex numbers in modulus-argument form.

Example

Use the compound angle formulae to find exact values for:

(i) $\sin 15°$

(ii) $\cos 75°$

Solution

(i) $\sin 15° = \sin(45° - 30°) = \sin 45°\cos 30° - \cos 45°\sin 30°$

$$= \frac{1}{\sqrt{2}} \times \frac{\sqrt{3}}{2} - \frac{1}{\sqrt{2}} \times \frac{1}{2}$$

$$= \frac{\sqrt{3}}{2\sqrt{2}} - \frac{1}{2\sqrt{2}}$$

$$= \frac{\sqrt{3}-1}{2\sqrt{2}} \text{ or } \frac{\sqrt{6}-\sqrt{2}}{4}$$

(ii) $\cos 75° = \cos(45° + 30°) = \cos 45°\cos 30° - \sin 45°\sin 30°$

$$= \frac{1}{\sqrt{2}} \times \frac{\sqrt{3}}{2} - \frac{1}{\sqrt{2}} \times \frac{1}{2}$$

This is the same as part (i) and so $\cos 75° = \dfrac{\sqrt{6}-\sqrt{2}}{4}$.

The exercise below is designed to familiarise you with these identities.

Exercise

① Use the compound angle formulae to write the following in surd form:

  (i) $\cos 15° = \cos(45° - 30°)$

  (ii) $\sin 105° = \sin(60° + 45°)$

  (iii) $\cos 105° = \cos(60° + 45°)$

  (iv) $\sin 165° = \sin(120° + 45°)$

② Simplify each of the following expressions, giving answers in surd form where possible:

  (i) $\sin 60° \cos 30° - \cos 60° \sin 30°$

  (ii) $\sin 40° \cos 50° + \cos 40° \sin 50°$

  (iii) $\cos 3\theta \cos \theta - \sin 3\theta \sin \theta$

  (iv) $\cos\left(\dfrac{\pi}{3}\right)\cos\left(\dfrac{\pi}{6}\right) + \sin\left(\dfrac{\pi}{3}\right)\sin\left(\dfrac{\pi}{6}\right)$

  (v) $2\sin\left(\dfrac{\pi}{4}\right)\cos\left(\dfrac{\pi}{6}\right) - 2\cos\left(\dfrac{\pi}{4}\right)\sin\left(\dfrac{\pi}{6}\right)$

  (vi) $\cos 47° \cos 13° - \sin 13° \sin 47°$

③ Expand and simplify the following expressions:

  (i) $\sin(\theta + 45°)$

  (ii) $\cos(2\theta - 30°)$

  (iii) $\sin\left(\theta - \dfrac{\pi}{6}\right)$

  (iv) $\cos\left(3\theta + \dfrac{\pi}{3}\right)$

Answers

Chapter 1

Discussion point (Page 1)

$\mathbb{R}$ Real numbers – any number which is not complex

$\mathbb{Q}$ Rational numbers – numbers which can be expressed exactly as a fraction

$\mathbb{Z}$ Integers – positive or negative whole numbers, including zero

$\mathbb{N}$ Natural numbers – non-negative whole numbers (although there is some debate amongst mathematicians as to whether zero should be included!)

Discussion point (Page 2)

Any real number is either rational or irrational. This means that all real numbers will either lie inside the set of rational numbers, or inside the set of real numbers but outside the set of rational numbers. Therefore no separate set is needed for irrational numbers.

The symbol $\overline{\mathbb{Q}}$ is used for irrational numbers – numbers which cannot be expressed exactly as a fraction, such as π.

Activity 1.1 (Page 2)

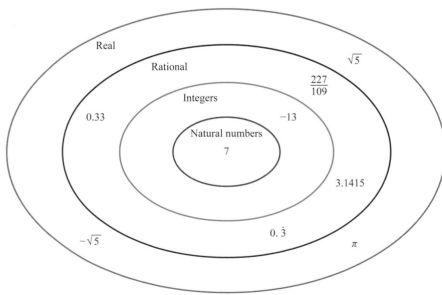

Activity 1.2 (Page 2)

(i) $x = 2$ Natural number (or integer)

(ii) $x = \dfrac{9}{7}$ Rational number

(iii) $x = \pm 3$ Integers

(iv) $x = -1$ Integer

(v) $x = 0, -7$ Integers

(vi) $\pm\sqrt{5}$ Irrational numbers

Discussion point (Page 3)

You know $i^2 = -1$

$i^3 = i^2 \times i = -1 \times i = -i$

$i^4 = i^2 \times i^2 = -1 \times -1 = 1$

$i^5 = i^4 \times i = 1 \times i = i$

$i^6 = i^5 \times i = i \times i = -1$

$i^7 = i^6 \times i = -1 \times i = -i$

The powers of i form a cycle:

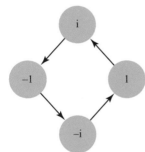

All numbers of the form i^{4n} are equal to 1.

All numbers of the form i^{4n+1} are equal to i.

All numbers of the form i^{4n+2} are equal to -1.

All numbers of the form i^{4n+3} are equal to $-i$.

Discussion point (Page 4)

$$\left(5 + \sqrt{-15}\right)\left(5 - \sqrt{-15}\right)$$
$$= 25 - 5\sqrt{-15} + 5\sqrt{-15} - (-15)$$
$$= 25 + 15$$
$$= 40$$

Discussion point (Page 4)

If the numerators and denominators of two fractions are equal then the fractions must also be equal.

However, it is possible for two fractions to be equal if the numerators and denominators are not equal, for example $\frac{3}{4} = \frac{6}{8}$.

Exercise 1.1 (Page 6)

1 (i) i   (ii) -1
   (iii) $-i$ (iv) 1
2 (i) $9 - i$ (ii) $-9 + 9i$
   (iii) $3 + 9i$ (iv) $-3 - i$
3 (i) $24 + 2i$ (ii) $-2 + 24i$
   (iii) $20 + 48i$ (iv) $38 - 18i$
4 (i) (a) 52   (b) 34   (c) 1768
   (ii) Multiplying a complex number by its
        conjugate gives a wholly real answer.
5 (i) $92 - 60i$ (ii) $-414 + 154i$
6 (i) $-1 \pm i$ (ii) $1 \pm 2i$ (iii) $2 \pm 3i$
   (iv) $-3 \pm 5i$ (v) $\frac{1}{2} \pm 2i$ (vi) $-2 \pm \sqrt{2}i$
7 $a = 1$ or $4, b = -1$ or 3
   The possible complex numbers are
   $1 + 9i$, $1 + i$, $16 + 9i$, $16 + i$
8 $a = 3$, $b = 5$ or $a = -3$, $b = -5$
9 (i) $\pm(2 + i)$ (ii) $\pm(7 - 3i)$

10 (i)

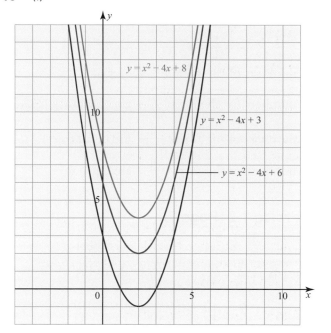

(ii) (a) $x = 1$, $x = 3$
      (b) $x = 2 \pm \sqrt{2}i$
      (c) $2 \pm 2i$
(iii) The roots all occur in pairs that are of the
       form $x = 2 \pm k$ for some value k where
       $k \in C$

11 $a = -7$, $b = 11$
    You cannot assume the second root is the
    conjugate of $2 + 3i$ as the coefficients of the
    equation are not real.
    The second root is $5 - 2i$.

Activity 1.3 (Page 7)

$z + z^{\star} = (x + yi) + (x - yi) = 2x$ which is real

$zz^{\star} = (x + yi)(x - yi) = x^2 - xyi + yxi - y^2i^2 = x^2 + y^2$
which is real

Discussion point (Page 8)

$\dfrac{1}{i} = \dfrac{1}{i} \times \dfrac{i}{i} = \dfrac{i}{-1} = -i$

$\dfrac{1}{i^2} = \dfrac{1}{i^2} \times \dfrac{i^2}{i^2} = \dfrac{-1}{1} = -1$

$$\frac{1}{i^3} = \frac{1}{i^3} \times \frac{i^3}{i^3} = \frac{-i}{-1} = i$$

$$\frac{1}{i^4} = \frac{1}{i^4} \times \frac{i^4}{i^4} = \frac{1}{1} = 1$$

All numbers of the form $\frac{1}{i^{4n}}$ are equal to 1.

All numbers for the form $\frac{1}{i^{4n+1}}$ are equal to $-i$.

All numbers of the form $\frac{1}{i^{4n+2}}$ are equal to -1.

All numbers of the form $\frac{1}{i^{4n+3}}$ are equal to i.

Exercise 1.2 (Page 9)

1 (i) $\frac{21}{50} + \frac{3}{50}i$ (ii) $\frac{21}{50} - \frac{3}{50}i$

   (iii) $-\frac{3}{50} + \frac{21}{50}i$ (iv) $\frac{3}{50} + \frac{21}{50}i$

2 (i) $-\frac{9}{13} + \frac{19}{13}i$ (ii) $-\frac{9}{34} - \frac{19}{34}i$

   (iii) $-\frac{9}{13} - \frac{19}{13}i$ (iv) $-\frac{9}{34} + \frac{19}{34}i$

3 (i) $\frac{94}{25} + \frac{158}{25}i$ (ii) $\frac{204}{625} + \frac{253}{625}i$

4 (i) 6   (ii) 85

   (iii) 12   (iv) 45

   (v) -4 (vi) 45

5 (i) 2   (ii) 3

   (iii) $2 - 3i$ (iv) $6 + 4i$

   (v) $8 + i$ (vi) $-4 - 7i$

6 (i) 0   (ii) 0

   (iii) -39 (iv) $-46 - 9i$

   (v) $-46 - 9i$ (vi) $52i$

7 (i) $\frac{348}{61} + \frac{290}{61}i$ (ii) $\frac{322}{29} - \frac{65}{29}i$

   (iii) $-\frac{600}{3721} + \frac{110}{3721}i$

8 (i) $2 - i$ (ii) 1

   (iii) $3 + i$ (iv) $-\frac{35}{34} + \frac{149}{34}i$

9 $a = -\frac{23}{13}$ $b = -\frac{15}{13}$

10 $a = 9,\ b = 11$

11 (i) $\frac{10}{89}$ (ii) $\frac{10}{89}$

12 $\frac{2x}{x^2 + y^2}$

14 $a = 2,\ b = 2$

15 $z = 0,\quad z = 2,\quad z = -1 \pm \sqrt{3}i$

16 $z = 8 - 6i,\ w = 6 - 5i$

Discussion point (Page 10)

A complex number has a real component and an imaginary component. It is not possible to illustrate two components using a single number line.

Activity 1.4 (Page 10)

(i)

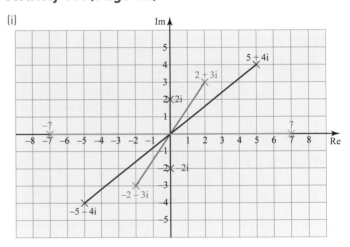

The points representing z and $-z$ have half turn rotational symmetry about the origin.

(ii)

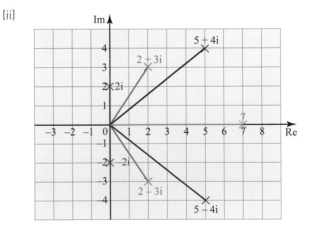

The points representing z and z^* are reflections of each other in the real axis.

Exercise 1.3 (Page 12)

1

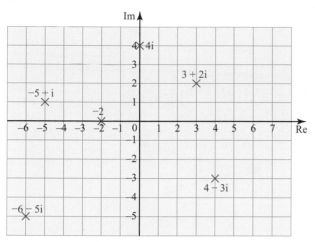

2

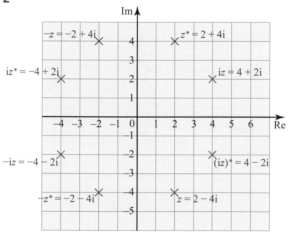

The point representing z^* is the reflection in the real axis of the point representing z.

3

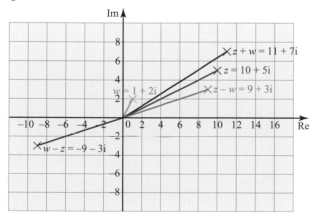

4 (i) $x^2 - 4x + 3$

(ii) $x^2 - 4x + 5$

(iii) $x^2 - 4x + 13$

(iv) All of the form $x^2 - 4x + k$ where $k \in \mathbb{R}$

5

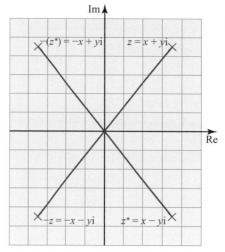

6 (i)

n	-1	0	1	2	3	4	5
z^n	$\frac{1}{2} - \frac{1}{2}i$	1	$1+i$	$2i$	$-2+2i$	-4	$-4-4i$

(ii)

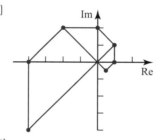

(iii)

n	-1	0	1	2	3	4	5
z^n	$\frac{1}{2} - \frac{1}{2}i$	1	$1+i$	$2i$	$-2+2i$	-4	$-4-4i$
Distance from origin	$\frac{1}{\sqrt{2}}$	1	$\sqrt{2}$	2	$2\sqrt{2}$	4	$4\sqrt{2}$

(iv) The half squares formed are enlarged by a factor of $\sqrt{2}$ and rotated through $45°$ each time.

7 (i) $r = \sqrt{a^2 + b^2}$

$zz^* = (a + bi)(a - bi) = a^2 + b^2 = r^2$

(ii) $s = \sqrt{c^2 + d^2}$

(iii) $zw = (a + bi)(c + di) = (ac - bd) + (bc + ad)i$

Distance from origin of zw is

$$\sqrt{(ac - bd)^2 + (bc + ad)^2} = \sqrt{a^2c^2 + b^2d^2 + b^2c^2 + a^2d^2}$$
$$= \sqrt{(a^2 + b^2)(c^2 + d^2)}$$
$$= \sqrt{a^2 + b^2}\sqrt{c^2 + d^2} = rs$$

Chapter 2

Discussion point (Page 15)

$3, 2, 1, 0$

Discussion point (Page 18)

When subtracting numbers, the order in which the numbers appear is important – changing the order changes the answer, for example: $3 - 6 \neq 6 - 3$. So subtraction of numbers is not commutative.

The grouping of the numbers is also important, for example $(13 - 5) - 2 \neq 13 - (5 - 2)$. Therefore subtraction of numbers is not associative.

Matrices follow the same rules for commutativity and associativity as numbers. Matrix addition is both commutative and associative, but matrix subtraction is not commutative or associative. This is true because addition and subtraction of each of the individual elements will determine whether the matrices are commutative or associative overall.

You can use more formal methods to prove these properties. For example, to show that matrix addition is commutative:

$$\begin{pmatrix} a & b \\ c & d \end{pmatrix} + \begin{pmatrix} e & f \\ g & h \end{pmatrix} = \begin{pmatrix} a+e & b+f \\ c+g & d+h \end{pmatrix} = \begin{pmatrix} e+a & f+b \\ g+c & h+d \end{pmatrix} = \begin{pmatrix} e & f \\ g & h \end{pmatrix} + \begin{pmatrix} a & b \\ c & d \end{pmatrix}$$

Addition of numbers is commutative

Exercise 2.1 (Page 18)

1 (i) 3×2 (ii) 3×3 (iii) 1×2
(iv) 5×1 (v) 2×4 (vi) 3×2

2 (i) $\begin{pmatrix} 5 & -8 \\ 2 & -3 \end{pmatrix}$ (ii) $\begin{pmatrix} 3 & 1 & -4 \\ 4 & 2 & 12 \end{pmatrix}$

(iii) $\begin{pmatrix} -8 & 2+3i \\ -2-i & 7 \end{pmatrix}$

(iv) Non-conformable (v) $\begin{pmatrix} -3 & -9 & 14 \\ 0 & 0 & 4 \end{pmatrix}$

(vi) $\begin{pmatrix} 4 \\ 12 \\ 20 \end{pmatrix}$ (vii) $\begin{pmatrix} 9 & 7 & -17 \\ 10 & 5 & 28 \end{pmatrix}$

(viii) Non-conformable

(ix) $\begin{pmatrix} -15 & 2+6i \\ -2-2i & 3 \end{pmatrix}$ (x) $\begin{pmatrix} 2 & 0 \\ -3 & 4 \end{pmatrix}$

(xi) $\begin{pmatrix} 3 & 2 \\ 5 & 1 \\ -9 & 4 \end{pmatrix}$ (xii) $\begin{pmatrix} 1 & 3 & 5 \end{pmatrix}$

3 (i) $\begin{pmatrix} 0 & 2 & 1 & 0 \\ 1 & 0 & 2 & 1 \\ 0 & 2 & 0 & 2 \\ 1 & 0 & 1 & 0 \end{pmatrix}$ (ii) $\begin{pmatrix} 0 & 0 & 2 & 2 \\ 1 & 0 & 0 & 0 \\ 2 & 0 & 0 & 1 \\ 0 & 0 & 2 & 0 \end{pmatrix}$

(iii)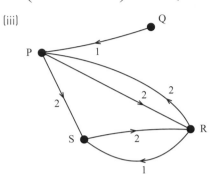

4 $w = 2, x = -6, y = -2, z = 2$

5 $p = 1$ or 6, $q = \pm\sqrt{5}$

6 (i) $\begin{pmatrix} 1 & 0 & 1 & 4 & 4 \\ 0 & 0 & 1 & 0 & 2 \\ 1 & 1 & 0 & 7 & 5 \\ 0 & 1 & 0 & 3 & 3 \end{pmatrix}$

$\begin{pmatrix} 3 & 1 & 1 & 10 & 7 \\ 0 & 0 & 4 & 2 & 10 \\ 3 & 1 & 1 & 11 & 8 \\ 1 & 2 & 1 & 8 & 6 \end{pmatrix}$

(ii) $\begin{pmatrix} 1 & 0 & 0 & 2 & 1 \\ 1 & 1 & 0 & 3 & 2 \\ 0 & 0 & 1 & 1 & 2 \\ 0 & 1 & 1 & 2 & 3 \end{pmatrix}$

City 2 vs United 1
Rangers 2 vs Town 1
Rangers 1 vs /United 1

7 (i) $\begin{pmatrix} 15 & 3 & 7 & 15 \\ 5 & 9 & 15 & -3 \\ 19 & 10 & 9 & 3 \end{pmatrix}$

The matrix represents the number of jackets left in stock after all the orders have been dispatched. The negative element indicates there was not enough of that type of jacket in stock to fulfil the order.

$$\text{(ii)} \quad \begin{pmatrix} 20 & 13 & 17 & 20 \\ 15 & 19 & 20 & 12 \\ 19 & 10 & 14 & 8 \end{pmatrix}$$

$$\text{(iii)} \quad \begin{pmatrix} 12 & 30 & 18 & 0 \\ 6 & 18 & 24 & 36 \\ 30 & 0 & 12 & 18 \end{pmatrix}$$

Discussion point (Page 22)

The dimensions of the matrices are **A** (3 × 3), **B** (3 × 2) and **C** (2 × 2). The conformable products are **AB** and **BC**. Both of these products would have dimension (3 × 2), even though the original matrices are not the same sizes.

Activity 2.1 (Page 23)

$$\mathbf{AB} = \begin{pmatrix} 2 & -1 \\ 3 & 4 \end{pmatrix}\begin{pmatrix} -4 & 0 \\ -2 & 1 \end{pmatrix} = \begin{pmatrix} -6 & -1 \\ -20 & 4 \end{pmatrix}$$

$$\mathbf{BA} = \begin{pmatrix} -4 & 0 \\ -2 & 1 \end{pmatrix}\begin{pmatrix} 2 & -1 \\ 3 & 4 \end{pmatrix} = \begin{pmatrix} -8 & 4 \\ -1 & 6 \end{pmatrix}$$

These two matrices are not equal and so matrix multiplication is not commutative. There are, however, some pairs of matrices for which CD=DC, for example if

$$\mathbf{C} = \begin{pmatrix} 2 & 0 \\ 0 & 2 \end{pmatrix} \text{ and } \mathbf{D} = \begin{pmatrix} 3 & 3 \\ -1 & -1 \end{pmatrix} \text{ then}$$

$$\mathbf{CD} = \mathbf{DC} = \begin{pmatrix} 6 & 6 \\ -2 & -2 \end{pmatrix}.$$

Activity 2.2 (Page 24)

(i) $\quad \mathbf{AB} = \begin{pmatrix} -6 & -1 \\ -20 & 4 \end{pmatrix}$

(ii) $\quad \mathbf{BC} = \begin{pmatrix} -4 & -8 \\ 0 & -1 \end{pmatrix}$

(iii) $\quad \mathbf{(AB)C} = \begin{pmatrix} -8 & -15 \\ -12 & -28 \end{pmatrix}$

(iv) $\quad \mathbf{A(BC)} = \begin{pmatrix} -8 & -15 \\ -12 & -28 \end{pmatrix}$

$(\mathbf{AB})\mathbf{C} = \mathbf{A}(\mathbf{BC})$ so matrix multiplication is associative in this case

To produce a general proof, use general matrices such as

$$\mathbf{A} = \begin{pmatrix} a & b \\ c & d \end{pmatrix}, \mathbf{B} = \begin{pmatrix} e & f \\ g & h \end{pmatrix} \text{ and}$$

$$\mathbf{C} = \begin{pmatrix} i & j \\ k & l \end{pmatrix}.$$

$$\mathbf{AB} = \begin{pmatrix} a & b \\ c & d \end{pmatrix}\begin{pmatrix} e & f \\ g & h \end{pmatrix} = \begin{pmatrix} ae + bg & af + bh \\ ce + dg & cf + dh \end{pmatrix},$$

$$\mathbf{BC} = \begin{pmatrix} e & f \\ g & h \end{pmatrix}\begin{pmatrix} i & j \\ k & l \end{pmatrix} = \begin{pmatrix} ei + fk & ej + fl \\ gi + hk & gj + hl \end{pmatrix}$$

and so

$$(\mathbf{AB})\mathbf{C} = \begin{pmatrix} ae + bg & af + bh \\ ce + dg & cf + dh \end{pmatrix}\begin{pmatrix} i & j \\ k & l \end{pmatrix}$$

$$\begin{pmatrix} aei + bgi + afk + bhk & aej + bgj + afl + bhl \\ cei + cfk + dgi + dhk & cej + cfl + dgj + dhl \end{pmatrix}$$

and

$$\mathbf{A}(\mathbf{BC}) = \begin{pmatrix} a & b \\ c & d \end{pmatrix}\begin{pmatrix} ei + fk & ej + fl \\ gi + hk & gj + hl \end{pmatrix}$$

$$= \begin{pmatrix} aei + afk + bgi + bhk & aej + afl + bgj + bhl \\ cei + dgi + cfk + dhk & cej + dgj + cfl + dhl \end{pmatrix}$$

Since $(\mathbf{AB})\mathbf{C} = \mathbf{A}(\mathbf{BC})$ matrix multiplication is associative and the product can be written without brackets as **ABC**.

Exercise 2.2 (Page 24)

1 (i) (a) 3 × 3 (b) 1 × 3 (c) 2 × 3 (d) 2 × 4
       (e) 2 × 1   (f) 3 × 5
   (ii) (a) non–conformable
       (b) 3 × 5
       (c) non–conformable
       (d) 2 × 3
       (e) non–conformable

2 (i) $\begin{pmatrix} 21 & 6 \\ 31 & 13 \end{pmatrix}$ (ii) $\begin{pmatrix} -30 & -15 \end{pmatrix}$

(iii) $\begin{pmatrix} -54 \\ -1 \end{pmatrix}$

3 $\mathbf{AB} = \begin{pmatrix} 3 & -56 \\ 20 & -73 \end{pmatrix}$, $\mathbf{BA} = \begin{pmatrix} -25 & 8 \\ 28 & -45 \end{pmatrix}$

$\mathbf{AB} \neq \mathbf{BA}$ so matrix multiplication is non-commutative.

4 (i) $\begin{pmatrix} -7 & 26 \\ 2 & 34 \end{pmatrix}$ (ii) $\begin{pmatrix} 5 & 25 \\ 16 & 22 \end{pmatrix}$

(iii) $\begin{pmatrix} 31 & 0 \\ 65 & 18 \end{pmatrix}$ (iv) $\begin{pmatrix} 26 & 37 & 16 \\ 14 & 21 & 28 \\ -8 & -11 & 2 \end{pmatrix}$

(v) non-conformable (vi) $\begin{pmatrix} 28 & -18 \\ 26 & 2 \\ 16 & 25 \end{pmatrix}$

5 (i) $\begin{pmatrix} 0 & 1 \\ -1 & 0 \end{pmatrix}$

(ii) $\begin{pmatrix} 0 & 1 \\ -1 & 0 \end{pmatrix}$

(iii) $\begin{pmatrix} -1-i & 1 \\ -2 & -1+i \end{pmatrix}$

(iv) $\begin{pmatrix} -1+i & 2 \\ -1 & 1(-1-i) \end{pmatrix}$

6 $\begin{pmatrix} -38 & -136 & -135 \\ 133 & 133 & 100 \\ 273 & 404 & 369 \end{pmatrix}$

7 (i) $\begin{pmatrix} 2x^2 + 12 & -9 \\ -4 & 3 \end{pmatrix}$ (ii) $x = 2$ or 3

(iii) $\mathbf{BA} = \begin{pmatrix} 8 & 12 \\ 8 & 15 \end{pmatrix}$ or $\begin{pmatrix} 18 & 18 \\ 12 & 15 \end{pmatrix}$

8 (i) (a) $\begin{pmatrix} 4 & 3 \\ 0 & 1 \end{pmatrix}$ (b) $\begin{pmatrix} 8 & 7 \\ 0 & 1 \end{pmatrix}$

(c) $\begin{pmatrix} 16 & 15 \\ 0 & 1 \end{pmatrix}$ (ii) $\begin{pmatrix} 2^n & 2^n - 1 \\ 0 & 1 \end{pmatrix}$

9 (i) $\begin{pmatrix} 1 & 1 & 2 & 0 \\ 1 & 0 & 1 & 0 \\ 1 & 1 & 0 & 2 \\ 0 & 0 & 1 & 0 \end{pmatrix}$

(ii) $\begin{pmatrix} 4 & 3 & 3 & 4 \\ 2 & 2 & 2 & 2 \\ 2 & 1 & 5 & 0 \\ 1 & 1 & 0 & 2 \end{pmatrix}$ $\mathbf{M}^2$ represents the number of two-stage routes between each pair of resorts.

(iii) $\mathbf{M}^3$ would represent the number of three-stage routes between each pair of resorts.

10 (i) $\begin{pmatrix} 8+4x & -20+x^2 \\ -8+x & -3-3x \end{pmatrix}$

(ii) $x = -3$ or 4

(iii) $\begin{pmatrix} -4 & -11 \\ -11 & 6 \end{pmatrix}$ or $\begin{pmatrix} 24 & -4 \\ -4 & -15 \end{pmatrix}$

11 (i) $\mathbf{D} = \begin{pmatrix} 1 & 1 & 1 & 1 \end{pmatrix}$

$\mathbf{DA} = \begin{pmatrix} 299 & 199 & 270 & 175 & 114 \end{pmatrix}$

(ii) $\mathbf{F} = \begin{pmatrix} 1 \\ 1 \\ 1 \\ 1 \\ 1 \end{pmatrix}$, $\mathbf{AF} = \begin{pmatrix} 229 \\ 231 \\ 263 \\ 334 \end{pmatrix}$

(iii) $\mathbf{S} = \begin{pmatrix} 1 \\ 0 \\ 0 \\ 0 \\ 1 \end{pmatrix}$, $\mathbf{DAS} = (413)$,

$\mathbf{C} = \begin{pmatrix} 0 \\ 1 \\ 1 \\ 1 \\ 0 \end{pmatrix}$, $\mathbf{DAC} = (644)$

(iv) $\mathbf{P} = \begin{pmatrix} 0.95 \\ 0.95 \\ 1.05 \\ 1.15 \\ 1.15 \end{pmatrix}$,

$\mathbf{DAP} = (1088.95) = £1088.95$

12 (i) $\begin{pmatrix} b \\ a \\ c \end{pmatrix}$ (ii) $\begin{pmatrix} 1 & 0 & 0 \\ 0 & 0 & 1 \\ 0 & 1 & 0 \end{pmatrix}$

(iii) $\begin{pmatrix} 0 & 1 & 0 \\ 0 & 0 & 1 \\ 1 & 0 & 0 \end{pmatrix}$, $\begin{pmatrix} b \\ c \\ a \end{pmatrix}$

(iv) $\begin{pmatrix} 0 & 0 & 1 \\ 1 & 0 & 0 \\ 0 & 1 & 0 \end{pmatrix}$, $\begin{pmatrix} c \\ a \\ b \end{pmatrix}$

(v) $\begin{pmatrix} 1 & 0 & 0 \\ 0 & 1 & 0 \\ 0 & 0 & 1 \end{pmatrix}$ The strands are back in the

original order at the end of Stage 6.

Discussion point (Page 31)

The image of the unit vector $\begin{pmatrix} 1 \\ 0 \end{pmatrix}$ is $\begin{pmatrix} a \\ c \end{pmatrix}$ and

the image of the unit vector $\begin{pmatrix} 0 \\ 1 \end{pmatrix}$ is $\begin{pmatrix} b \\ d \end{pmatrix}$.

Activity 2.3 (Page 31)

The diagram below shows the unit square with two of its sides along the unit vectors **i** and **j**. It is rotated by 45° about the origin.

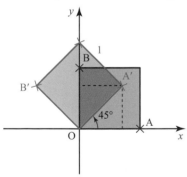

You can use trigonometry to find the images of the unit vectors **i** and **j**.

For A′, the x-coordinate satisfies $\cos 45 = \frac{x}{1}$ so

$x = \cos 45 = \frac{1}{\sqrt{2}}$.

In a similar way, the y-coordinate of A′ is $\frac{1}{\sqrt{2}}$.

For B′, the symmetry of the diagram shows that the

x-coordinate is $-\frac{1}{\sqrt{2}}$ and the y-coordinate is $\frac{1}{\sqrt{2}}$.

Hence, the image of $\begin{pmatrix} 1 \\ 0 \end{pmatrix}$ is $\begin{pmatrix} \frac{1}{\sqrt{2}} \\ \frac{1}{\sqrt{2}} \end{pmatrix}$ and the

image of $\begin{pmatrix} 0 \\ 1 \end{pmatrix}$ is

$\begin{pmatrix} -\frac{1}{\sqrt{2}} \\ \frac{1}{\sqrt{2}} \end{pmatrix}$ and so the matrix representing an

anticlockwise rotation of

45° about the origin is $\begin{pmatrix} \frac{1}{\sqrt{2}} & -\frac{1}{\sqrt{2}} \\ \frac{1}{\sqrt{2}} & \frac{1}{\sqrt{2}} \end{pmatrix}$.

Rotations of 45° clockwise about the origin and 135° anticlockwise about the origin are also represented by matrices involving $\pm\frac{1}{\sqrt{2}}$.

This is due to the symmetry about the origin.

(i) The diagram for a 45° clockwise rotation about the origin is shown below.

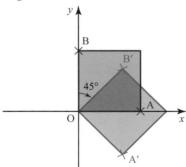

The image of $\begin{pmatrix} 1 \\ 0 \end{pmatrix}$ is $\begin{pmatrix} \frac{1}{\sqrt{2}} \\ -\frac{1}{\sqrt{2}} \end{pmatrix}$ and the image

of $\begin{pmatrix} 0 \\ 1 \end{pmatrix}$ is $\begin{pmatrix} \frac{1}{\sqrt{2}} \\ \frac{1}{\sqrt{2}} \end{pmatrix}$ and so the matrix

representing a clockwise rotation of

45° about the origin is $\begin{pmatrix} \frac{1}{\sqrt{2}} & \frac{1}{\sqrt{2}} \\ -\frac{1}{\sqrt{2}} & \frac{1}{\sqrt{2}} \end{pmatrix}$.

(ii) The diagram for a 135° anticlockwise rotation about the origin is shown below.

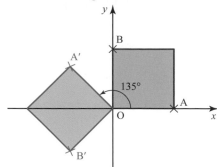

The image of $\begin{pmatrix} 1 \\ 0 \end{pmatrix}$ is $\begin{pmatrix} -\dfrac{1}{\sqrt{2}} \\ \dfrac{1}{\sqrt{2}} \end{pmatrix}$ and the image of

$\begin{pmatrix} 0 \\ 1 \end{pmatrix}$ is $\begin{pmatrix} -\dfrac{1}{\sqrt{2}} \\ -\dfrac{1}{\sqrt{2}} \end{pmatrix}$ and so the matrix representing

an anticlockwise rotation of 45° about the origin is

$\begin{pmatrix} -\dfrac{1}{\sqrt{2}} & -\dfrac{1}{\sqrt{2}} \\ \dfrac{1}{\sqrt{2}} & -\dfrac{1}{\sqrt{2}} \end{pmatrix}.$

Discussion point (Page 32)

The matrix for a rotation of $\theta°$ clockwise about the origin is $\begin{pmatrix} \cos\theta & \sin\theta \\ -\sin\theta & \cos\theta \end{pmatrix}$

Activity 2.4 (Page 33)

(i) The diagram below shows the effect of the matrix $\begin{pmatrix} 2 & 0 \\ 0 & 1 \end{pmatrix}$ on the unit vectors **i** and **j**.

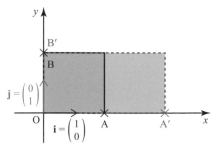

You can see that the vector **i** has image $\begin{pmatrix} 2 \\ 0 \end{pmatrix}$ and the vector **j** is unchanged. Therefore this matrix represents a stretch of scale factor 2 parallel to the x-axis.

(ii) The diagram below shows the effect of the matrix

$\begin{pmatrix} 1 & 0 \\ 0 & 5 \end{pmatrix}$ on the unit vectors **i** and **j**.

You can see that the vector **i** is unchanged and the vector **j** has image $\begin{pmatrix} 0 \\ 5 \end{pmatrix}$. Therefore this matrix represents a stretch of scale factor 5 parallel to the y-axis.

The matrix $\begin{pmatrix} m & 0 \\ 0 & 1 \end{pmatrix}$ represents a stretch of scale factor m

parallel to the x-axis.

The matrix $\begin{pmatrix} 1 & 0 \\ 0 & n \end{pmatrix}$ represents a stretch of scale factor n

parallel to the y-axis.

Activity 2.5 (Page 34)

Point A: $6 \div 2 = 3$

Point B: $6 \div 2 = 3$

Point C: $3 \div 1 = 3$

Point D: $3 \div 1 = 3$

The ratio is equal to 3 for each point.

Exercise 2.3 (Page 38)

1 (i) (a)

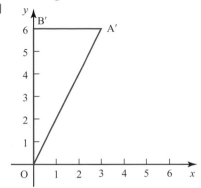

(b) $A' = (3, 6)$, $B' = (0, 6)$

(c) $x' = 3x$, $y' = 3y$

(d) $\begin{pmatrix} 3 & 0 \\ 0 & 3 \end{pmatrix}$

(ii) (a)

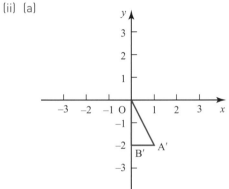

(b) $A' = (1, -2)$, $B' = (0, -2)$

(c) $x' = x$, $y' = -y$

(d) $\begin{pmatrix} 1 & 0 \\ 0 & -1 \end{pmatrix}$

(iii) (a)

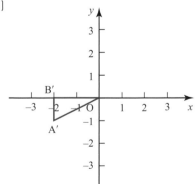

(b) $A' = (-2, -1)$, $B' = (-2, 0)$

(c) $x' - y$ $y' = -x$

(d) $\begin{pmatrix} 0 & -1 \\ -1 & 0 \end{pmatrix}$

(iv) (a)

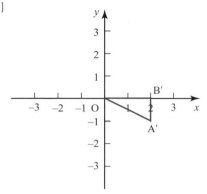

(b) $A' = (2, -1)$, $B' = (2, 0)$

(c) $x' = y$, $y' = -x$

(d) $\begin{pmatrix} 0 & 1 \\ -1 & 0 \end{pmatrix}$

(v) (a)

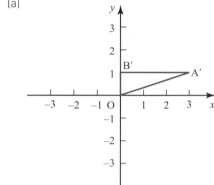

(b) $A' = (3, 1)$, $B' = (0, 1)$

(c) $x' = 3x$, $y' = \frac{1}{2}y$

(d) $\begin{pmatrix} 3 & 0 \\ 0 & \frac{1}{2} \end{pmatrix}$

2 (i) Reflection in the x-axis

(ii) Reflection in the line $y = -x$

(iii) Stretch of factor 2 parallel to the x-axis and stretch factor 3 parallel to the y-axis

(iv) Enlargement, scale factor 4, centre the origin

(v) Rotation of 90° clockwise (or 270° anticlockwise) about the origin

3 (i) Rotation of 60° anticlockwise about the origin

(ii) Rotation of 55° anticlockwise about the origin

(iii) Rotation of 135° clockwise about the origin

(iv) Rotation of 150° anticlockwise about the origin

4 (i)

$$\begin{pmatrix} 1 & 4 \\ 0 & 1 \end{pmatrix}\begin{pmatrix} 1 & 1 & -1 & -1 \\ 1 & -1 & -1 & 1 \end{pmatrix} = \begin{pmatrix} 5 & -3 & -5 & 3 \\ 1 & -1 & -1 & 1 \end{pmatrix}$$

so the transformed square would look like this:

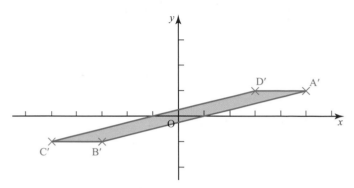

(ii) The transformation is a shear with the
x-axis invariant and the point A(1, 1) has
image A′(5, 1).

5 (i) (a) The image of the unit square has vertices
(0, 0), (1, 5), (0, 1), (1, 6) as shown in the
diagram below.

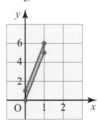

(b) The image of the unit square has vertices
(0, 0), (1, 0), (0.5, 1), (1.5, 1) as shown in
the diagram below.

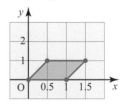

(ii) Matrix **A** represents a shear with the y-axis
invariant; the point (1, 1) has image (1, 6). **A**
has shear factor 5.
Matrix **B** represents a shear with the x-axis
invariant; the point (1, 1) has image (1.5, 1).
B has shear factor 0.5.

6 (i) $\begin{pmatrix} 0 & -1 & 0 \\ 1 & 0 & 0 \\ 0 & 0 & 1 \end{pmatrix}$ (ii) $\begin{pmatrix} 1 & 0 & 0 \\ 0 & -1 & 0 \\ 0 & 0 & 1 \end{pmatrix}$

(iii) $\begin{pmatrix} 1 & 0 & 0 \\ 0 & -1 & 0 \\ 0 & 0 & -1 \end{pmatrix}$ (iv) $\begin{pmatrix} 0 & 0 & -1 \\ 0 & 1 & 0 \\ 1 & 0 & 0 \end{pmatrix}$

(v) $\begin{pmatrix} \dfrac{1}{\sqrt{2}} & -\dfrac{1}{\sqrt{2}} & 0 \\ \dfrac{1}{\sqrt{2}} & \dfrac{1}{\sqrt{2}} & 0 \\ 0 & 0 & 1 \end{pmatrix}$ (vi) $\begin{pmatrix} 1 & 0 & 0 \\ 0 & \dfrac{1}{2} & -\dfrac{\sqrt{3}}{2} \\ 0 & \dfrac{\sqrt{3}}{2} & \dfrac{1}{2} \end{pmatrix}$

(vii) $\begin{pmatrix} -\dfrac{1}{2} & 0 & -\dfrac{\sqrt{3}}{2} \\ 0 & 1 & 0 \\ \dfrac{\sqrt{3}}{2} & 0 & -\dfrac{1}{2} \end{pmatrix}$

7 (i) A′(2√3 − 1, 2)   (ii) $\begin{pmatrix} 1 & \sqrt{3} \\ 0 & 1 \end{pmatrix}$

8 A′(4, 5), B′(7, 9), C′(3, 4). The original square
and the image both have an area of one square
unit.

9 (i)

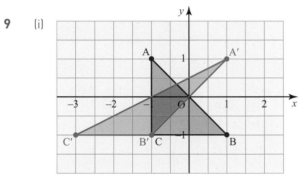

(ii) The gradient of A′C′ is $\frac{1}{2}$, which is the
reciprocal of the top right-hand entry of the
matrix **M**.

10 (i) Rotation of 90° clockwise about the x-axis
(ii) Enlargement scale factor 3, centre (0, 0)
(iii) Reflection in the plane z = 0
(iv) Rotation of 36.9° anticlockwise about the
y-axis

11 (i) $\begin{pmatrix} -1 & 0 & 0 \\ 0 & 1 & 1 \\ 0 & 0 & 1 \end{pmatrix}$ (ii) $\begin{pmatrix} -1 & 0 & 0 \\ 0 & 1 & 0 \\ 0 & 0 & -1 \end{pmatrix}$

12 $(x, y) \rightarrow (x, x)$

The matrix for the transformation is $\begin{pmatrix} 1 & 0 \\ 1 & 0 \end{pmatrix}$.

13 (i) Any matrix of the form $\begin{pmatrix} 5 & 0 \\ 0 & k \end{pmatrix}$ or

$\begin{pmatrix} k & 0 \\ 0 & 5 \end{pmatrix}$.

If $k = 5$ the rectangle would be a square.

(ii) $\begin{pmatrix} \sqrt{2} & 1 \\ 0 & 1 \end{pmatrix}, \begin{pmatrix} 1 & 0 \\ 1 & \sqrt{2} \end{pmatrix}$,

$\begin{pmatrix} 1 & \sqrt{2} \\ 1 & 0 \end{pmatrix}$ or $\begin{pmatrix} 0 & 1 \\ \sqrt{2} & 1 \end{pmatrix}$

(iii) $\begin{pmatrix} 7 & \dfrac{3\sqrt{3}}{2} \\ 0 & \dfrac{3}{2} \end{pmatrix}, \begin{pmatrix} 0 & \dfrac{3}{2} \\ 7 & \dfrac{3\sqrt{3}}{2} \end{pmatrix}$,

$\begin{pmatrix} \dfrac{3\sqrt{3}}{2} & 7 \\ \dfrac{3}{2} & 0 \end{pmatrix}$ or $\begin{pmatrix} \dfrac{3}{2} & 0 \\ \dfrac{3\sqrt{3}}{2} & 7 \end{pmatrix}$

Discussion point (Page 41)

(i) **BA** represents a reflection in the line $y = x$

(ii) The transformation **A** is represented by the

matrix $\mathbf{A} = \begin{pmatrix} 1 & 0 \\ 0 & -1 \end{pmatrix}$ and the transformation

B is represented by the matrix

$\mathbf{B} = \begin{pmatrix} 0 & -1 \\ 1 & 0 \end{pmatrix}$. The matrix product

$\mathbf{BA} = \begin{pmatrix} 0 & -1 \\ 1 & 0 \end{pmatrix}\begin{pmatrix} 1 & 0 \\ 0 & -1 \end{pmatrix} = \begin{pmatrix} 0 & 1 \\ 1 & 0 \end{pmatrix}$.

This is the matrix which represents a reflection in
the line $y = x$.

Activity 2.6 (Page 42)

(i) $\mathbf{P'} = \begin{pmatrix} a & b \\ c & d \end{pmatrix}\begin{pmatrix} x \\ y \end{pmatrix} = \begin{pmatrix} ax + by \\ cx + dy \end{pmatrix}$

(ii) $\mathbf{P''} = \begin{pmatrix} p & q \\ r & s \end{pmatrix}\begin{pmatrix} ax + by \\ cx + dy \end{pmatrix}$

$= \begin{pmatrix} pax + pby + qcx + qdy \\ rax + rby + scx + sdy \end{pmatrix}$

(iii)

$\mathbf{U} = \begin{pmatrix} p & q \\ r & s \end{pmatrix}\begin{pmatrix} a & b \\ c & d \end{pmatrix} = \begin{pmatrix} pa + qc & pb + qd \\ ra + sc & rb + sd \end{pmatrix}$

and so

$\mathbf{UP} = \begin{pmatrix} pa + qc & pb + qd \\ ra + sc & rb + sd \end{pmatrix}\begin{pmatrix} x \\ y \end{pmatrix}$

$\begin{pmatrix} pax + qcx + pby + qdy \\ rax + scx + rby + sdy \end{pmatrix}$. Therefore $\mathbf{UP = P''}$

Discussion point (Page 42)

AB represents 'carry out transformation **B** followed
by transformation **A**.

(**AB**)**C** represents 'carry out transformation **C**
followed by transformation **AB**, i.e. 'carry out **C**
followed by **B** followed by **A**'.

BC represents 'carry out transformation **C** followed
by transformation **B**'.

A(**BC**) represents 'carry out transformation **BC**
followed by transformation **A**, i.e. carry out **C**
followed by **B** followed by **A**'.

Activity 2.7 (Page 43)

(i) $\mathbf{A} = \begin{pmatrix} \cos\theta & -\sin\theta \\ \sin\theta & \cos\theta \end{pmatrix}$,

$\mathbf{B} = \begin{pmatrix} \cos\phi & -\sin\phi \\ \sin\phi & \cos\phi \end{pmatrix}$

(ii)

$\mathbf{BA} = \begin{pmatrix} \cos\theta\cos\phi - \sin\theta\sin\phi & -\sin\theta\cos\phi - \cos\theta\sin\phi \\ \sin\theta\cos\phi + \cos\theta\sin\phi & -\sin\theta\sin\phi + \cos\theta\cos\phi \end{pmatrix}$

(iii) $\mathbf{C} = \begin{pmatrix} \cos(\theta + \phi) & -\sin(\theta + \phi) \\ \sin(\theta + \phi) & \cos(\theta + \phi) \end{pmatrix}$

(iv) $\sin(\theta + \phi) = \sin\theta\cos\phi + \cos\theta\sin\phi$

$\cos(\theta + \phi) = \cos\theta\cos\phi - \sin\theta\sin\phi$

(v) A rotation through angle θ followed by rotation
through angle ϕ has the same effect as a rotation
through angle ϕ followed by angle θ.

Exercise 2.4 (Page 44)

1 (i) **A**: enlargement centre (0,0), scale factor 3
B: rotation 90° anticlockwise about (0,0)
C: reflection in the x-axis
D: reflection in the line $y = x$

(ii) $\mathbf{BC} = \begin{pmatrix} 0 & 1 \\ 1 & 0 \end{pmatrix}$, reflection in the line $y = x$

$\mathbf{CB} = \begin{pmatrix} 0 & -1 \\ -1 & 0 \end{pmatrix}$, reflection in the line $y = -x$

$\mathbf{DC} = \begin{pmatrix} 0 & -1 \\ 1 & 0 \end{pmatrix}$, rotation 90° anticlockwise about (0, 0)

$\mathbf{A}^2 = \begin{pmatrix} 9 & 0 \\ 0 & 9 \end{pmatrix}$, enlargement centre (0, 0), scale factor 9

$\mathbf{BCB} = \begin{pmatrix} 1 & 0 \\ 0 & -1 \end{pmatrix}$, reflection in the x-axis

$\mathbf{DC}^2\mathbf{D} = \begin{pmatrix} 1 & 0 \\ 0 & 1 \end{pmatrix}$ returns the object to its original position

(iii) For example, $\mathbf{B}^4$, $\mathbf{C}^2$ or $\mathbf{D}^2$

2 (i) $\mathbf{X} = \begin{pmatrix} 1 & 0 \\ 0 & -1 \end{pmatrix}$ $\mathbf{Y} = \begin{pmatrix} -1 & 0 \\ 0 & 1 \end{pmatrix}$

(ii) $\mathbf{XY} = \begin{pmatrix} -1 & 0 \\ 0 & -1 \end{pmatrix}$, rotation of 180° about the origin

(iii) $\mathbf{YX} = \begin{pmatrix} -1 & 0 \\ 0 & -1 \end{pmatrix}$

(iv) When considering the effect on the unit vectors **i** and **j**, as each transformation only affects one of the unit vectors the order of the transformations is not important in this case.

3 (i) $\mathbf{P} = \begin{pmatrix} -1 & 0 \\ 0 & -1 \end{pmatrix}$ $\mathbf{Q} = \begin{pmatrix} 0 & 1 \\ 1 & 0 \end{pmatrix}$

(ii) $\mathbf{PQ} = \begin{pmatrix} 0 & -1 \\ -1 & 0 \end{pmatrix}$, reflection in the line $y = -x$

(iii) $\mathbf{QP} = \begin{pmatrix} 0 & -1 \\ -1 & 0 \end{pmatrix}$

(iv) The matrix **P** has the effect of making the coordinates of any point the negative of their original values,

i.e. $(x, y) \rightarrow (-x, -y)$

The matrix **Q** interchanges the coordinates,

i.e. $(x, y) \rightarrow (y, x)$

It does not matter what order these two transformations occur as the result will be the same

4 (i) $\begin{pmatrix} 1 & 0 & 0 \\ 0 & 1 & 0 \\ 0 & 0 & -1 \end{pmatrix}$ (ii) $\begin{pmatrix} 1 & 0 & 0 \\ 0 & 0 & -1 \\ 0 & 1 & 0 \end{pmatrix}$

(iii) $\begin{pmatrix} -1 & 0 & 0 \\ 0 & 1 & 0 \\ 0 & 0 & 1 \end{pmatrix}$ (iv) $\begin{pmatrix} 0 & 0 & -1 \\ 0 & 1 & 0 \\ 1 & 0 & 0 \end{pmatrix}$

(v) $\begin{pmatrix} 1 & 0 & 0 \\ 0 & 3 & 0 \\ 0 & 0 & 1 \end{pmatrix}$ (vi) $\begin{pmatrix} \frac{1}{2} & -\frac{1}{2}\sqrt{3} & 0 \\ \frac{1}{2}\sqrt{3} & \frac{1}{2} & 0 \\ 0 & 0 & 1 \end{pmatrix}$

5 (i) $\begin{pmatrix} 8 & -4 \\ -3 & 12 \end{pmatrix}$ (ii) $(32, -33)$

6 Possible transformations are $\mathbf{B} = \begin{pmatrix} 0 & 1 \\ -1 & 0 \end{pmatrix}$, which is a rotation of 90° clockwise about the origin, followed by

$\mathbf{A} = \begin{pmatrix} 3 & 0 \\ 0 & 1 \end{pmatrix}$, which is a stretch of scale factor 3 parallel to the x-axis. The order of these is important as performing **A** followed by **B** leads

to the matrix $\begin{pmatrix} 0 & 1 \\ -3 & 0 \end{pmatrix}$. Could also have

$\mathbf{B} = \begin{pmatrix} 1 & 0 \\ 0 & 3 \end{pmatrix}$, which represents a stretch of factor 3 parallel to the y-axis, followed by

$\mathbf{A} = \begin{pmatrix} 0 & 1 \\ -1 & 0 \end{pmatrix}$, which represents a rotation of 90° clockwise about the origin; again the order is important.

7 (i) $\mathbf{PQ} = \begin{pmatrix} 1 & 0 \\ -3 & -1 \end{pmatrix}$

(ii) $\mathbf{P} = \begin{pmatrix} 1 & 0 \\ 0 & -1 \end{pmatrix}$ represents a reflection in

the x-axis.

$\mathbf{Q} = \begin{pmatrix} 1 & 0 \\ 3 & 1 \end{pmatrix}$ represents a shear with the

y-axis fixed; point B(1,1) has image (1,−4).

8 $\mathbf{X} = \begin{pmatrix} \dfrac{1}{\sqrt{2}} & \dfrac{1}{\sqrt{2}} \\ \dfrac{-1}{\sqrt{2}} & -\dfrac{1}{\sqrt{2}} \end{pmatrix}$

A matrix representing a rotation about the

origin has the form $\begin{pmatrix} \cos\theta & -\sin\theta \\ \sin\theta & \cos\theta \end{pmatrix}$ and so

the entries on the leading diagonal would be
equal. That is not true for matrix $\mathbf{X}$ and so this
cannot represent a rotation.

9 (i) Stretch in the z-direction, scale factor 2.5
(ii) Rotation of 30° clockwise about the
z-axis

10 (i) $\begin{pmatrix} 1 & 0 \\ 0 & 2 \end{pmatrix}$

(ii) A reflection in the x-axis and a stretch of
scale factor 5 parallel to the x-axis

(iii) $\begin{pmatrix} 5 & 0 \\ 0 & -2 \end{pmatrix}$

Reflection in the x-axis; stretch of scale
factor 5 parallel to the x-axis; stretch of scale
factor 2 parallel to the y-axis. The outcome
of these three transformations would be the
same regardless of the order in which they are
applied. There are six different possible orders.

(iv) $\begin{pmatrix} \dfrac{1}{5} & 0 \\ 0 & -\dfrac{1}{2} \end{pmatrix}$

11 (i) $\begin{pmatrix} 1 & -R_1 \\ 0 & 1 \end{pmatrix}$ (ii) $\begin{pmatrix} 1 & 0 \\ -\dfrac{1}{R_2} & 1 \end{pmatrix}$

(iii) $\begin{pmatrix} 1 & -R_1 \\ -\dfrac{1}{R_2} & \dfrac{R_1}{R_2} + 1 \end{pmatrix}$ (iv) $\begin{pmatrix} 1 + \dfrac{R_1}{R_2} & -R_1 \\ -\dfrac{1}{R_2} & 1 \end{pmatrix}$

The effect of Type B followed by Type A
is different from that of Type A followed by
Type B.

12 $a = \sqrt{\dfrac{\sqrt{2} + 2}{4}}$ and $b = \sqrt{\dfrac{1}{2\left(\sqrt{2} + 2\right)}}$

$\mathbf{D}$ represents an anticlockwise rotation of 22.5°
about the origin.

By comparison to the matrix

$\begin{pmatrix} \cos\theta & -\sin\theta \\ \sin\theta & \cos\theta \end{pmatrix}$ for an anticlockwise

rotation of θ about the origin, a and b are
the exact values of $\cos 22.5°$ and $\sin 22.5°$
respectively.

13 (i) $\mathbf{P} = \begin{pmatrix} \dfrac{1}{2} & \dfrac{\sqrt{3}}{2} \\ \dfrac{\sqrt{3}}{2} & -\dfrac{1}{2} \end{pmatrix}$ $Q = \begin{pmatrix} -\dfrac{1}{2} & \dfrac{\sqrt{3}}{2} \\ \dfrac{\sqrt{3}}{2} & \dfrac{1}{2} \end{pmatrix}$

(ii) $\mathbf{QP} = \begin{pmatrix} \dfrac{1}{2} & -\dfrac{\sqrt{3}}{2} \\ \dfrac{\sqrt{3}}{2} & \dfrac{1}{2} \end{pmatrix}$, which represents

a rotation of 60° anticlockwise about the
origin.

(iii) $\mathbf{PQ} = \begin{pmatrix} \dfrac{1}{2} & \dfrac{\sqrt{3}}{2} \\ -\dfrac{\sqrt{3}}{2} & \dfrac{1}{2} \end{pmatrix}$, which represents a

rotation of 60° clockwise about the origin.

14 A reflection in a line followed by a second
reflection in the same line returns a point to its
original position.

Discussion point (Page 47)

In a reflection, all points on the mirror line map to
themselves.

In a rotation, only the centre of rotation maps to itself.

Exercise 2.5 (Page 49)

1 (i) Points of the form $(\lambda, -2\lambda)$

(ii) $(0, 0)$

(iii) Points of the form $(\lambda, -3\lambda)$

(iv) Points of the form $(2\lambda, 3\lambda)$

2 (i) x-axis, y-axis, lines of the form $y = mx$

(ii) x-axis, y-axis, lines of the form $y = mx$

(iii) no invariant lines

(iv) $y = x$, lines of the form $y = -x + c$

(v) $y = -x$, lines of the form $y = x + c$

(vi) x-axis

3 (i) Any points on the line $y = \frac{1}{2}x$, for example $(0, 0)$, $(2, 1)$ and $(3, 1.5)$

(ii) $y = \frac{1}{2}x$

(iii) Any line of the form $y = -2x + c$

(iv) Using the method of Example 1.11 leads to the equations

$2m^2 + 3m - 2 = 0 \Rightarrow m = 0.5 \text{ or } -2$

$(4 + 2m)c = 0 \Rightarrow m = -2 \text{ or } c = 0$

If $m = 0.5$ then $c = 0$ so $y = \frac{1}{2}x$ is invariant.

If $m = -2$ then c can take any value and so $y = -2x + c$ is an invariant line.

4 (i) Solving $\begin{pmatrix} 4 & 11 \\ 11 & 4 \end{pmatrix} \begin{pmatrix} x \\ y \end{pmatrix} = \begin{pmatrix} x \\ y \end{pmatrix}$ leads to the equations $y = -\frac{3x}{11}$ and $y = -\frac{11x}{3}$.

The only point that satisfies both of these is $(0, 0)$.

(ii) $y = x$ and $y = -x$

5 (i) $y = x$, $y = -\frac{9}{4}x$

(ii)

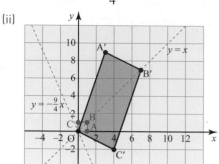

6 (i) $y = x$ (ii) $y = x$

(iii)

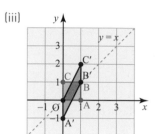

9 (i) $A = \begin{pmatrix} 1 & 0 & 0 \\ 0 & \frac{1}{\sqrt{2}} & -\frac{1}{\sqrt{2}} \\ 0 & \frac{1}{\sqrt{2}} & \frac{1}{\sqrt{2}} \end{pmatrix}$, $B = \begin{pmatrix} \frac{1}{\sqrt{2}} & -\frac{1}{\sqrt{2}} & 0 \\ \frac{1}{\sqrt{2}} & \frac{1}{\sqrt{2}} & 0 \\ 0 & 0 & 1 \end{pmatrix}$

(ii) $\begin{pmatrix} \frac{1}{\sqrt{2}} & -\frac{1}{2} & \frac{1}{2} \\ \frac{1}{\sqrt{2}} & \frac{1}{2} & -\frac{1}{2} \\ 0 & \frac{1}{\sqrt{2}} & \frac{1}{\sqrt{2}} \end{pmatrix}$

(iv) $\begin{pmatrix} \frac{1}{\sqrt{2}} - \frac{1}{2} \\ \frac{1}{\sqrt{2}} + \frac{1}{2} \\ -\frac{1}{\sqrt{2}} \end{pmatrix}$

11 (i) $x' = x + a$, $y' = y + b$

(iii) (c) $a = -2b$

Chapter 3

Discussion point (Page 55)

$4x^3 + x^2 - 4x - 1 = 0$

Looking at the graph you may suspect that $x = 1$ is a root. Setting $x = 1$ verifies this. The factor theorem tells you that $(x - 1)$ must be a factor, so factorise the cubic $(x - 1)(4x^2 + 5x + 1) = 0$. Now factorise the remaining quadratic factor: $(x - 1)(4x + 1)(x + 1) = 0$, so the roots are $x = 1, -\frac{1}{4}, -1$.

$4x^3 + x^2 + 4x + 1 = 0$

This does not have such an obvious starting point, but the graph suggests only one real root. Comparing with previous example, you may spot that $x = -\frac{1}{4}$ might work, so you can factorise giving $(4x + 1)(x^2 + 1) = 0$. From this you can see that the other roots must be complex. $x^2 = -1$, so the three roots are $x = -\frac{1}{4}, \pm i$.

Activity 3.1 (Page 56)

Equation	Two roots	Sum of roots	Product of roots
(i) $z^2 - 3z + 2 = 0$	1, 2	3	2
(ii) $z^2 + z - 6 = 0$	2, −3	−1	−6
(iii) $z^2 - 6z + 8 = 0$	2, 4	6	8
(iv) $z^2 - 3z - 10 = 0$	−2, 5	3	−10
(v) $2z^2 - 3z + 1 = 0$	$\frac{1}{2}$, 1	$\frac{3}{2}$	$\frac{1}{2}$
(vi) $z^2 - 4z + 5 = 0$	$2 \pm i$	4	5

Discussion point (Page 56)

If the equation is $ax^2 + bx + c = 0$, the sum appears to be $-\frac{b}{a}$ and the product appears to be $\frac{c}{a}$.

Discussion point (Page 57)

You get back to the original quadratic equation.

Exercise 3.1 (Page 59)

1 (i) $\alpha + \beta = -\frac{7}{2}, \quad \alpha\beta = 3$

(ii) $\alpha + \beta = \frac{1}{5}, \quad \alpha\beta = -\frac{1}{5}$

(iii) $\alpha + \beta = 0, \quad \alpha\beta = \frac{2}{7}$

(iv) $\alpha + \beta = -\frac{24}{5}, \quad \alpha\beta = 0$

(v) $\alpha + \beta = -11, \quad \alpha\beta = -4$

(vi) $\alpha + \beta = -\frac{8}{3}, \quad \alpha\beta = -2$

2 (i) $z^2 - 10z + 21 = 0$

(ii) $z^2 - 3z - 4 = 0$

(iii) $2z^2 + 19z + 45 = 0$

(iv) $z^2 - 5z = 0$

(v) $z^2 - 6z + 9 = 0$

(vi) $z^2 - 6z + 13 = 0$

3 (i) $2z^2 + 15z - 81 = 0$

(ii) $2z^2 - 5z - 9 = 0$

(iii) $2z^2 + 13z + 9 = 0$

(iv) $z^2 - 7z - 12 = 0$

4 (i) Roots are real, distinct and negative (since $\alpha\beta > 0 \Rightarrow$ same signs and $\alpha + \beta < 0 \Rightarrow$ both <0)

(ii) $\alpha = -\beta$

(iii) One of the roots is zeros and the other is $-\frac{b}{a}$.

(iv) The roots are of opposite signs.

5 Let $az^2 + bz + c = 0$ have roots α and 2α.

Sum of roots $\alpha + 2\alpha = 3\alpha = -\frac{b}{a}$ so $\alpha = -\frac{b}{3a}$

Product of roots $\alpha \times 2\alpha = 2\alpha^2 = \frac{c}{a}$ so

$2 \times \left(-\frac{b}{3a}\right)^2 = \frac{c}{a}$

Then $2b^2 = 9ac$ as required.

6 (i) $az^2 + bkz + ck^2 = 0$

(ii) $az^2 + (b - 2ka)z + (k^2a - kb + c) = 0$

7 (ii) $z^2 - (5 + 2i) + (9 + 7i) = 0$

Exercise 3.2 (Page 63)

1 (i) $-\frac{3}{2}$

(ii) $-\frac{1}{2}$

(iii) $-\frac{7}{2}$

2 (i) $z^3 - 7z^2 + 14z - 8 = 0$

(ii) $z^3 - 3z^2 - 4z + 12 = 0$

(iii) $2z^3 + 7z^2 + 6z = 0$

(iv) $2z^3 - 13z^2 + 28z - 20 = 0$

(v) $z^3 - 19z - 30 = 0$

(vi) $z^3 - 5z^2 + 9z - 5 = 0$

3 (i) $z = 2, 5, 8$

(ii) $z = -\dfrac{2}{3}, \dfrac{2}{3}, 2$

(iii) $z = 2 - 2\sqrt{3}, 2, 2 + 2\sqrt{3}$

(iv) $z = \dfrac{2}{3}, \dfrac{7}{6}, \dfrac{5}{3}$

4 (i) $z = w - 3$

(ii) $(w - 3)^3 + (w - 3)^2 + 2(w - 3) - 3 = 0$

(iii) $w^3 - 8w^2 + 23w - 27 = 0$

(iv) $\alpha + 3, \beta + 3, \gamma + 3$

5 $w^3 - 4w^2 + 4w - 24 = 0$

6 (i) $2w^3 - 16w^2 + 37w - 27 = 0$

(ii) $2w^3 + 24w^2 + 45w + 37 = 0$

7 The roots are $\dfrac{3}{2}, 2, \dfrac{5}{2}$ $k = \dfrac{47}{2}$

8 $z = \dfrac{1}{4}, \dfrac{1}{2}, -\dfrac{3}{4}$

9 $\alpha = -1, p = 7, q = 8$ or $\alpha = p = q = 0$

10 Roots are $-p$ and $\pm\sqrt{-q}$ (note $\pm\sqrt{-q}$ is not necessarily imaginary, since q is not necessarily > 0)

11 (i) $p = -8\left(\alpha + \dfrac{1}{2\alpha} + \beta\right)$

$q = 8\left(\dfrac{1}{2} + \alpha\beta + \dfrac{\beta}{2\alpha}\right)$

$r = -4\beta$

(iii) $r = 9; x = 1, \dfrac{1}{2}, -\dfrac{9}{4}$

$r = -6; x = -2, -\dfrac{1}{4}, \dfrac{3}{2}$

12 $z = \dfrac{3}{7}, \dfrac{7}{3}, -2$

13 $ac^3 = b^3 d$

$z = \dfrac{1}{2}, \dfrac{3}{2}, \dfrac{9}{2}$

Exercise 3.3 (Page 66)

1 (i) $-\dfrac{3}{2}$

(ii) 3

(iii) $\dfrac{5}{2}$

(iv) 2

2 (i) $z^4 - 6z^3 + 7z^2 + 6z - 8 = 0$

(ii) $4z^4 + 20z^3 + z^2 - 60z = 0$

(iii) $4z^4 + 12z^3 - 27z^2 - 54z + 81 = 0$

(iv) $z^4 - 5z^2 + 10z - 6 = 0$

3 (i) $z^4 + 4z^3 - 6z^2 - 4z + 48 = 0$

(ii) $2z^4 + 12z^3 + 21z^2 + 13z + 8 = 0$

4 (i) Let $w = x + 1$ then $x = w - 1$

new quartic: $x^4 - 6x^2 + 9$

(ii) Solutions to new quartic are $x = \pm\sqrt{3}$ (each one repeated), solutions to original quartic are therefore: $\alpha = \beta = \sqrt{3} - 1$ and $\gamma = \delta = -\sqrt{3} - 1$.

5 (i) $\alpha = -1, \ \beta = \sqrt{3}$

(ii) $p = 4$ and $q = -9$

(iii) Use substitution $y = x - 3\alpha$ (i.e. $y = x + 3$ then $x = y - 3$) and $y^3 - 8y^2 + 18y - 12 = 0$

6 (i)
$\alpha + \beta + \gamma + \delta + \varepsilon = -\dfrac{b}{a}$

$\alpha\beta + \alpha\gamma + \alpha\delta + \alpha\varepsilon + \beta\gamma + \beta\delta + \beta\varepsilon + \gamma\delta + \gamma\varepsilon + \delta\varepsilon = \dfrac{c}{a}$

$\alpha\beta\gamma + \alpha\beta\delta + \alpha\beta\varepsilon + \alpha\gamma\delta + \alpha\gamma\varepsilon + \alpha\delta\varepsilon + \beta\gamma\delta + \beta\gamma\varepsilon + \beta\delta\varepsilon + \gamma\delta\varepsilon = -\dfrac{d}{a}$

$\alpha\beta\gamma\delta + \beta\gamma\delta\varepsilon + \gamma\delta\varepsilon\alpha + \delta\varepsilon\alpha\beta + \varepsilon\alpha\beta\gamma = \dfrac{e}{a}$

$\alpha\beta\gamma\delta\varepsilon = -\dfrac{f}{a}$

$\sum\alpha = -\dfrac{b}{a}$

$\sum\alpha\beta = \dfrac{c}{a}$

$\sum\alpha\beta\gamma = -\dfrac{d}{a}$

$\sum\alpha\beta\gamma\delta = \dfrac{e}{a}$

$\sum\alpha\beta\gamma\delta\varepsilon = -\dfrac{f}{a}$

Exercise 3.4 (Page 70)

1   4 + 5i is the other root.

     The equation is $z^2 - 8z + 41 = 0$.

2 $2 - i, -3$

3 $7, 4 \pm 2i$

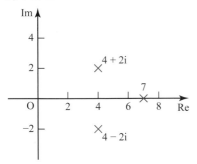

4   (i) $z = -3$

     (ii) $z = -3, \dfrac{5}{2} \pm \dfrac{\sqrt{11}}{2}i$

5 $k = 36$, other roots are $-\dfrac{3}{2} \pm \dfrac{3\sqrt{3}}{2}i$

6 $p = 4, q = -10$, other roots are $1 + i$ and -6

7 $z^3 - z - 6 = 0$

8 $z = 3 \pm 2i, 2 \pm i$

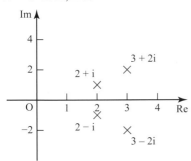

9   (i) $w^2 = -2i, w^3 = -2 - 2i, w^4 = -4$

     (ii) $p = -4, q = 2$

     (iii) $z = -4, -1, 1 \pm i$

10   (i) $z = \pm 3, \pm 3i$

     (ii)

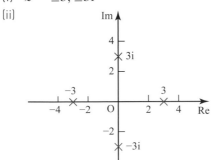

11   (i) $\alpha^2 = -3 - 4i, \alpha^3 = 11 - 2i$

     (ii) $z = -1 - 2i, -5$

     (iii)

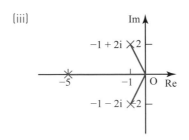

12   A false, B true, C true, D true

13 $a = 2, b = 2, z = -2 \pm i, 1 \pm 2i$

14 $z = \pm 3i, 4 \pm \sqrt{5}$

15   (i) $\alpha^2 = -8 - 6i, \alpha^3 = 26 - 18i$

     (ii) $\mu = 20$

     (iii) $z = -1 \pm 3i, -\dfrac{2}{3}$

     (iv)

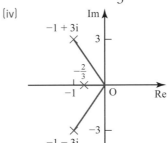

16 $a = 1, b = -9, c = 44, d = -174, e = 448,$
        $f = -480$

Chapter 4

Discussion point (Page 74)

If she was 121 last year then it would be fine, but we don't know if this is true. If she were able to provide any evidence of her age at a particular point then we could work from there, but we need a starting point.

Activity 4.1 (Page 74)

$$\begin{pmatrix} 1 & 2 \\ 0 & 1 \end{pmatrix}, \begin{pmatrix} 1 & 3 \\ 0 & 1 \end{pmatrix}, \begin{pmatrix} 1 & 4 \\ 0 & 1 \end{pmatrix}$$

Exercise 4.1 (Page 80)

10   (ii) $n_0 = 9$

13   (i) $\mathbf{M}^2 = \begin{pmatrix} 7 & 0 \\ 0 & 7 \end{pmatrix},$

         $\mathbf{M}^3 = \begin{pmatrix} -7 & 14 \\ 21 & 7 \end{pmatrix}, \mathbf{M}^4 = \begin{pmatrix} 49 & 0 \\ 0 & 49 \end{pmatrix}$

     (ii) $\mathbf{M}^{2m} = 7^m \begin{pmatrix} 1 & 0 \\ 0 & 1 \end{pmatrix}, \mathbf{M}^{2m+1} = 7^m \begin{pmatrix} -1 & 2 \\ 3 & 1 \end{pmatrix}$

Practice questions Pure Further Mathematics 1 (Page 82)

1 (i) Points plotted at $1 + 2i$, $-3 + 4i$, $4i$, $\frac{2}{5}$

[1], [1], [1], [2]

(ii) w^2, $w - w^\star$ [1]

2 *Either*

Cubic has real coefficients [1]

so $3 - i$ a root [1]

Sum of $3 + i$ and $3 - i$ is 6; sum of all 3 roots is 9 [1]

so real root is 3 [1]

Or

$z = 3$ a root by trying factors of 30 [1]

Factor theorem $(z - 3)$ a factor of cubic [1]

$z^3 - 9z^2 + 28z - 30 = (z - 3)(z^2 - 6z + 10)$ [1]

Roots of quadratic are $3 + i$, $3 - i$ [1]

3 $= \dfrac{-6 \pm \sqrt{36 - 20}}{2(2 + i)}$ [1]

$= \dfrac{-5}{2 + i}$ or $\dfrac{-1}{2 + i}$ [1]

$= \dfrac{-5(2 - i)}{(2 + i)(2 - i)}$ or $\dfrac{-(2 - i)}{(2 + i)(2 - i)}$ [1]

$= (2 - i)$ or $= -\dfrac{1}{5}(2 - i)$: both solutions are in the form $\lambda(2 - i)$ with $\lambda = -1$ and $\lambda = -\dfrac{1}{5}$ [1]

4 (i) $\alpha + 1, \beta + 1, \gamma + 1$ satisfy

$(y - 1)^3 + 3(y - 1)^2 - 6(y - 1) - 8 = 0$ [1]

$y^3 - 3y^2 + 3y - 1 + 3y^2 - 6y + 3 - 6y + 6 - 8 = 0$ [1], [1]

$y^3 - 9y = 0$ [1]

(ii) $y(y^2 - 9) = 0$ [1]

$y(y - 3)(y + 3) = 0$ [1]

$y = 0, 3, -3$ [1]

(iii) $x = -1, 2, -4$ [2]

5 (i) $x^3 + 4x^2 - 4x - 16 = 0$ [3]

(ii) $(a, b, c) = (2, 2, -4)$ in any order [5]

6 $\delta + (\delta + 1) = -\dfrac{b}{a} \Rightarrow b^2 = a^2(\delta + (\delta + 1))^2$

$= a^2(\delta^2 + 2\delta(\delta + 1) + (\delta + 1)^2)$

$= a^2(4\delta^2 + 4\delta + 1)$ [1]

$\delta(\delta + 1) = \dfrac{c}{a} \Rightarrow ac$

$= a^2(\delta(\delta + 1))$

$= a^2(\delta^2 + \delta)$ [1]

LHS $= b^2 - 4ac$

$= a^2(4\delta^2 + 4\delta + 1 - 4(\delta^2 + \delta))$

$= a^2(1)$ [1]

$= a^2$ [1]

$=$ RHS [complete argument, well set out]

7 (i) $3, 6, 11, 20, 37$ [1]

(ii) To prove $u_n = 2^n + n$

When

$n = 1$, LHS $= 3$, RHS $= 2^1 + 1$

$= 2 + 1 = 3$ [1]

So it is true for $n = 1$

Assume it is true for $n = k$, so

$u_k = 2^k + k$ [1]

Want to show that $u_{k+1} = 2^{k+1} + k + 1$.

$u_{k+1} = 2u_k - k + 1$

$= 2(2^k + k) - k + 1$ [1]

$= 2^{k+1} + 2k - k + 1$

$= 2^{k+1} + k + 1$ as required [1]

So, if the result is true for $n = k$ then it is true for $n = k + 1$ [1]

Since it is true for $n = 1$, by induction it is true for all positive integers n. [1]

8 (i) Calculations or image correct for three points [1]

Totally correct plot of $(0, 0)$ $(-0.6, 0.8)$ $(0.2, 1.4)$ $(0.8, 0.6)$ [1]

(ii) $\begin{pmatrix} -\dfrac{3}{5} & \dfrac{4}{5} \\ \dfrac{4}{5} & \dfrac{3}{5} \end{pmatrix} \begin{pmatrix} x \\ y \end{pmatrix} = \begin{pmatrix} x \\ y \end{pmatrix}$

$-\dfrac{3}{5}x + \dfrac{4}{5}y = x$ [1]

$\dfrac{4}{5}x + \dfrac{3}{5}y = y$

$\left.\begin{array}{l} y = 2x \\ y = 2x \end{array}\right\}$ from both equations [1]

$y = 2x$ is equation of line of invariant points. [1]

(iii) Perpendicular line to this, through origin, is
$$y = -\frac{1}{2}x$$

$$\begin{pmatrix} -\frac{3}{5} & \frac{4}{5} \\ \frac{4}{5} & \frac{3}{5} \end{pmatrix} \begin{pmatrix} x \\ -\frac{1}{2}x \end{pmatrix} = \begin{pmatrix} -\frac{3}{5}x - \frac{2}{5}x \\ \frac{4}{5}x - \frac{3}{10}x \end{pmatrix}$$

$$= \begin{pmatrix} -x \\ \frac{1}{2}x \end{pmatrix} = -\begin{pmatrix} x \\ -\frac{1}{2}x \end{pmatrix}$$ [1]

So $y = -\frac{1}{2}x$ is an invariant line, and is perpendicular to line of invariant points, and both go through the origin. [1]

(iv) Two points marked, where image of unit square intersects unit square, at $(0, 0)$ and $(0.5, 1)$. [1],[1]

9 (i) $\begin{pmatrix} 0 & 2 \\ 2 & 0 \end{pmatrix}$ (ii) $\begin{pmatrix} 2^n & 0 \\ 0 & 2^n \end{pmatrix}$ [1],[2]

Chapter 5

Discussion point (Page 86)

It is not true that $\arg(z)$ is given by $\arctan\left(\dfrac{y}{x}\right)$. For example the complex number $-1 + i$ has argument $\dfrac{3\pi}{4}$ but $\arctan\left(\dfrac{1}{-1}\right) = -\dfrac{\pi}{4}$. A diagram is needed to ensure the correct angle is calculated.

Activity 5.1 (Page 89)

	$\frac{\pi}{6}$	$\frac{\pi}{4}$	$\frac{\pi}{3}$
sin	$\frac{1}{2}$	$\frac{1}{\sqrt{2}}$	$\frac{\sqrt{3}}{2}$
cos	$\frac{\sqrt{3}}{2}$	$\frac{1}{\sqrt{2}}$	$\frac{1}{2}$
tan	$\frac{1}{\sqrt{3}}$	1	$\sqrt{3}$

Exercise 5.1 (Page 91)

1   $z_1 = 4$ or $4(\cos 0 + i \sin 0)$

   $z_2 = -2 + 4i$ or $2\sqrt{5}(\cos 2.03 + i \sin 2.03)$

   $z_3 = 1 - 3i$ or
   $\sqrt{10}\left(\cos(-1.25) + i \sin(-1.25)\right)$

2   (i) $\left[\sqrt{13}, 0.588\right]$

   (ii) $\left[\sqrt{29}, 2.76\right]$

   (iii) $\left[\sqrt{13}, -2.55\right]$

   (iv) $\left[\sqrt{29}, -1.19\right]$

3   $|z_1| = \sqrt{13}$ $\arg(z_1) = 0.588$

   $|z_2| = \sqrt{13}$ $\arg(z_2) = -0.588$

   $|z_3| = \sqrt{13}$ $\arg(z_3) = -2.16$

   $|z_4| = \sqrt{13}$ $\arg(z_4) = 2.16$

   $z_1 \to z_2$ Reflection in real axis

   $z_1 \to z_4$ Reflection in the line $y = -x$

   $z_1 \to z_3$ Rotation of 90° anticlockwise about the origin

4   (i) $-4i$

   (ii) $-\dfrac{7}{\sqrt{2}} + \dfrac{7}{\sqrt{2}}i$

   (iii) $-\dfrac{3\sqrt{3}}{2} + \dfrac{3}{2}i$

   (iv) $\dfrac{5\sqrt{3}}{2} - \dfrac{5}{2}i$

5   (i) $[1, 0]$

   (ii) $[2, \pi]$

   (iii) $[3, \dfrac{\pi}{2}]$

   (iv) $[4, -\dfrac{\pi}{2}]$

6   (i) $\sqrt{2}\left(\cos\dfrac{\pi}{4} + i \sin\dfrac{\pi}{4}\right)$

   (ii) $\sqrt{2}\left(\cos\dfrac{3\pi}{4} + i \sin\dfrac{3\pi}{4}\right)$

   (iii) $\sqrt{2}\left(\cos\left(\dfrac{-3\pi}{4}\right) + i \sin\left(\dfrac{-3\pi}{4}\right)\right)$

   (iv) $\sqrt{2}\left(\cos\left(\dfrac{-\pi}{4}\right) + i \sin\left(\dfrac{-\pi}{4}\right)\right)$

7 $7\left(\cos\dfrac{\pi}{3} + i\sin\dfrac{\pi}{3}\right)$, $2\left(\cos\dfrac{\pi}{3} + i\sin\dfrac{\pi}{3}\right)$

8 (i) $12\left(\cos\dfrac{\pi}{6} + i\sin\dfrac{\pi}{6}\right)$

(ii) $5\left(\cos(-0.927) + i\sin(-0.927)\right)$

(iii) $13\left(\cos 2.75 + i\sin 2.75\right)$

(iv) $\sqrt{65}\left(\cos 1.05 + i\sin 1.05\right)$

(v) $\sqrt{12\,013}\left(\cos(-2.13) + i\sin(-2.13)\right)$

9 (i) $\dfrac{1}{5}\sqrt{10}\left(\cos 0.322 + i\sin 0.322\right)$

(ii) $\dfrac{\sqrt{130}}{10}\left(\cos(-0.266) + i\sin(-0.266)\right)$

(iii) $\dfrac{\sqrt{290}}{10}\left(\cos(-1.63) + i\sin(-1.63)\right)$

10 (i) $z = 2i$ or $0 + 2i$

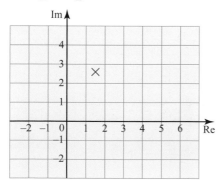

(ii) $z = \dfrac{3}{2} + \dfrac{3\sqrt{3}}{2}i$

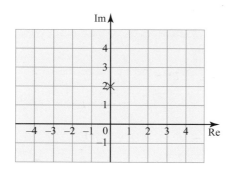

(iii) $z = -\dfrac{7\sqrt{3}}{2} + \dfrac{7}{2}i$

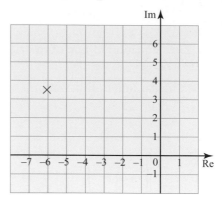

(iv) $z = \dfrac{1}{\sqrt{2}} - \dfrac{1}{\sqrt{2}}i$

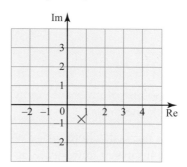

(v) $z = -\dfrac{5}{2} - \dfrac{5\sqrt{3}}{2}i$

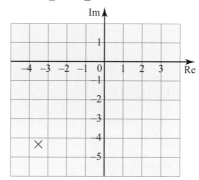

(vi) $z = -2.50 - 5.46i$

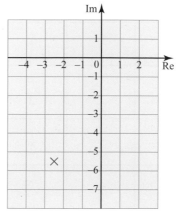

11 (i) $-(\pi - \alpha)$ or $\alpha - \pi$ (ii) $-\alpha$

   (iii) $\pi - \alpha$ (iv) $\dfrac{\pi}{2} - \alpha$

   (v) $\dfrac{\pi}{2} + \alpha$

12 $\sqrt{3}\left(\cos\dfrac{\pi}{6} + i\sin\dfrac{\pi}{6}\right)$

13 $4\sqrt{3}\left(\cos\dfrac{4\pi}{15} + i\sin\dfrac{4\pi}{15}\right)$,

   $4\left(\cos\dfrac{7\pi}{30} - i\sin\dfrac{7\pi}{30}\right)$

14 $8.92(\cos 0.877 + i\sin 0.877)$

15 (i) $|z_1| = 5$ $\arg(z_1) = 0.927$

     $|z_2| = \sqrt{2}$ $\arg(z_2) = \dfrac{3\pi}{4}$

  (ii) (a) $z_1 z_2 = -7 - i$ $\dfrac{z_1}{z_2} = \dfrac{1}{2} - \dfrac{7}{2}i$

     (b) $|z_1 z_2| = 5\sqrt{2}$ $\arg(z_1 z_2) = -3.00$

       $\left|\dfrac{z_1}{z_2}\right| = \dfrac{5\sqrt{2}}{2}$ $\arg\left(\dfrac{z_1}{z_2}\right) = -1.43$

  (iii) $|z_1 z_2| = |z_1||z_2|$ and $\left|\dfrac{z_1}{z_2}\right| = \dfrac{|z_1|}{|z_2|}$

    $\arg(z_1) + \arg(z_2) = 3.28$ which is greater than π,
    but is equivalent to -3.00

    i.e. $\arg(z_1) + \arg(z_2) = \arg(z_1 z_2)$

    $\arg(z_1) - \arg(z_2) = \arg\left(\dfrac{z_1}{z_2}\right)$

Activity 5.3 (Page 93)

(i) Rotation of 90° anticlockwise about the origin

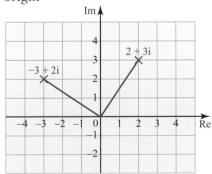

(ii) Rotation of 90° anticlockwise about the origin and enlargement of scale factor 2

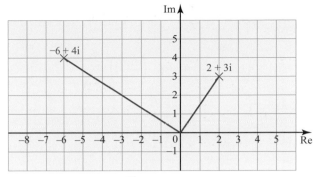

(iii) Rotation of $\dfrac{\pi}{4}$ anticlockwise and enlargement of scale factor $\sqrt{2}$

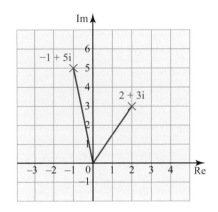

Exercise 5.2 (Page 95)

1 (i) $|w| = \sqrt{2}$ $\arg(w) = \dfrac{\pi}{4}$

     $|z| = 2$ $\arg(z) = -\dfrac{\pi}{3}$

  (ii) (a) $|wz| = 2\sqrt{2}$ $\arg(wz) = -\dfrac{\pi}{12}$

     (b) $\left|\dfrac{w}{z}\right| = \dfrac{1}{\sqrt{2}}$ $\arg\left(\dfrac{w}{z}\right) = \dfrac{7\pi}{12}$

  (iii)

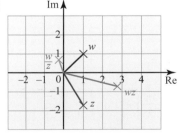

2 (i) $6\left(\cos\dfrac{7\pi}{12} + i\sin\dfrac{7\pi}{12}\right)$

  (ii) $\dfrac{3}{2}\left(\cos\left(\dfrac{\pi}{12}\right) + i\sin\left(\dfrac{\pi}{12}\right)\right)$

(iii) $\dfrac{2}{3}\left(\cos\left(-\dfrac{\pi}{12}\right) + i\sin\left(-\dfrac{\pi}{12}\right)\right)$

(iv) $\dfrac{1}{2}\left(\cos\left(-\dfrac{\pi}{4}\right) + i\sin\left(-\dfrac{\pi}{4}\right)\right)$

3 (i) $\dfrac{2\pi}{3}$ (ii) 6

  (iii) $\dfrac{\pi}{2}$ (iv) 108

4 (i) $4\left(\cos\left(-\dfrac{\pi}{2}\right) + i\sin\left(-\dfrac{\pi}{2}\right)\right)$

  (ii) $7776\left(\cos\left(\dfrac{5\pi}{6}\right) + i\sin\left(\dfrac{5\pi}{6}\right)\right)$

  (iii) $10368\left(\cos\left(-\dfrac{\pi}{12}\right) + i\sin\left(-\dfrac{\pi}{12}\right)\right)$

  (iv) $30\left(\cos\left(\dfrac{2\pi}{3}\right) + i\sin\left(\dfrac{2\pi}{3}\right)\right)$

  (v) $2\sqrt{2}\left(\cos 0 + i\sin 0\right)$

5 (i) Multiplication scale factor $\dfrac{\sqrt{377}}{13}$, angle of rotation -1.36 radians (i.e. 1.36 radians clockwise)

  (ii) Multiplication scale factor $\dfrac{3}{\sqrt{17}}$, angle of rotation -1.33 radians (i.e. 1.33 radians clockwise)

6 $\arg\left(\dfrac{w}{z}\right) = \arg(w) - \arg(z) \Rightarrow \arg\left(\dfrac{1}{z}\right)$

$= \arg(1) - \arg(z) = 0 - \arg(z) = -\arg(z)$

The exceptions are the complex number $z = 0$ (since $\arg 0$ is not defined), and complex numbers for which both $\mathrm{Im}(z) = 0$ and $\mathrm{Re}(z) \leq 0$ (since $-\pi < \arg(z) \leq \pi$)

7 (i) Real part $= \dfrac{-1 + \sqrt{3}}{4}$

    Imaginary part $= \dfrac{1 + \sqrt{3}}{4}$

  (ii) $\dfrac{\sqrt{2}\left(\cos\left(\dfrac{3\pi}{4}\right) + i\sin\left(\dfrac{3\pi}{4}\right)\right)}{2\left(\cos\left(\dfrac{\pi}{3}\right) + i\sin\left(\dfrac{\pi}{3}\right)\right)}$

(iii)

$\dfrac{-1 + i}{1 + \sqrt{3}i} = \dfrac{\sqrt{2}\left(\cos\left(\dfrac{3\pi}{4}\right) + i\sin\left(\dfrac{3\pi}{4}\right)\right)}{2\left(\cos\left(\dfrac{\pi}{3}\right) + i\sin\left(\dfrac{\pi}{3}\right)\right)}$

$= \dfrac{1}{\sqrt{2}}\left(\cos\left(\dfrac{5\pi}{12}\right) + i\sin\left(\dfrac{5\pi}{12}\right)\right)$

$= \dfrac{-1 + \sqrt{3}}{4} + \dfrac{1 + \sqrt{3}}{4}i$

$\Rightarrow \cos\left(\dfrac{5\pi}{12}\right) = \dfrac{\sqrt{3} - 1}{2\sqrt{2}} \quad \sin\left(\dfrac{5\pi}{12}\right) = \dfrac{\sqrt{3} + 1}{2\sqrt{2}}$

8 For the complex numbers
$w = r_1\left(\cos\theta_1 + i\sin\theta_1\right)$ and
$z = r_2\left(\cos\theta_2 + i\sin\theta_2\right)$ we have proven that
$wz = r_1 r_2\left[(\cos(\theta_1 + \theta_2) + i\sin(\theta_1 + \theta_2)\right]$
So,

$wzp = r_1 r_2[(\cos(\theta_1 + \theta_2) + i\sin(\theta_1 + \theta_2)] \times r_3\left(\cos\theta_3 + i\sin\theta_3\right)$

$= r_1 r_2 r_3[\cos(\theta_1 + \theta_2)\cos\theta_3 + i\sin(\theta_1 + \theta_2)\sin\theta_3 +$
$i\sin(\theta_1 + \theta_2)\cos\theta_3 + i^2\sin(\theta_1 + \theta_2)\sin\theta_3]$

$= r_1 r_2 r_3\{[\cos(\theta_1 + \theta_2)\cos\theta_3 - \sin(\theta_1 + \theta_2)\sin\theta_3]$
$+ i[\cos(\theta_1 + \theta_2)\sin\theta_3 + \sin(\theta_1 + \theta_2)\cos\theta_3]\}$

$= r_1 r_2 r_3\{\cos[(\theta_1 + \theta_2) + \theta_3] + i\sin[(\theta_1 + \theta_2) + \theta_3]\}$

Therefore, $|wzp| = |w|\,|z|\,|p|$ and
$\arg(wzp) = \arg(z) + \arg(w) + \arg(p)$.

Activity 5.4 (Page 100)

(i)

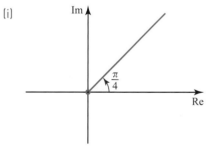

$\arg(z) = \dfrac{\pi}{4}$ represents a half line. The locus is a half line of points, with the origin as the starting point.
$-2 - 2i$ has argument $-\dfrac{3\pi}{4}$ and so it is not on this half line.

(ii) Calculating $z - 2$ for each point and finding the argument of $(z - 2)$ gives:

(a) $z = 4$ $z - 2 = 2$ $\arg(z - 2) = 0$

(b) $z = 3 + i$ $z - 2 = 1 + i$ $\arg(1 + i) = \dfrac{\pi}{4}$

(c) $z = 4i$ $z - 2 = 4i - 2$ $\arg(-2 + 4i) = 2.03$

(d) $z = 8 + 6i$ $z - 2 - 6 + 6i$ $\arg(6 + 6i) = \dfrac{\pi}{4}$

(e) $z = 1 - i$ $z - 2 = -1 - i$ $\arg(-1 - i) = -\dfrac{\pi}{4}$

So $\arg(z - 2) = \dfrac{\pi}{4}$ is satisfied by $z = 3 + i$ and $z = 8 + 6i$.

(iii) $z - 2$ represents a line between the point z and the point with coordinates $(2, 0)$.

So $\arg(z - 2) = \dfrac{\pi}{4}$ represents a line of points from $(2, 0)$ with an argument of $\dfrac{\pi}{4}$. This is a half line of points as shown.

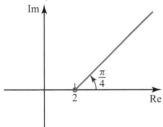

The line is a half line because points on the other half of the line would have an argument of $-\dfrac{\pi}{4}$ as was the case in part (ii)(e).

Activity 5.5 (Page 103)

The condition can be written as
$\left|z - (3 + 4i)\right| = \left|z - (-1 + 2i)\right|$.
$\left|z - (3 + 4i)\right|$ is the distance of point z from the point $3 + 4i$ (point A) and $\left|z - (-1 + 2i)\right|$ is the distance of point z from the point $-1 + 2i$ (point B).

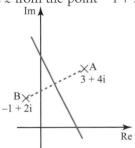

These distances are equal if z is on the perpendicular bisector of AB.

1 (i)

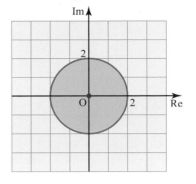

(ii)

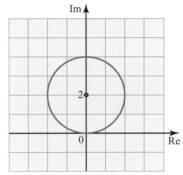

(iii)

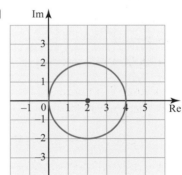

(iv)

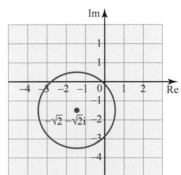

2 (i)

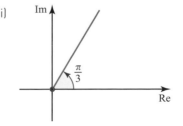

(ii)

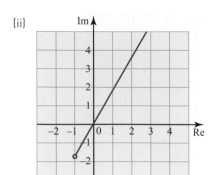

(iii)

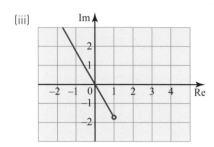

(iv)

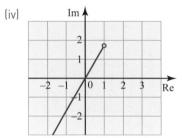

(v)

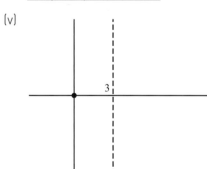

(vi)

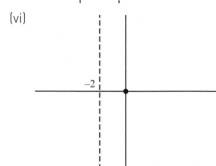

(vii)

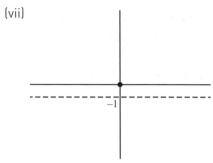

(viii)

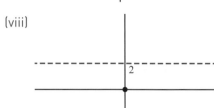

3 (i)

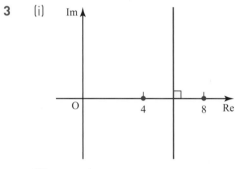

(ii)

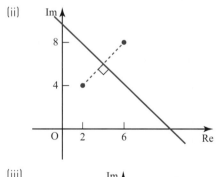

(iii)

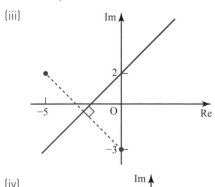

(iv)

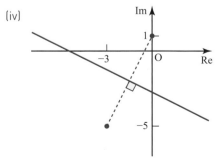

4 (i) $|z - (1 + i)| = 3$

(ii) $\arg(z + 2i) = \dfrac{3\pi}{4}$

(iii) $|z + 1| = |z - (3 + 2i)|$

5 (i) $|z - (4 + i)| \leq |z - (1 + 6i)|$

(ii) $-\dfrac{\pi}{4} \leq \arg(z + 2 - i) < 0$

(iii) $|z - (-2 + 3i)| < 4$

6

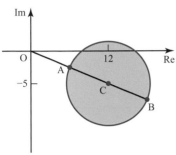

$|z|$ is least at A and greatest at B. Using Pythagoras' theorem, the distance OC is $\sqrt{(-5)^2 + 12^2} = 13$. We know AC = 7 and so OA = 13 − 7 = 6.
So, minimum value of $|z|$ is OA = 6 and maximum value of $|z|$ is OB = 6 + 14 = 20.

7 (i)

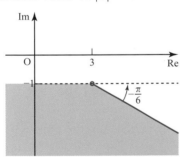

(ii)

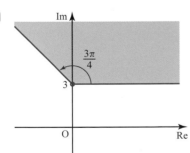

(iii)

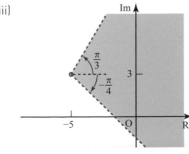

8 (i)

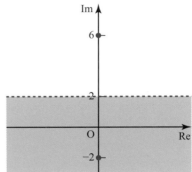

(ii)

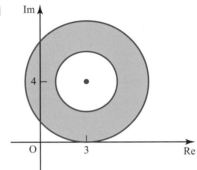

(iii)

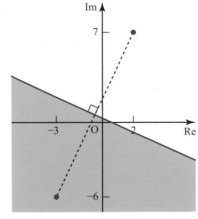

(iv)

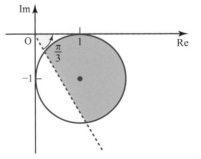

9

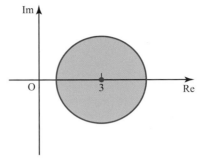

10 (i) (a) $|z + 1 + 2i| = 3$

(b) $|z + 6| = |z + 4i|$

(ii) $|z + 1 + 2i| \leq 3$ and $|z + 6| \geq |z + 4i|$

11

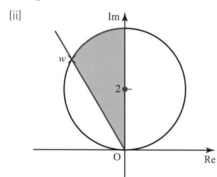

12 (i) $\dfrac{2\pi}{3}, 2$

(ii)

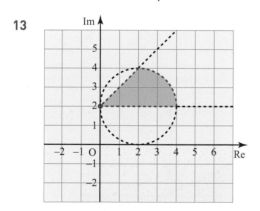

13

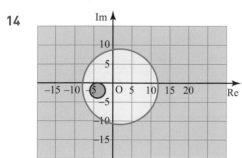

14

There are no values of z which satisfy both regions simultaneously.

15 The diagram shows $|z - 5 + 4i| = 3$. The minimum value is 7 and the maximum value is 13.

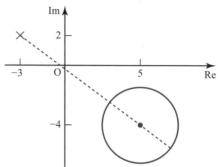

16 (i) Centre is $(3, -12)$, radius 6

(ii)

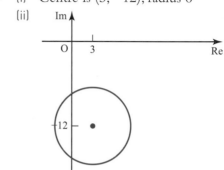

17 (i) Straight line, $\text{Im}(z) = 2$, excluding w_1 and w_2

(ii) Circle, centre $2i$, radius 3, excluding w_1 and w_2

Chapter 6

Discussion point (Page 110)

The triangles are all congruent to each other.
256 yellow triangles make up the purple triangle.

Activity 6.1 (Page 111)

The diagram shows the image of the unit square OABC under the transformation with matrix

$$\begin{pmatrix} a & b \\ c & d \end{pmatrix}.$$

The point $A(1, 0)$ is transformed to the point A' (a, c); the point $C(0, 1)$ is transformed to the point C' (b, d). B' has coordinates $(a + b, c + d)$.

The area of the parallelogram is given by the area of the whole rectangle minus the area of the rectangles and triangles.

Area of rectangle $= b \times c$

Area of first triangle $= \frac{1}{2} \times b \times d$

Area of second triangle $= \frac{1}{2} \times a \times c$

Area of whole rectangle $= (a + b) \times (c + d)$

Therefore the area of the parallelogram is

$(a + b) \times (c + d) - 2\left(bc + \frac{1}{2}bd + \frac{1}{2}ac\right) = ad - bc.$

Discussion point (Page 113)

(i) A rotation does not reverse the order of the vertices, e.g. for $\mathbf{A} = \begin{pmatrix} 0 & -1 \\ 1 & 0 \end{pmatrix}$,

$\det(\mathbf{A}) = 1$ which is positive.

(ii) A reflection reverses the order of the vertices,

e.g. for $\mathbf{B} = \begin{pmatrix} 1 & 0 \\ 0 & -1 \end{pmatrix}$,

$\det(\mathbf{B}) = -1$ which is negative.

(iii) An enlargement does not reverse the order of the vertices, e.g. for $\mathbf{C} = \begin{pmatrix} 2 & 0 \\ 0 & 2 \end{pmatrix}$,

$\det(\mathbf{C}) = 4$ which is positive

Discussion point (Page 115)

A 3×3 matrix with zero determinant will produce an image which has no volume, i.e. the points are all mapped to the same plane.

Exercise 6.1 (Page 115)

1 (i) (a)

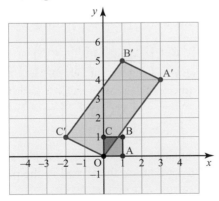

  (b) Area of parallelogram = 11
  (c) 11

(ii) (a)

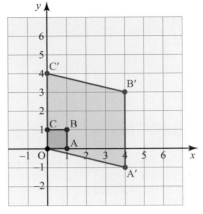

  (b) Area of parallelogram = 16
  (c) 16

(iii) (a)

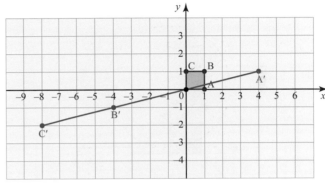

  (b) area of parallelogram = 0
  (c) 0

(iv) (a)

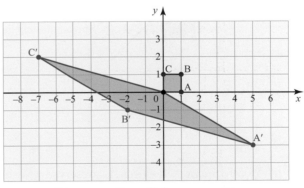

  (b) area of parallelogram = 11
  (c) −11

2    $x = 2, x = 6$

3 (i) $\mathbf{A} = \begin{pmatrix} 1 & 0 \\ 0 & -1 \end{pmatrix}$ $\mathbf{C} = \begin{pmatrix} 0 & 1 \\ 1 & 0 \end{pmatrix}$

$\mathbf{B} = \begin{pmatrix} -1 & 0 \\ 0 & 1 \end{pmatrix}$ $\mathbf{D} = \begin{pmatrix} 0 & -1 \\ -1 & 0 \end{pmatrix}$

(iii) A

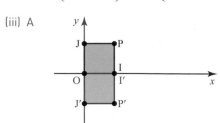

B

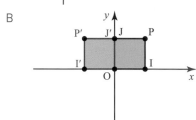

C

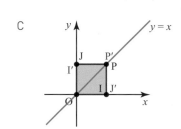

D

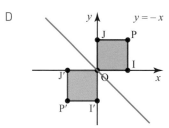

4 $66\,\text{cm}^2$

5 $ad = 1$

6 (i) $\begin{pmatrix} 1 & 3 \\ 0 & 1 \end{pmatrix}$

(ii) determinant = 1 so area is preserved

7 determinant = 6 so volume of image
$6 \times 5 = 30\,\text{cm}^3$

8 (i) $\det(\mathbf{M}) = -2,$ $\det(\mathbf{N}) = 7$

(ii) $\mathbf{MN} = \begin{pmatrix} 9 & 13 \\ 8 & 10 \end{pmatrix},$ $\det(\mathbf{MN}) = -14$
and $-14 = -2 \times 7$

9 (i)

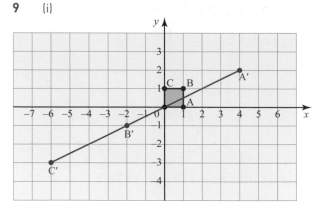

(ii) The image of all points lie on the line.
$y = \frac{1}{2}x$ The determinant of the matrix is zero which shows that the image will have zero area.

10 (i) $\begin{pmatrix} 5p - 10q \\ -p + 2q \end{pmatrix}$

(ii) $y = -\frac{1}{5}x$

(iii) $\det(\mathbf{N}) = 0$ and so the image has zero area

11 (i) $\mathbf{T} = \begin{pmatrix} 1 & 2 \\ 3 & 6 \end{pmatrix},$

$\det(\mathbf{T}) = (1 \times 6) - (3 \times 2) = 0$

(ii) $\begin{pmatrix} x' \\ y' \end{pmatrix} = \begin{pmatrix} 1 & 2 \\ 3 & 6 \end{pmatrix} \begin{pmatrix} x \\ y \end{pmatrix}$

$\Rightarrow \begin{matrix} x' = x + 2y \\ y' = 3x + 6y \end{matrix} \Rightarrow y' = 3x'$

(iii) $(3, 9)$

12 $\begin{pmatrix} x' \\ y' \end{pmatrix} = \begin{pmatrix} a & b \\ c & d \end{pmatrix} \begin{pmatrix} x \\ y \end{pmatrix} \Rightarrow \begin{pmatrix} x' \\ y' \end{pmatrix}$

$= \begin{pmatrix} ax + by \\ cx + dy \end{pmatrix} \Rightarrow \begin{matrix} x' = ax + by \\ y' = cx + dy \end{matrix}$

Solving simultaneously and using the fact
$ad - bc = 0$ gives the result.

13 (i) $y = 3x - 3s + t$

(ii) $P'\left(\frac{9}{8}s - \frac{3}{8}t, \frac{3}{8}s - \frac{1}{8}t\right)$

(iii) $\begin{pmatrix} \frac{9}{8} & -\frac{3}{8} \\ \frac{3}{8} & -\frac{1}{8} \end{pmatrix}$ which has determinant

$\left(\frac{9}{8} \times -\frac{1}{8}\right) - \left(\frac{3}{8} \times -\frac{3}{8}\right) = 0$

Activity 6.2 (Page 118)

(i) $\mathbf{P} = \begin{pmatrix} 1 & 0 \\ 0 & -1 \end{pmatrix}$

(ii) $\mathbf{P^2} = \begin{pmatrix} 1 & 0 \\ 0 & 1 \end{pmatrix}$

(iii) Reflecting an object in the x-axis twice takes it back to the starting position and so the final image is the same as the original object. Hence the matrix for the combined transformation is $\mathbf{I}$.

Activity 6.3 (Page 119)

$$\begin{pmatrix} a & b \\ c & d \end{pmatrix}\begin{pmatrix} d & -b \\ -c & a \end{pmatrix} = \begin{pmatrix} ad - bc & 0 \\ 0 & ad - bc \end{pmatrix}$$

To turn this into the identity matrix it would need to be divided by $ad - bc$ which is the value $|M|$.

Therefore $\mathbf{M}^{-1} = \dfrac{1}{ad - bc}\begin{pmatrix} d & -b \\ -c & a \end{pmatrix}$

Activity 6.4 (Page 120)

(i) $\mathbf{AA^{-1}} = \dfrac{1}{4}\begin{pmatrix} 11 & 3 \\ 6 & 2 \end{pmatrix}\begin{pmatrix} 2 & -3 \\ -6 & 11 \end{pmatrix}$

$$= \dfrac{1}{4}\begin{pmatrix} 4 & 0 \\ 0 & 4 \end{pmatrix} = \mathbf{I}$$

$\mathbf{A^{-1}A} = \dfrac{1}{4}\begin{pmatrix} 2 & -3 \\ -6 & 11 \end{pmatrix}\begin{pmatrix} 11 & 3 \\ 6 & 2 \end{pmatrix}$

$$= \dfrac{1}{4}\begin{pmatrix} 4 & 0 \\ 0 & 4 \end{pmatrix} = \mathbf{I}$$

(ii) $\mathbf{M}^{-1} = \dfrac{1}{ad - bc}\begin{pmatrix} d & -b \\ -c & a \end{pmatrix}$

$\mathbf{MM^{-1}} = \begin{pmatrix} a & b \\ c & d \end{pmatrix}\dfrac{1}{ad - bc}\begin{pmatrix} d & -b \\ -c & a \end{pmatrix}$

$$= \dfrac{1}{ad - bc}\begin{pmatrix} a & b \\ c & d \end{pmatrix}\begin{pmatrix} d & -b \\ -c & a \end{pmatrix}$$

$$= \dfrac{1}{ad - bc}\begin{pmatrix} ad - bc & -ab + ab \\ cd - dc & -cb + ad \end{pmatrix}$$

$$= \dfrac{1}{ad - bc}\begin{pmatrix} ad - bc & 0 \\ 0 & ad - bc \end{pmatrix} = \begin{pmatrix} 1 & 0 \\ 0 & 1 \end{pmatrix} = \mathbf{I}$$

$\mathbf{M^{-1}M} = \dfrac{1}{ad - bc}\begin{pmatrix} d & -b \\ -c & a \end{pmatrix}\begin{pmatrix} a & b \\ c & d \end{pmatrix}$

$$= \dfrac{1}{ad - bc}\begin{pmatrix} da - bc & db - bd \\ -ca + ac & -cb + ad \end{pmatrix}$$

$$= \dfrac{1}{ad - bc}\begin{pmatrix} ad - bc & 0 \\ 0 & ad - bc \end{pmatrix}$$

$$= \begin{pmatrix} 1 & 0 \\ 0 & 1 \end{pmatrix} = \mathbf{I}$$

Discussion point (Page 120)

First reverse the reflection by using the transformation with the inverse matrix of the reflection. Secondly, reverse the rotation by using the transformation with the inverse matrix of the rotation.

$(\mathbf{MN})^{-1} = \mathbf{N^{-1}M^{-1}}$

Activity 6.5 (Page 120)

$\det(\mathbf{A}) = (1 \times 3) - (-2 \times 4) = 11$

$\det(\mathbf{B}) = (3 \times 2) - (2 \times 1) = 4$

$\mathbf{AB} = \begin{pmatrix} 1 & 4 \\ -2 & 3 \end{pmatrix}\begin{pmatrix} 3 & 1 \\ 2 & 2 \end{pmatrix} = \begin{pmatrix} 11 & 9 \\ 0 & 4 \end{pmatrix}$

$\det(\mathbf{AB}) = 44 = 11 \times 4 = \det(\mathbf{A}) \times \det(\mathbf{B})$

Exercise 6.2 (Page 121)

1 (i) $(10, -6)$

(ii) $-\dfrac{1}{2}\begin{pmatrix} 0 & 1 \\ 2 & 5 \end{pmatrix}$

(iii) $(1, 2)$

2 (i) non-singular, $\dfrac{1}{24}\begin{pmatrix} 2 & -3 \\ 4 & 6 \end{pmatrix}$

(ii) singular

(iii) non-singular, $\dfrac{1}{112}\begin{pmatrix} 11 & -3 \\ -3 & 11 \end{pmatrix}$

(iv) singular

(v) singular

(vi) singular

(vii) non-singular, $\dfrac{1}{16(1 - ab)}\begin{pmatrix} -8 & -4a \\ -4b & -2 \end{pmatrix}$

(viii) non-singular, $\dfrac{1}{2}\begin{pmatrix} 1 & -i \\ -i & 1 \end{pmatrix}$

3 (i) $\dfrac{1}{3}\begin{pmatrix} 3 & -6 \\ -2 & 5 \end{pmatrix}$ (ii) $\dfrac{1}{2}\begin{pmatrix} -1 & -5 \\ 2 & 8 \end{pmatrix}$

(iii) $\begin{pmatrix} 28 & 19 \\ 10 & 7 \end{pmatrix}$ (iv) $\begin{pmatrix} 50 & 63 \\ -12 & -15 \end{pmatrix}$

(v) $\dfrac{1}{6}\begin{pmatrix} 7 & -19 \\ -10 & 28 \end{pmatrix}$ (vi) $\dfrac{1}{6}\begin{pmatrix} -15 & -63 \\ 12 & 50 \end{pmatrix}$

(vii) $\dfrac{1}{6}\begin{pmatrix} -15 & -63 \\ 12 & 50 \end{pmatrix}$ (viii) $\dfrac{1}{6}\begin{pmatrix} 7 & -19 \\ -10 & 28 \end{pmatrix}$

4 (i) $\dfrac{1}{8}\begin{pmatrix} 2 & 2 \\ -3 & 1 \end{pmatrix}$

(ii) $\mathbf{M}^{-1}\mathbf{M} = \dfrac{1}{8}\begin{pmatrix} 2 & 2 \\ -3 & 1 \end{pmatrix}\begin{pmatrix} 1 & -2 \\ 3 & 2 \end{pmatrix} = \mathbf{I}$

5 $k = 2$ or $k = 3$

6 $\begin{pmatrix} 2 & 1 & 0 & -1 \\ 1 & 0 & -3 & 4 \end{pmatrix}$

7 (i) $(3, 1), (1, 1)$ and $(-6, -2)$

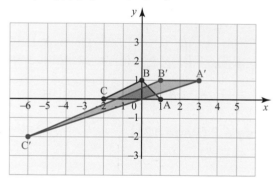

(ii) ratio of area T' to T is 3 : 1.5 or 2 : 1

This is equal to the determinant of the matrix $\mathbf{M}$.

(iii) $\mathbf{M}^{-1} = \dfrac{1}{2}\begin{pmatrix} 1 & -1 \\ -1 & 3 \end{pmatrix}$

8 (ii) $\mathbf{M}^n = (a + d)^{n-1}\mathbf{M}$

9

(iii) $\begin{pmatrix} 0 & \dfrac{1}{5} \\ \dfrac{1}{6} & -\dfrac{11}{10} \end{pmatrix}$ (iv) $\begin{pmatrix} 33 & 6 \\ 5 & 0 \end{pmatrix}$

Activity 6.6 (Page 122)

(i) $\begin{pmatrix} 2 & -2 & 3 \\ 5 & 1 & -1 \\ 3 & 4 & -2 \end{pmatrix}\begin{pmatrix} x \\ y \\ z \end{pmatrix} = \begin{pmatrix} 4 \\ -6 \\ 1 \end{pmatrix}$

$\begin{pmatrix} x \\ y \\ z \end{pmatrix} = \begin{pmatrix} 2 & -2 & 3 \\ 5 & 1 & -1 \\ 3 & 4 & -2 \end{pmatrix}^{-1}\begin{pmatrix} 4 \\ -6 \\ 1 \end{pmatrix}$

$\Rightarrow x = -1,\ y = 3,\ z = 4$

(ii) $\begin{pmatrix} 2 & -2 & 3 \\ 5 & 1 & -1 \\ 3 & 3 & -4 \end{pmatrix}\begin{pmatrix} x \\ y \\ z \end{pmatrix} = \begin{pmatrix} 4 \\ -6 \\ 1 \end{pmatrix}$

$\begin{pmatrix} x \\ y \\ z \end{pmatrix} = \begin{pmatrix} 2 & -2 & 3 \\ 5 & 1 & -1 \\ 3 & 3 & -4 \end{pmatrix}^{-1}\begin{pmatrix} 4 \\ -6 \\ 1 \end{pmatrix}$

The equations cannot be solved as the determinant of the matrix is zero, so the inverse matrix does not exist. Using an algebraic method results in inconsistent equations, which have no solutions.

Exercise 6.3 (Page 127)

1 (i) non-singular, $\dfrac{1}{140}$ $\begin{pmatrix} 21 & 10 & 27 \\ -7 & -50 & -9 \\ 14 & 20 & -2 \end{pmatrix}$

(ii) singular

(iii) non-singular, $\dfrac{1}{121}$ $\begin{pmatrix} -17 & 15 & 6 \\ -91 & -2 & 25 \\ 46 & -5 & -2 \end{pmatrix}$

2 (i) (a) 5 (b) 5
(ii) (a) −5 (b) −5

Interchanging the rows and columns has not changed the determinant.

(iii) (a) 0 (b) 0

If a matrix has a repeated row or column the determinant will be zero.

3 (i) $\dfrac{1}{3}\begin{pmatrix} 3 & 0 & 6 \\ -4 & 2 & 3 \\ 2 & -1 & 0 \end{pmatrix}$

(ii) matrix is singular

(iii) $\begin{pmatrix} -0.06 & -0.1 & -0.1 \\ 0.92 & 0.2 & 0.7 \\ 0.66 & 0.1 & 0.6 \end{pmatrix}$

(iv) $\dfrac{1}{21}\begin{pmatrix} 34 & 11 & 32 \\ 9 & 6 & 6 \\ -38 & -16 & -37 \end{pmatrix}$

4    $\dfrac{1}{7}\begin{pmatrix} 2 & 18 & -11 \\ 2 & 39 & -25 \\ 3 & 41 & -27 \end{pmatrix}$; $x = 8, y = 4, z = -3$

5    $\mathbf{M}^{-1} = \dfrac{1}{28 - 10k}\begin{pmatrix} 4 & -10 & 12 \\ -(4k-8) & 8 & -(4+2k) \\ -k & 7 & -3k \end{pmatrix}$

     ; $k = 2.8$

6   (i)   The columns of the matrix have been moved one place to the right, with the final column moving to replace the first. This is called **cyclical interchange** of the columns.

      (ii) $\det(\mathbf{A}) = \det(\mathbf{B}) = \det(\mathbf{C}) = -26$

         Cyclical interchange of the columns leaves the determinant unchanged.

7    $x = \dfrac{-1 \pm \sqrt{41}}{2}$

8    $x = 1, x = 4$

9    $1 < k < 5$

10   (i)   Let $\mathbf{X} = (\mathbf{PQ})^{-1}$ so $\mathbf{X}(\mathbf{PQ}) = \mathbf{1}$

           $\Rightarrow \mathbf{X} = (\mathbf{PQ})\mathbf{Q}^{-1} = \mathbf{1}\mathbf{Q}^{-1} = \mathbf{Q}^{-1}$

           $\Rightarrow \mathbf{XP}(\mathbf{QQ}^{-1}) = \mathbf{XP}^{-1} = \mathbf{Q}^{-1}$

           $\Rightarrow \mathbf{XPP}^{-1} = \mathbf{Q}^{-1}\mathbf{P}^{-1}$

           $\Rightarrow \mathbf{X} = \mathbf{Q}^{-1}\mathbf{P}^{-1}$

      (ii)

$\mathbf{P}^{-1}\begin{pmatrix} -\dfrac{1}{9} & \dfrac{1}{6} & -\dfrac{4}{9} \\ \dfrac{2}{9} & \dfrac{1}{6} & -\dfrac{1}{9} \\ -\dfrac{1}{3} & \dfrac{1}{2} & -\dfrac{1}{3} \end{pmatrix}$ $\mathbf{Q}^{-1} = \begin{pmatrix} \dfrac{3}{2} & -4 & \dfrac{1}{2} \\ 1 & -2 & 0 \\ -\dfrac{3}{2} & 5 & -\dfrac{1}{2} \end{pmatrix}$

$(\mathbf{PQ})^{-1} = \mathbf{Q}^{-1}\mathbf{P}^{-1} = \begin{pmatrix} -\dfrac{11}{9} & -\dfrac{1}{6} & -\dfrac{7}{18} \\ -\dfrac{5}{9} & -\dfrac{1}{6} & -\dfrac{2}{9} \\ \dfrac{13}{9} & \dfrac{1}{3} & \dfrac{5}{18} \end{pmatrix}$

11   (ii)   Multiplying only the first column by k equates to a stretch of scale factor k in one direction, so only multiplies the volume by k.

      (iii)   Multiplying any column by k multplies the determinant by k.

12   (i) $10 \times 43 = 430$

      (ii) $4 \times 5 \times -7 \times 43 = -6020$

      (iii) $x \times 2 \times y \times 43 = 86xy$

      (iv) $x \times \dfrac{1}{2x} \times 4y \times 43 = 86y$

13   (i) $\begin{pmatrix} 18 & -9 & 4 \\ 1 & -7 & 2 \\ -1 & -4 & 1 \end{pmatrix}$

      (ii) $\begin{pmatrix} 1 & a+7 & b+7c+4 \\ 0 & 1 & c+2 \\ 0 & 0 & 1 \end{pmatrix}$

      (iii) $\begin{pmatrix} 1 & -7 & 10 \\ 0 & 1 & -2 \\ 0 & 0 & 1 \end{pmatrix}$

      (iv) $\begin{pmatrix} 1 & 0 & 0 \\ -3 & 1 & 0 \\ -11 & 4 & 1 \end{pmatrix}$

      (v) $\begin{pmatrix} 1 & -7 & 10 \\ -3 & 22 & -32 \\ -11 & 81 & -117 \end{pmatrix}$

14   $k = 3$

Exercise 6.4 (Page 132)

1   (i) $\dfrac{1}{11}\begin{pmatrix} 3 & 1 \\ -2 & 3 \end{pmatrix}$

     (ii) $x = 1, \; y = 1$

2   (i) $x = 2, \; y = -1$

     (ii) $x = 4, \; y = 1.5$

3   (i) $\begin{pmatrix} 0.5 & 0 & -0.5 \\ -0.8 & -0.2 & 1.4 \\ 0.3 & 0.2 & 0.1 \end{pmatrix}$

     (ii) $x = -2, \; y = 4.6, \; z = -0.6$

4 $\dfrac{1}{5}\begin{pmatrix} 3 & -i \\ -2i & 1 \end{pmatrix}$

$x = 1 + i, \ y = 1 - i$

5 $x = 4, \ y = -1, \ z = 1$

6   (i)   Single point of intersection at $(8.5, -1.5)$

        (ii)   Lines are coincident. There are an infinite number of solutions of the form $(6 - \lambda, \ \lambda)$.

        (iii)   Lines are parallel and therefore there are no solutions.

7 $k = 4$, infinite number of solutions

      $k = -4$, no solutions

8   (i) $\begin{pmatrix} k-1 & 0 & 0 \\ 0 & k-1 & 0 \\ 0 & 0 & k-1 \end{pmatrix}$ so

$\mathbf{A}^{-1} = \dfrac{1}{k-1}\begin{pmatrix} -1 & 3k+8 & 4k+10 \\ -2 & 2k+20 & 3k+25 \\ 1 & -11 & -14 \end{pmatrix}$

        where $k \neq 1$

        (ii) $x = 8, \ y = 6, \ z = 0$

Chapter 7

Discussion point (Page 130)

Could also draw lines perpendicular to the x-axis to the points P and Q as shown.

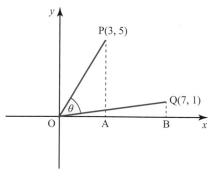

Using trigonometry on the two right-angled triangles, find $\angle POA$ and $\angle QOB$ and calculate the difference between these values, which equals θ.

Activity 7.1 (Page 131)

$$\cos\theta = \dfrac{\left|\overrightarrow{OA}\right|^2 + \left|\overrightarrow{OB}\right|^2 - \left|\overrightarrow{AB}\right|^2}{2 \times \left|\overrightarrow{OA}\right| \times \left|\overrightarrow{OB}\right|}$$

$$\Rightarrow \cos\theta = \dfrac{\left(a_1^2 + a_2^2\right) + \left(b_1^2 + b_2^2\right) - \left[(b_1 - a_1)^2\right] + \left[(b_2 - a_2)^2\right]}{2\left(a_1^2 + a_2^2\right)\left(b_1^2 + b_2^2\right)}$$

$$\Rightarrow \cos\theta = \dfrac{2\left(a_1 b_1 + a_2 b_2\right)}{2\sqrt{\left(a_1^2 + a_2^2\right)}\sqrt{\left(b_1^2 + b_2^2\right)}} = \dfrac{a_1 b_1 + a_2 b_2}{|\mathbf{a}||\mathbf{b}|}$$

Discussion point (Page 133)

$$\overrightarrow{BA} = \begin{pmatrix} 2 \\ -2 \\ -4 \end{pmatrix} \qquad \overrightarrow{BC} = \begin{pmatrix} 8 \\ -7 \\ 0 \end{pmatrix}$$

$$\begin{pmatrix} 2 \\ -2 \\ -4 \end{pmatrix} \cdot \begin{pmatrix} 8 \\ -7 \\ 0 \end{pmatrix} = 30 \quad \text{which is the same answer as in Example 7.2}$$

Exercise 7.1 (Page 140)

1   (i) -4 (iii) 1

     (ii) 4 (iv) 7

2 $64.7°$

3   (i) $66.6°$

     (ii) $113.4°$

     (iii) $113.4°$

4   (i) 0; vectors are parallel

     (ii) $180°$; vectors are anti-parallel

6 -17

7 $-2, -3$

8 $s = 3, \ t = -2$

9 $52.2°, 33.2°, 94.6°$ which add up to $180°$

10 $35.8°, 71.1°, 60.9°$

11 $(-2, 3, -2), \sqrt{86}$

12   (i) $(0, 4, 3)$

      (ii) $\begin{pmatrix} -5 \\ 4 \\ 3 \end{pmatrix}, 5\sqrt{2} \approx 7.07$

      (iii) $25.1°$

13 (i) A(4, 0, 0); C(0, 5, 0); H(0, 5, 3)

(ii) No; trapezium

(iii) $-\frac{1}{3}$; $\sqrt{8}$

(iv) 39.8°

Activity 7.2 (Page 136)

(ii)

$$\begin{pmatrix} -2 \\ -9 \end{pmatrix}, \begin{pmatrix} 0 \\ -5 \end{pmatrix}, \begin{pmatrix} 2 \\ -1 \end{pmatrix}, \begin{pmatrix} 3 \\ 1 \end{pmatrix}, \begin{pmatrix} 3\frac{1}{2} \\ 2 \end{pmatrix}, \begin{pmatrix} 6 \\ 7 \end{pmatrix}, \begin{pmatrix} 8 \\ 11 \end{pmatrix}$$

(iv) (a) between A and B

(b) beyond/above/right of B

(c) before/below/left of A

Activity 7.3 (Page 138)

(i) $x = a_1 + \lambda d_1$, $y = a_2 + \lambda d_2$

(ii) $\lambda = \dfrac{x - a_1}{d_1} = \dfrac{y - a_2}{d_2}$

(iii) $y = \dfrac{d_2}{d_1}x + \dfrac{a_2 d_1 - a_1 d_2}{d_1}$

Activity 7.4 (Page 144)

$\dfrac{x}{2} = \dfrac{y-3}{1}$ and $\dfrac{x-3}{1} = \dfrac{y-1}{-3}$; for example, use gradients to give angles between lines and the positive x-direction. This gives $\tan^{-1} 2 = 63.4°$ and $\tan^{-1}(-\frac{1}{3}) = -18.4°$. Subtracting gives an angle of 81.9°.

Exercise 7.2 (Page 145)

[Throughout this exercise, other answers can be expected.]

1 (i) $\mathbf{r} = \begin{pmatrix} 3 \\ 1 \end{pmatrix} + \lambda \begin{pmatrix} 5 \\ -2 \end{pmatrix}$

(ii) $\mathbf{r} = \begin{pmatrix} 5 \\ -1 \end{pmatrix} + \lambda \begin{pmatrix} 0 \\ 4 \end{pmatrix}$

(iii) $\mathbf{r} = \begin{pmatrix} -2 \\ 4 \end{pmatrix} + \lambda \begin{pmatrix} 1 \\ 1 \end{pmatrix}$

(iv) $\mathbf{r} = \begin{pmatrix} 0 \\ 8 \end{pmatrix} + \lambda \begin{pmatrix} -2 \\ -11 \end{pmatrix}$

2 (i) $\mathbf{r} = \begin{pmatrix} 2 \\ 4 \\ -1 \end{pmatrix} + \lambda \begin{pmatrix} 3 \\ 6 \\ 4 \end{pmatrix}$

(ii) $\mathbf{r} = \begin{pmatrix} 1 \\ 0 \\ -1 \end{pmatrix} + \lambda \begin{pmatrix} 1 \\ 0 \\ 0 \end{pmatrix}$

(iii) $\mathbf{r} = \begin{pmatrix} 1 \\ 0 \\ 4 \end{pmatrix} + \lambda \begin{pmatrix} 5 \\ 3 \\ -6 \end{pmatrix}$

(iv) $\mathbf{r} = \begin{pmatrix} 0 \\ 0 \\ 1 \end{pmatrix} + \lambda \begin{pmatrix} 2 \\ 1 \\ 3 \end{pmatrix}$

3 (i) $\dfrac{x-2}{3} = \dfrac{y-4}{6} = \dfrac{z+1}{4}$

(ii) $\dfrac{x-1}{1} = \dfrac{y}{3} = \dfrac{z+1}{4}$

(iii) $\dfrac{x-3}{1} = \dfrac{z-4}{2}, y = 0$

(iv) $\dfrac{x}{2} = \dfrac{z-1}{4}, y = 4$

4 (i) $\mathbf{r} = \begin{pmatrix} 3 \\ -2 \\ 1 \end{pmatrix} + \lambda \begin{pmatrix} 5 \\ 3 \\ 4 \end{pmatrix}$

(ii) $\mathbf{r} = \begin{pmatrix} 0 \\ 0 \\ -1 \end{pmatrix} + \lambda \begin{pmatrix} 1 \\ 2 \\ 3 \end{pmatrix}$

(iii) $\mathbf{r} = \begin{pmatrix} 0 \\ 0 \\ 0 \end{pmatrix} + \lambda \begin{pmatrix} 1 \\ 1 \\ 1 \end{pmatrix}$

(iv) $\mathbf{r} = \begin{pmatrix} 2 \\ 0 \\ 0 \end{pmatrix} + \lambda \begin{pmatrix} 0 \\ 1 \\ 1 \end{pmatrix}$

5 $\mathbf{r} = \begin{pmatrix} 3 \\ -5 \\ 2 \end{pmatrix} + \lambda \begin{pmatrix} 0 \\ 1 \\ 0 \end{pmatrix}, x = 3, z = 2$

6 (i) $\begin{pmatrix} 4 \\ 1 \end{pmatrix}$

(ii) $\begin{pmatrix} 5 \\ 5 \end{pmatrix}$

(iii) $\begin{pmatrix} -5 \\ 6 \end{pmatrix}$

7 (i) Intersect at $(3, 2, -13)$

(ii) Skew

(iii) Parallel

(iv) Intersect at $(4, -7, 11)$

(v) Skew

8 (i) 81.9°
(ii) 56.3°
(iii) 53.6°
(iv) 81.8°

9 No

10 $9, 6, \sqrt{77}$

11 (i) $\begin{pmatrix} -0.25 \\ 0 \\ 0 \end{pmatrix}$

(ii) $(0, 0.05, 1.1)$

(iii) $\mathbf{r} = \begin{pmatrix} -0.25 \\ 0 \\ 1 \end{pmatrix} + \lambda \begin{pmatrix} 1 \\ 0 \\ 0 \end{pmatrix}$,

$\mathbf{r} = \begin{pmatrix} 0.25 \\ 0 \\ 1 \end{pmatrix} + \lambda \begin{pmatrix} 0 \\ 1 \\ 2 \end{pmatrix}$

12 (i) $(1, 0.5, 0)$
(ii) 41.8°
(iii) 027°
(iv) $(2, 2.5, 2)$
(v) $t = 2$
(vi) 2.24 km (3 sf)

13 (i) $(7, 7, 10)$; $(5, -3, 4)$; $(-5, 3, -4)$
(iii) $\sqrt{1746} = 41.8$ (3 sf)

14 (i) $(4 + 2t, -2 + 3t, 9 - 5t)$
(ii) $(3 + 2t - s)\mathbf{i} + (3t - 1)\mathbf{j} + (4 - 5t + s)\mathbf{k}$
(iii) $-1 + 7t - 2s = 0; -17 + 38t - 7s = 0$
(iv) $t = 1, s = 3; A(4, -1, 2); B(6, 1, 4)$
(v) $2\sqrt{3}$, shortest distance between the lines

Discussion point (Page 151)

Use the scalar product to check that the vector $\mathbf{a} \times \mathbf{b}$ is perpendicular to both $\mathbf{a}$ and $\mathbf{b}$:

$(\mathbf{a} \times \mathbf{b}).\mathbf{a} = \begin{pmatrix} 24 \\ -1 \\ -14 \end{pmatrix} \cdot \begin{pmatrix} 3 \\ 2 \\ 5 \end{pmatrix} = (24 \times 3) + (-1 \times 2)$

$+ (-14 \times 5) = 0$

$(\mathbf{a} \times \mathbf{b}).\mathbf{b} = \begin{pmatrix} 24 \\ -1 \\ -14 \end{pmatrix} \cdot \begin{pmatrix} 1 \\ -4 \\ 2 \end{pmatrix} = (24 \times 1) +$

$(-1 \times -4) + (-14 \times 2) = 0$

Activity 7.5 (Page 159)

$\mathbf{j} \times \mathbf{i} = -\mathbf{k} \qquad \mathbf{j} \times \mathbf{j} = 0$
$\mathbf{j} \times \mathbf{k} = \mathbf{i}$
$\mathbf{k} \times \mathbf{i} = \mathbf{j} \qquad \mathbf{k} \times \mathbf{k} = 0$
$\mathbf{k} \times \mathbf{j} = -\mathbf{i}$

Exercise 7.3 (Page 154)

1 (i) $\begin{pmatrix} -23 \\ 13 \\ 2 \end{pmatrix}$ (ii) $\begin{pmatrix} 37 \\ 41 \\ 19 \end{pmatrix}$

(iii) $\begin{pmatrix} -8 \\ 34 \\ 27 \end{pmatrix}$ (iv) $\begin{pmatrix} 21 \\ -29 \\ 9 \end{pmatrix}$

2 (i) $\begin{pmatrix} 5 \\ 19 \\ -2 \end{pmatrix}$ (ii) $\begin{pmatrix} 14 \\ -62 \\ -9 \end{pmatrix}$

(iii) $\begin{pmatrix} -3 \\ -2 \\ 3 \end{pmatrix}$ (iv) $\begin{pmatrix} -18 \\ 57 \\ 47 \end{pmatrix}$

3 (i) $\overrightarrow{AB} = \begin{pmatrix} 1 \\ -4 \\ 3 \end{pmatrix}, \overrightarrow{AC} = \begin{pmatrix} 4 \\ -1 \\ 0 \end{pmatrix}$,

(ii) $\begin{pmatrix} 3 \\ 12 \\ 15 \end{pmatrix}$ or $\begin{pmatrix} 1 \\ 4 \\ 5 \end{pmatrix}$

4 $\dfrac{1}{\sqrt{635}} \begin{pmatrix} 19 \\ 15 \\ -7 \end{pmatrix}$

5 $\sqrt{74}$

6 (i) $-8\mathbf{j}$
(ii) $6\mathbf{j} - 4\mathbf{k}$
(iii) $2\mathbf{i} - 12\mathbf{j}$
(iv) $6\mathbf{i} + 14\mathbf{j} - 2\mathbf{k}$

8 (i) $\sqrt{38}, \sqrt{21}, \sqrt{41}; \frac{1}{2}\sqrt{717}$
(ii) $\sqrt{717}$
(iii) The area of the triangle is given by $\frac{1}{2}|\mathbf{a}| \times |\mathbf{b}| \times \sin C$.

Answers

Practice questions Pure Further Mathematics 2 (Page 163)

1. $(s = 2, t = -1); 83.0°$ [6]

2. (i) Reflection in the line $y = 0$. [1]

   (ii) Reflection in the line $x = 0$. [1]

   (iii) $\mathbf{BA} = \begin{pmatrix} -1 & 0 \\ 0 & -1 \end{pmatrix}$. [1]

   It represents rotation of $180°$ about the origin. [1]

   (iv) $(\mathbf{BA})^{-1} = \begin{pmatrix} -1 & 0 \\ 0 & -1 \end{pmatrix} = \mathbf{BA}$. [1], [1]

   A rotation of 180° about the origin followed by another rotation of 180° about the origin. Is equivalent to one full turn about the origin, which has no effect. This means, the inverse of a rotation of 180° about the origin is another rotation of 180° about the origin. [1]

3. (i) $z_1 z_2 = (a + bi)(c + di)$
   $= ac - bd + (ad + bc)i$ [1], [1]

   (ii) $|z_1| = \sqrt{a^2 + b^2}, |z_1| = \sqrt{c^2 + d^2}$ [1]

   (iii) $|z_1 z_2| = \sqrt{(ac - bd)^2 + (ad + bc)^2}$ [1]

   $= \sqrt{a^2 c^2 - 2abcd + b^2 d^2 + a^2 d^2 + 2abcd + b^2 c^2}$

   $= \sqrt{a^2 c^2 + b^2 d^2 + a^2 d^2 + b^2 c^2}$ [1]

   $|z_1||z_2| = \sqrt{a^2 + b^2} \sqrt{c^2 + d^2}$

   $= \sqrt{(a^2 + b^2)(c^2 + d^2)}$

   $= \sqrt{a^2 c^2 + b^2 d^2 + a^2 d^2 + b^2 c^2}$ [1]

   $\Rightarrow |z_1 z_2| = |z_1||z_2|$ [1]

4. (i) $|z - 3 - 3i| = 3$ [1], [1]

   (ii) $\arg(z - 3 - 3i) = \dfrac{\pi}{3}$ [1], [1]

   (iii) $\dfrac{1}{2} r^2 \theta = \dfrac{3\pi}{8}$

   $r = 3 \Rightarrow \theta = \dfrac{\pi}{12}$

   $\Rightarrow \arg(z - 3 - 3i) = \dfrac{\pi}{3} + \dfrac{\pi}{12} = \dfrac{5\pi}{12}$

So the half-line has equation

$\arg(z - 3 - 3i) = \dfrac{5\pi}{12}$. [1]

5. (i) $\dfrac{1}{6k + 24} \begin{pmatrix} 2k + 8 & -2 & k + 8 \\ 0 & 6 & -12 \\ 0 & 6 & 3k \end{pmatrix}$ [3]

   (ii) $(1.5, 0, 0.5)$ [3]

6. (i) $\mathbf{r} = -4\mathbf{i} + s(7\mathbf{i} + 2\mathbf{j} + 5\mathbf{k})$ [2]

   (ii) $(4, 0, 0)$ [4]

   (iii) $4\sqrt{29}$ [4]

7. (ii) $\mathbf{i} - 2\mathbf{j} + 2\mathbf{k}$ or any multiple.

   (iii) $(2, -4, 4)$ and $(-2, 4, -4)$

8. (ii) $\begin{pmatrix} 0.3 & -0.1 \\ -0.2 & 0.4 \end{pmatrix}$

   (iii) $42\mathbf{M} - 70\mathbf{I} = \begin{pmatrix} 98 & 42 \\ 84 & 56 \end{pmatrix}$

An introduction to radians
Exercise (Page 159)

1. (i) $\dfrac{\pi}{3}$ (ii) $\dfrac{\pi}{4}$ (iii) $\dfrac{5\pi}{6}$

   (iv) $\dfrac{10\pi}{9}$ (v) 0.775^C (3 s.f.) (vi) $\dfrac{9\pi}{4}$

   (vii) $\dfrac{3\pi}{2}$ (viii) 1.73^C (3 s.f.) or $\dfrac{11\pi}{20}$

   (ix) $\dfrac{5\pi}{3}$ (x) 4π

   (xi) $\dfrac{\pi}{12}$ (xii) $\dfrac{\pi}{60}$ or 0.0524^C (3 s.f.)

2. (i) $20°$ (ii) $24°$

   (iii) $229°$ (3 s.f.) (iv) $300°$

   (v) $25.7°$ (3 s.f.) (vi) $9°$

   (vii) $103°$ (3 s.f.) (viii) $220°$

   (ix) $630°$ (x) $900°$

   (xi) $405°$ (xii) $255°$

The identities $\sin(\theta \pm \phi)$ and $\cos(\theta \pm \phi)$
Exercise (Page 163)

1 (i) $\dfrac{1 + \sqrt{3}}{2\sqrt{2}}$ (ii) $\dfrac{1 - \sqrt{3}}{2\sqrt{2}}$

(iii) $\dfrac{1 - \sqrt{3}}{2\sqrt{2}}$ (iv) $\dfrac{\sqrt{3} - 1}{\sqrt{2}}$

2 (i) $\dfrac{1}{2}$ (ii) 1

(iii) $\cos 4\theta$ (iv) $\dfrac{\sqrt{3}}{2}$

(v) $\dfrac{\sqrt{3} - 1}{\sqrt{2}}$ (vi) $\dfrac{1}{2}$

3 (i) $\dfrac{1}{\sqrt{2}}(\sin\theta + \cos\theta)$

(ii) $\dfrac{\sqrt{3}}{2}\cos 2\theta + \dfrac{1}{2}\sin 2\theta$

(iii) $\dfrac{\sqrt{3}}{2}\sin\theta - \dfrac{1}{2}\cos\theta$

(iv) $\dfrac{1}{2}\cos 3\theta - \dfrac{\sqrt{3}}{2}\sin 3\theta$

Index